DISCOURSES ON RELIGIOUS DIVERSITY

Ashgate AHRC/ESRC Religion and Society Series

Series Editors:

Linda Woodhead, University of Lancaster, UK
Rebecca Catto, University of Lancaster, UK

This book series emanates from the largest research programme on religion in Europe today – the AHRC/ESRC Religion and Society Programme which has invested in over seventy-five research projects. Thirty-two separate disciplines are represented looking at religion across the world, many with a contemporary and some with an historical focus. This international, multi-disciplinary and interdisciplinary book series will include monographs, paperback textbooks and edited research collections drawn from this leading research programme.

Other titles in the series:

Understanding Muslim Chaplaincy
Sophie Gilliat-Ray, Stephen Pattison and Mansur Ali

Social Identities Between the Sacred and the Secular
Edited by Abby Day, Giselle Vincett and Christopher R. Cotter

Religion in Consumer Society
Brands, Consumers and Markets
Edited by François Gauthier and Tuomas Martikainen

Contesting Secularism
Comparative Perspectives
Edited by Anders Berg-Sørensen

Religion in the Neoliberal Age
Political Economy and Modes of Governance
Edited by Tuomas Martikainen and François Gauthier

Discourses on Religious Diversity

Explorations in an Urban Ecology

MARTIN D. STRINGER
University of Birmingham, UK

ASHGATE

In Memoriam
Lowell Livezey

Discourses on Religious Diversity
Explorations in an Urban Ecology

Martin Stringer has produced a fascinating "bottom-up" account of the discourses about religious diversity now flowing through Birmingham's urban culture. Focusing on four arenas in which religious difference becomes manifest – clothing, buildings, festivals, and current event news items – Stringer charts the different ways in which people confront or ignore diversity, and the ways in which difference is downplayed or attributed to ethnic culture, or religion. The result is an insightful analysis of the ways in which religion, culture and politics become intertwined and how the latent can be as problematic as the manifest. Through it all there is keen attention to the latest currents in urban social theory, making this a book for students of cities, of religion, of immigration, and of contemporary modern society.

Rhys H. Williams, Loyola University Chicago, USA

Religious diversity is an ever-present, and increasingly visible, reality in cities across the world. It is an issue of immediate concern to city leaders and members of religious communities, but do we really know what ordinary members of the public, the people who live in the city, really think about it? Major news items, inter-religious violence and notorious public events often lead to negative views being expressed, especially among those who would not consider themselves to have a religious identity of their own.

Martin Stringer explores the highly complex series of discourses around religion and religious diversity that are held by ordinary members of the city; discourses that are often contradictory in themselves and discourses that show that attitudes to religion vary considerably depending on context and wider local or national narratives. Drawing on examples from the UK (particularly Birmingham, one of the UK's most diverse cities), Europe and the United States, Stringer offers some practical suggestions for ways in which discourses of religious diversity can be managed in the future. Students in the fields of religious studies, sociology, anthropology and urban studies; practitioners involved in inter-religious debates; and church and other faith leaders and politicians should all find this book an invaluable addition to ongoing debates.

Published by
Ashgate Publishing Limited
Wey Court East
Union Road
Farnham
Surrey, GU9 7PT
England

Ashgate Publishing Company
110 Cherry Street
Suite 3-1
Burlington, VT 05401-3818
USA

www.ashgate.com

British Library Cataloguing in Publication Data
A catalogue record for this book is available from the British Library

The Library of Congress has cataloged the printed edition as follows:
Stringer, Martin D.
  Discourses on religious diversity : explorations in an urban ecology / by Martin D. Stringer.
      pages cm. -- (Ashgate AHRC/ESRC religion and society series)
  Includes bibliographical references and index.
  ISBN 978-1-4724-1174-7 -- ISBN 978-1-4724-1175-4 (pbk) -- ISBN 978-1-4724-1176-1 (ebook) -- ISBN 978-1-4724-1177-8 (epub) 1. Religious pluralism. 2. Cities and towns--Religious aspects. 3. Cultural pluralism--Religious aspects. I. Title.
  BL85.S75 2013
  201'.5--dc23

                                                                                          2013000813

ISBN 9781472411747 (hbk)
ISBN 9781472411754 (pbk)
ISBN 9781472411761 (ebk – PDF)
ISBN 9781472411778 (ebk – ePUB)

Printed and bound in Great Britain by
TJ International Ltd, Padstow, Cornwall.

Contents

List of Tables

Acknowledgements

In the mid 1990s a group of colleagues from the Department of Theology and Religion in Birmingham was invited to engage in an exchange of ideas and people with colleagues in the Department of Religious Studies in DePaul University in Chicago. It was during these discussions that I first met Lowell Livezey who, at that time, was a member of the faculty at the University of Illinois, Chicago, and was head of the Religion in Urban America Project. I was fascinated by the project which aimed to provide a detailed ethnographic study of religion and public life in a wide range of neighbourhoods across the city. I desperately wanted to replicate this study in Birmingham although it was clear that there were no funders at that time who would have provided the kind of sums necessary for the multi-site work undertaken in Chicago. As an alternative I encouraged a number of potential PhD students to come and join me in Birmingham, each engaged in their own detailed, local ethnographic studies. I gave the overall title of the Worship in Birmingham Project to this work, reflecting my own interest at the time in liturgical study as well as congregational and neighbourhood studies. In hindsight that was probably something of a misnomer as the work that was undertaken on worship tended to be outside of Birmingham and the work within Birmingham tended to be on other issues. I was, however, able to attract just over 20 MPhil and PhD students to the project over 10 years and these students have produced an interesting and detailed body of ethnographic work on religion in a range of communities, both in Birmingham and beyond.

In the meantime I continued my collaboration with Lowell and we began to explore, with the support of Grace Davie and others, the possibility of developing a detailed comparative study of religion in 10 global cities under the title of Religion and Urban Modernities. To this end Lowell, Grace and I arranged a series of streams at international sociology of religion conferences on the theme of religion and the urban ecology. Through this process we developed a network of colleagues around the world with very similar interests and came close to submitting a grant application for a major global study. Unfortunately Lowell became very ill in 2010 and died at the end of the year. This was a great personal tragedy for many friends and colleagues and a significant loss for the discipline. This book emerged out of that process and many of the chapters were first presented as papers within the various streams that we organised. I am very grateful for all the support and encouragement that Lowell offered to the project and to me personally over this time. I miss his wisdom and insight on these issues and have dedicated this work to his memory as the book clearly would not have existed without him.

As each chapter emerged within a conference or seminar series I am also grateful to the many other scholars who have engaged me in conversation and responded both positively and critically to the work over the years:

- A preliminary draft of Chapter 1 was presented to the Urban Theology Forum at the University of Birmingham in November 2007.
- Chapter 2 is based on a paper that I gave at the 19th Congress of the International Association for the History of Religion in Tokyo in April 2005.
- The ideas behind Chapter 3 were first presented at a conference of the International Society for the Sociology of Religion in Zagreb, July 2005.
- The outline of Chapter 5 was presented as a paper at the 19th Nordic Conference in Sociology of Religion held in Turku, Finland, in August 2008
- Chapter 6 was presented as part of the Religion and Cities strand of the American Academy of Religion in San Diego, November 2007.
- The ideas behind Chapter 7 were presented as part of a paper at a conference of Research Committee for the Sociology of Religion, from the International Sociological Association mid-term Conference in January 2007 in Manila.
- A section from the draft of the final Chapter was presented at an International Conference on 'From Religious Diversity to Religious Pluralism' in the University of Padua, February 2012.

I would also like to offer my thanks the people of Birmingham, and especially of Highgate and Handsworth, who, entirely unknowingly, have contributed so much to this work through the fieldwork that I have undertaken to bring the ideas together and to test the various hunches and ideas that have been developed in the various papers outlined above.

Finally I am very grateful for all the support that Sarah Lloyd and her colleagues at Ashgate Publishing have offered, the very professional service that all those involved in the publication of this book have provided, to Linda Woodhead and Rebecca Catto as editors of the series within which this book has been published, and to David, as ever for all his support and encouragement.

Chapter 1
Religion and Urban Theory

A couple of years ago I had some work done by a local plumber. He did his job and then, as he was leaving, we got to chatting. He asked me what I did for a living and I told him that I taught at Birmingham University. 'What do you teach?' he asked. I replied 'Religion', one of many alternatives I can use, but probably the most general and the most widely understood. 'Oh', he said, 'I was at the house of a Muslim the other day, nice chap, had a large picture of a man with a turban just inside his front door'.

I get all kinds of responses when I tell people what I do. Religion is one of those subjects that people feel that they ought to have some kind of opinion about. This response, however, was unusual and led, somewhat indirectly to the writing of this book. What I have been interested in was the way in which ordinary people of the city, particularly of Birmingham, Britain's second city, understand, react to, and talk about the religious diversity around them. This plumber personalised his sense of religious diversity through his account of an encounter with a Sikh client (the merging of Sikhs and Muslims in the popular imagination became very clear following 9/11 when turban-wearing Sikhs suffered more persecution because of their visibility than most of the Muslim population). Others respond with different kinds of comments, different images and assumptions that are held within society and different models of diversity. What follows, therefore, and what is essential to this book, is an analysis of the way in which ordinary individuals begin to manage their responses to religious diversity, and in some sense actually begin to manage that diversity, through their different responses.

Much of the discussion about religious diversity, or interreligious relations in the academic literature, tends to begin either from the perspective of philosophy/ theology, or from an understanding of religions as distinct and definable social groupings within society. So, for example, there is considerable theological and philosophical material debating the finer points of whether it is possible to engage creatively between the religions at all (see e.g. Hedges 2010, Cheetham 2011). Or, more usually, whether it is possible to hold a position that acknowledges any truth in one religion while holding firmly to the truth of another, and so on (Cornille 2008). This is not a debate that I wish to enter into.

From a more sociological, and increasingly from a political science-based perspective, the debate about religious diversity has assumed that there are things called 'religions' out there that are interacting, and that that interaction needs to be either studied or managed. When we explore in more detail what these 'things' called religions actually are, then in most cases the assumption being made is that a 'religion' is primarily a group of people, more or less organised, who share a common belief system and who engage in a common set of rituals. It is also assumed that these people see their 'religion' as a central element of their own identity and so can define themselves relatively unproblematically as 'Christian', 'Buddhist', 'Muslim' or whatever. Some writers, such as Gerd Baumann (1996), have questioned this basic assumption, and talk of 'discourses' rather than social groupings, but the ultimate effect is actually very much the same. Almost all authors working in this field assume that 'religions' are a social fact and that the real question is 'how do they, or how should they, interact?'

I want to question this assumption and I want to do this by starting somewhere very different. I do not wish to address the question of 'what is a religion', or even to begin with any assumptions about what a religion is. I covered those kinds of questions in a previous book looking at the role of specifically religious discourses within contemporary Britain (2004). Rather, I want to begin by listening to the people who live within the city and to hear how they are talking about religion, religions, and religious diversity and to identify the kind of assumptions that they are making within their conversations. More significantly, however, I want to ask where these assumptions may have come from and how they interact with the changing reality of the city itself.

For some years now I have been working within a number of different communities in the inner-urban areas of Birmingham, and before that I worked very closely with similar communities in Manchester. I also have a number of research students who have worked in different inner-urban communities and been involved in detailed ethnographic work in these areas. I therefore began this project with a great deal of circumstantial data. I did not, however, have the kind of detailed data on religion and religious diversity that I would have liked to collect to answer the kind of questions I was interested in. I therefore explored a number of different kinds of approach and different potential frameworks to see what makes most sense of the data that I had already collected and what further data could be collected to address the specific issues of religious diversity.

I want to develop the specifically methodological issues surrounding this study in Chapter 2 when I begin to talk about the kind of data that I collected and the different ways in which it could be approached. In this chapter, therefore, I want to stand back somewhat from the more specific issue of religious diversity, and the language used to express that diversity, to explore the range of theoretical frameworks within which the study of religion and the city have been understood in the past and so, as it were, to set my own study within this wider theoretical context.

Mapping Urban Theory

Urban theory can cover so much, from so many different disciplines including anthropology, sociology, political science, and urban geography among others. I am not going to be exhaustive in my survey of how religion interacts with urban theory; rather I am going to attempt to map the field to provide a sense of the range of theoretical frameworks available. In doing this I will aim to explore the various theories under consideration through a grid. On the vertical axis I wish to see a continuum from 'top down' to 'bottom up' reflecting the stance of the theory in relation to the population of the city. On the horizontal axis I will suggest a similar continuum from 'macro' to 'micro' representing the scope of the theoretical framework. Both of these axes should be seen as continua, but for the purposes of this discussion I want to suggest that this grid can provide four categories which can then be used to look more closely at the theories themselves. These categories are top down–macro, top down–micro, bottom up–macro, bottom up–micro. I will look at each of these in turn and explore the kind of theoretical frame and wider assumptions that are present in the work of the authors placed in each category. I will then look at how these authors, or others working within the same frame, have engaged with religion within their theories. In order to simplify the discussion I will provide only two or three examples of the kind of theories that are present in each quadrant of the grid.

Top Down–Macro

Any top down–macro study will be seen primarily as a classic bird's-eye view of the city. In other words all those writers who begin with the geographical positioning of the city and its overall shape and structure would belong to this category. Much of the work that deals with the history of the city or the city as an idea (whether real or fictional) can also be fitted into this quadrant, which probably reflects the vast majority of theoretical writing on the city itself. For the purposes of this discussion I am going to look at two kinds of theory. The first deals with the concept of 'morphology' and looks at the role religion plays in the mapping of the city and its development over time. The second will focus much more on governance and questions about the role of religion as a category in the political economy of the city. These are both issues that, in one way or another, will be picked up in the following chapters, but it is perhaps the governance issue that I will focus on most clearly and I will come back to this in Chapter 8.

The classic work on the working class by Friedrich Engels (1987 originally published 1844) clearly opens this kind of analysis. Based in Manchester, Engels notes the way the emerging industrial city has developed with an inner commercial core, a band of worker's slums surrounding it 'stretching like a girdle, averaging a mile and a half in breadth' and beyond that a buffer of lower middle class before the 'remote villas with gardens' of the upper middle class in 'wholesome country air' (1987, 86). What struck Engels in particular was that 'the members of this money aristocracy can take the shortest road through the middle of all the labouring districts to their places of business, without ever seeing that they are in the midst of the grimy misery that lurks to the right and the left' (1987, 86). Of course Engels goes beyond a simple mapping exercise to outline the economic and power relationships built into this model, but it is clearly the city as a whole that is his concern.

This essentially morphological approach to the city, seeing it in terms of concentric rings, was picked up 80 years later by the Chicago School of sociology writing in the 1920s and 1930s. The Chicago School developed analyses that fit into both the top down–macro and the bottom up–micro quadrants of the grid. In an early paper, outlining his vision for the study of Chicago, the founder of the school, Robert Park, laid out an agenda that included both broad city wide approaches and specific neighbourhood studies (1952, 13–51, originally published in 1916). When looking at the city-wide context, Park's concern was both with the movement of people within the city over time and with what he calls the 'moral order' of the city. The movement of people can be seen both in the gradual movement of whole populations from inner-urban areas outwards as their economic base improves, but also in the movement of individuals, which can run counter to the movement of populations; 'as individuals rise or sink in the struggle for status in the community they invariably move from one region to another; go up to the Gold Coast, or down to the slum, or perhaps occupy a tolerable position somewhere between the two' (1952, 80).

Drawing on Darwinian ideas, advances in animal and plant ecology, and the work of Spencer on the 'super-organism', the image that Park chose to describe his investigation of the city was that of an 'urban ecology' (1952, 118, 146). This leads to the idea that the forces for growth, and the rules governing that growth, are in some ways independent of the individuals and populations involved: 'it is rather a product of natural forces, extending its own boundaries more or less independently of the limits imposed upon it for political or administrative purposes' (1952, 167). McKenzie and Burgess built on Park's basic ideas to develop the classic 'bulls eye' model of the city with concentric rings through which the different populations moved over the course of time as part of this organic process of growth (McKenzie 1933, 173–8, Park 1952, 171, 194, Burgess 1967, 51).

In terms of religion, or religious diversity, then the best this kind of analysis can achieve is to note some kind of connection between certain ethnic groups and specific religions, such as that between the Irish or the Italians and Catholicism or the Germans and Lutheranism, and then to use the movement or mixing of the ethnic populations as a proxy for the movement of religious communities. This is something that Lowell Livezey and his colleagues do to a certain extent in the Religion and Urban America Project at the end of the last century (Livezey 2000a). This project is rooted in the Chicago tradition of sociological analysis, although it recognises how far the methodological questions have developed and is able to build on these developments to provide a more nuanced account than is seen in Park, McKenzie and Burgess. The project also recognises that the nature of religion, and the place of religion in American society as a whole, has also developed in the second half of the twentieth century, what Robert Wuthnow describes as the 'restructuring of American religion' (1998). Livezey relates this religious restructuring to a corresponding restructuring of the urban context and a refocusing of the moral culture (2000a, 3–23). The question of religious diversity, however, only really comes to the fore in relation to the city as a whole and when that whole is viewed from a bird's-eye perspective.

Writers in the mid twentieth century provided a wide range of critiques of the Chicago school and its ecological model. Perhaps the most substantial begins by saying that the ecological language of the model takes no account of the forces, political and economic, and more specifically the people, the political leaders, business leaders and city managers, that were needed to make the model work (Thorns 2002, 28–30). The organic growth of the city, these critiques suggest, does not happen of its own accord; it is managed by the city authorities and is the result of many different decisions, most of which are political and economic. David Thorns identifies the 'managerial approach' as the first major critique of the Chicago School in chronological terms and identifies this specifically with the work of John Rex and Robert Moore who investigated ethnicity and housing in an inner urban area of Birmingham in the 1960s (Rex and Moore 1967). Rex and Moore, however, focussed almost entirely on local, or middle, managers and so probably should fit within a micro quadrant of my model. It was the Marxist inspired work of political theorists in the 1970s, therefore, that began to offer a more serious alternative to the Chicago School at the macro level with their analysis of the political economy of cities as a whole (Castells 1977, Harvey 1973).

The analysis of the city through the lens of political economy focuses on the way in which political and economic decisions affect the growth and development of the city. In this view all economic decisions are political in that they are made to forward a political, and often a class, agenda. It is the political elite, those Engels refers to as the 'Big-Wigs', who have control of this system, and the same elite are also in control of the means of production, as well as the process of consumption, within the capitalist economy (Harvey 1973, 130–36). The decisions, therefore, are not neutral, or organic as Park suggested, they serve a particular ruling sector of society. An interesting recent example of this kind of approach comes from the work of Dolores Hayden looking at the development of suburbs at the outer edges of US cities (2006). Here the conventional narrative has always been one of 'private enterprise' and 'market forces' such that people were said to want to leave the cities and move to areas which were more open and with more land. The developers, therefore, built large uniform suburbs in places like Levittown on Long Island, because that is what the market demanded. What Hayden demonstrates is that this is far from the truth. In the 1930s the Roosevelt administration chose to subsidise, through tax breaks and beneficial land deals, the building of large cheap estates on the outer edges of cities (often without the infrastructure of roads and sewerage etc. to support them) and because of a lack of viable alternatives in the inner urban areas individual families were forced to buy properties and move out to these edge of city estates, at which point the political authorities were forced in turn to provide the infrastructure, providing yet another form of subsidy to the developers. This kind of pattern can be reproduced across the world where politicians and developers work round local legal systems to provide profit for themselves.

More recently the work of Saskia Sassen and others on 'global cities' builds on both the Chicago School and the political economy theorists to look at how global capitalism has led to a specific form of the urban experience (Sassen 1991). While Sassen does deal in passing with questions of migration, immigration and ethnicity within the cities she is focussing on (1991, 299–317) there is no direct reference to religion. The point she does make, however, is to note the way in which London, New York and Tokyo (the only three cities at the time she was writing that met her criteria of 'global cities'), despite having very different histories, governance structures, economies and cultures, have all responded in parallel ways in terms of economic base, spatial organisation and social structure to the global economic and political forces of the last 30 years (1991, 4). This suggests that much of what I am proposing within this text may be equally true for many other cities across the world, although that would, of course, have to be tested empirically.

We could perhaps compare Sassen's work, at least in its global vision, with that of Hugh McLeod, who looked at the role of religion within the development of London, Berlin and New York in the second half of the nineteenth century (1996). McLeod does see commonalities between these three cities, but also identifies a number of significant differences. He situates them at different stages in relation to the alienation of the working class from religion. At the turn of the twentieth century New York represented the first stage, the loosening of ties with the church, London represented the second stage, the decline in attendance at regular church services, and Berlin represented the third, the 'widespread repudiation even of the Christian rites of passage' (1996, 207). This should at least warn us that globalization is not a recent phenomena and also that there are numerous texts available on the historical place of religion within the city. Most of these historical accounts, however, as with that of McLeod, tend to focus on one religion, most normally Christianity, as the level of religious diversity found in a city such as Birmingham today is a very recent phenomena, a product in part of the processes of migration and immigration that Sassen discusses.

Top Down–Micro

With the top down–micro quadrant we move onto what has been referred to as 'city cultures' (Miles, Hall and Borden 2004). The top down element means that we are still concerned with work that treats the city in a holistic fashion, theorising about the city as a unit, or perhaps even more specifically in this context, as an ecology, although picking up a different understanding of 'ecology' from that which is usually associated with Park's work. One element of Park's ecology was associated with Darwinism and the idea of the city as an organism. Another built on the idea of the particular locality, and the idea of a specific ecology for a particular riverbank or hedgerow for example (1952, 146, McKenzie 1967). From the top down–micro perspective, therefore, I am thinking of ecology in the sense of an environment, the range of organisms living within a specific niche that interact and co-exist to form a single unit. The micro, however, also focuses our attention on the individual or the smaller social groups within the city and the way in which these are affected by the possibility of a wider urban ecology.

In focussing on the top down–micro quadrant I want to look first at those theories that see the urban context as alienating in some way, as separating the individual off from the wider community. The classic work in this area is Louis Wirth's essay 'Urbanism as a Way of Life' (1938) although many modern theorists prefer to look back beyond this to Georg Simmel's work that covers a very similar area but with much more depth and sophistication (1950, originally published 1903). This kind of approach has underpinned much of the debate throughout the twentieth century on secularisation, and the role of 'urbanisation' within this process, and I will touch on some of this literature below. The second set of theories I wish to pick up are those related to religion in the public sphere, built on ideas of civic society and the work of Jürgen Habermas (1991) among others. This has been developed in a number of different ways by those specifically concerned with the role of religion in civic society and will provide a strong theme within the rest of this book.

Both Wirth and Simmel were interested in the effect of urbanisation on the individual. Simmel was concerned primarily with what he conceived of as the psychological impact of the city, or metropolis, on individual citizens (1950, 409–10). This impact can be seen in a number of often contradictory, or even conflicting, ways. Simmel picks up, for example, the way in which the increased pace of life within the city leads to a more intellectual, even objective approach to others rather than one based on emotion and subjectivity (1950, 410). On the other hand the metropolis also enabled a certain level of freedom for the individual to develop their own personality and to reconstruct themselves (1950, 413–14). In both cases it is individualism that is at the core of the impact of the city, and it is this increasing focus on the individual, either negatively or positively, that is identified as the essential experience of the metropolis. For Simmel it is also important to note the role of money both in the development of the different understandings of individualisation and in the sustaining of those states within the metropolis (1950, 411, 1990, originally published 1907).

Wirth develops a very similar argument, building on Simmel's own work alongside that of Weber, Durkheim and other late-nineteenth-century scholars (1938). He begins by following a Weberian methodology and proposing two ideal types that represent rural and urban contexts (1938, 3). The rural is focussed on community and tradition while the urban, following Simmel, focuses on the individual. The drivers for the focus on the individual are not quite the same for Wirth as they are for Simmel, with more emphasis being placed on the size and density of the city rather than the pace of life and nature of human interactions as such. However, it is still the individualisation of the urban ecology that Wirth wants to highlight in opposition to the communal nature of rural life. The other difference between Wirth and Simmel is that Wirth does not emphasise the positive elements of 'freedom' to anything like the same extent and he sees the negative as all pervasive. Building on ideas of size and density he draws on

Durkheim to emphasise the division of labour, individual isolation, and *anomie* and it is this that Wirth identifies as the primary experience of the city (1938, 13). Individualisation, therefore, leads to isolation and to alienation and this, in turn, leads to many of the social ills that are associated with city life. With both Wirth and Simmel, therefore, the picture that was developed was of the isolated individual, largely alienated from those around them and existing in something of a social vacuum.

Sitting behind both Simmel and Wirth, in their different ways, are the distinction that Ferdinand Tönnies develops between *gemeinschaft* and *gesellschaft* (Tönnies 2001, originally published 1887). These German terms became central to twentieth-century sociology and underpin the distinction that Wirth, for example, makes between the urban and the rural. *Gemeinschaft*, or community, is seen by Tönnies to be the historic state of human society, focussing on small villages, low role differentiation, dense networks and strong familial ties (2001, 22–51). It is arguable that this ideal, almost romanticised view of the small community, the rural village or 'folk society' to use Wirth's term (1938, 3), is the 'other' against which the understanding of the city was developed. If the rural community epitomises *gemeinschaft* then the city must represent *gesellschaft*, the state of isolation and alienation that Tönnies, like Simmel and Wirth, argued was growing in modern, industrial or urban societies. The 'culture' of the city, therefore, must reflect this *gesellschaft* and it is this that Simmel and Wirth claim to be the essential experience of urban ecologies. A number of recent commentators on the 'postmodern' condition (Bauman 2001, Beck and Beck-Gernsheim 2002) have also picked up a similar set of dichotomies, although as Beck and Beck-Gersheim say 'the main difference is that today people are not discharged from corporate religious-cosmological certainties into the world of industrial society, but are transplanted from the national industrial societies of the first modernity into the transnational turmoil of world-risk society' (Beck and Beck-Gersheim 2002, 26). Once again this is related to economic factors, with more focus on consumerism than is present in Wirth, or even perhaps in Simmel, and once again with an ambiguity between the positive features associated with 'freedom' and the negative elements associated with 'alienation' or 'isolation'.

All these theories imply that there is something about the urban context, be it size, pace of life, complexity, industrialisation or whatever that leads to what might be called an 'urban culture', a particular mode of being that highlights the individual apart from community. Manuel Castells, among others, argues that the empirical evidence does not suggest such a clear deterministic link and so suggests that the idea of 'urban culture' is itself a myth. If something others define as 'urban culture', with its emphasis on the individual and alienation, does exist then, Castells suggests, it is probably representative of capitalist society as a whole and not just the city (1977, 75–85). This would, in fact, be fully supported by Simmel's argument that it is the role of money within the urban context that leads to the development of individualisation. Castells' criticism, however, suggests only one approach to the idea of urban, or city, culture, that focuses on the idea of 'culture' in the singular. Many authors wish, rather, to talk of 'city cultures' in the plural, either suggesting a range of different cultures, whether defined geographically or by ethnicity, class or some other element, or, to follow Sharon Zukin, to suggest a critical dialogue between the ideas of the 'urban' and of 'cultures' as understood in a range of different discourses (as art, as creative communities, as space, as particular activities such as shopping or eating in a restaurant, etc.) (1995).

The theories of Simmel and Wirth, and those of Marx and Weber on which they were based in different ways, formed one of the mainstays of the classic theories of secularisation in the middle of the twentieth century (Aldridge 2000, 56–86). With urbanisation came alienation and with alienation came a drift away from religion, or so the theory went. The accepted outcome of urbanisation and the growth of cities therefore, should have been a decline in religion and hence of religious diversity. For many decades the English and Scottish evidence appeared to support this theory. However, in recent years, and through the work of Callum Brown and others on religion in Victorian cities, we have seen that the alienation associated with the first contact with the urban environment often led to an increase in religious attendance as it was the churches, and later with the arrival of immigrants of other religious persuasions, the mosques and the temples, that provided the focus for community among the first generation of urban dwellers (Brown 2001, 145–9). Brown argues that our perception that religion declined in cities, to be replaced by corruption and moral pollution comes ultimately from the work of Thomas Chalmers in the 1840s who railed against the working people in towns of his own day with only limited evidence (2001, 18–30). Underlying this discourse, and the evangelical discourse of 'darkest London' that followed for much of the next century, was, according to Brown, a romantic nostalgia for the rural ideal rather than any specific evidence from the cities themselves. This romantic nostalgia can also be seen in the work of Simmel and Wirth but it is arguable that some kind of evidence does exist to support a very similar theory emerging in very different contexts (see McLeod 1996). Urbanisation and the growth or decline of religion, at a macro level, therefore, continue to be keen debating points, but theories of urban alienation and their role in religious attendance have ceased to hold a strong place within the sociology of religions.

The second area I wish to look at under this quadrant comes from a slightly different direction and picks up some of the work that has been undertaken on the idea of the 'public sphere' and more specifically on the role of religion within civic society. This kind of analysis traces its roots back to the classic texts by Alexis de Tocqueville on *Democracy in America* published in two volumes in 1835 and 1840 (2003) and Max Weber on *The Protestant Ethic and the Spirit of Capitalism* (2001, originally published 1904). From there the most common reference is to the work of Jürgen Habermas who traced the development of what he calls 'the bourgeois public sphere' from the enlightenment through to contemporary public opinion and democratic processes, although he plays down the possible place of religion within this public sphere (1991). Much of this discussion is not specifically focussed on the city. As with Castells' critique of 'urban culture', the 'public sphere' is generally considered to be a product of modernity and of capitalism more generally. However, as with Simmel's and Wirth's understanding of individual alienation, the public sphere is generally accepted to be present primarily within the urban context and in many discussions of the idea the city is implied if not stated explicitly.

José Casanova's work on *Public Religions in the Modern World* develops directly out of this kind of analysis, although Casanova is keen to distance himself from Habermas and to some extent to provide an alternative view that recognises the role of religion within the public sphere (1994). For Casanova the primary concept is 'deprivitisation' and he offers a number of case studies from Europe and America to illustrate his position. Casanova was writing before the real emergence of political Islam and opens his book with an analysis of religion in the 1980s (1994, 3–6). More recent contributions to the debate recognise the rise of Islam within the public sphere in a number of different ways and take the argument away from a purely Christian, or even Western, context. David Herbert, for example challenges the idea of the 'cross-cultural legitimization of liberal ideas such as civil society, the public sphere and human rights' and uses the model of intercultural communication derived from the work of Alisdair MacIntyre (1985) to 'articulate between recent developments in liberal thinking on cultural diversity and Muslim responses to liberal ideas and institutions' (2003, 153). I will return to some of these ideas in my final Chapter.

Bringing the ideas of this quadrant together, James Donald opens a discussion of urban ethics with a review of the work of one of the founders of Cultural Studies, Raymond Williams. In this analysis he shows that Williams, like Park and Redfield, maintained an ideal understanding of community (*gemeinschaft*) based on a romantic rural model, although in Williams' case this is his home village in the Black Mountains of Wales (1999, 147–52). Donald moves on from this to discuss the concepts of community, consensus and toleration with reference to various communitarian theorists and the idea of the public square. The public square in this argument is both a physical reality, a space 'surrounded by a mix of public and private buildings: government offices, museums, lecture and concert hall, churches, shops, cafes, residences' (Walzer 1995, 323), and a conceptual tool based on the idea of the agora in the ancient Greek polis and therefore the sense of the public sphere as discussed by Habermas and others (Donald 1999, 167). For Donald the public square is the space of community, the place where ethics and politics are both played out, the essential space of the city. It is, arguably, within this kind of 'public square' (both physical and conceptual) that I have generated the data that forms the basis for this text and I will return to these discussions in subsequent chapters.

Bottom Up–Macro

If we now turn to what the city might look like from the bottom up we get a very different series of theories. First I want to discuss theories that I am describing as bottom up–macro. These are theories that take the view point of the ordinary citizen but in some way try to capture the whole city experience. There are two sets of theories that I wish to focus on specifically. The first relates to theories of conflict and difference, theories that highlight differences of race, ethnicity, gender or wealth. Many of these focus on the experience of the poor and oppressed and look at the nature of oppression in some way. The second picks up the concept of flow, and look more specifically at the way in which people move around the city. While there are many studies of urban religion that focus on issues of difference and boundaries much less has been written about flow and interactions between communities. It is probably the latter, however, that will have most resonance with the ideas of this book.

In an important text David Sibley explores what he defines as 'geographies of exclusion', that is the ways in which our use and understanding of space explicitly and implicitly excludes certain members of society (1995). This inevitably focuses on borders of one kind or another and is closely related to Anthony Cohen's anthropological work on the symbolic construction of community where the deployment of symbols relating to borders also leads to exclusion (Cohen 1985). However, Sibley is keen to note that the boarders he is interested in can be both physical and conceptual. There is also a great deal of subversion of these borders, or leakage between things kept either side of the boarders, leading to what Mary Douglas defines as 'pollution' that is 'things out of place' (Douglas 1966). This is an interesting analysis and one that I will be relating to some discussions of religion, especially in Chapter 4. In the second half of his book, however, Sibley shows how the work of the Chicago School itself almost completely excluded the voices of ethnic minority and women scholars (1995, 115–86, DuBois 1996, original published 1899, Sandercock 1998). Other writers and theories were also exclusionary in their own way although there have been a number of significant attempts to redress this balance in the last quarter of the twentieth century.

One example of a scholar who challenges exclusion in both of Sibley's senses is Leonie Sandercock, an urban planner from Australia who has worked in Vancouver in Canada and Birmingham in the UK among other places (1998, 2003). Sandercock's practical experience and academic study have led her to become disillusioned with the history and practice of urban planning. Part of her aim is to rewrite the history, focussing much more on the roles of women, on the partnerships between planners and communities, and on the radical features of many contemporary planning practices. However, it is her re-envisioning of the city as what she calls a 'mongrel city' or 'cosmopolis' that provides her major contribution to the field of urban studies (1998, 2003). Sandercock's primary focus is on 'difference'. The contemporary city, through processes of migration, diversification and the recognition of many internally marginalised communities, has become a space of difference. That difference can lead to fear – in Sandercock's analysis, it is important to recognise and analyse that fear. However, it is through working together and confronting the fear in new co-operative planning processes, involving the local people, city authorities and professionals as equal parties, that, in Sandercock's view, the future of the city can be developed (2003). Sandercock has little specifically to say about religion. However, she is absolutely committed to radical practice and it is her vision of the city as a place of difference, where many diverse peoples can meet, mingle and interact that leads to some of her most important insights. It is these, and the focus on the specific, the local and the other, that will inform much of the discussion within this text.

Chris Baker's work from Manchester also picks up the same range of ideas, although from a much more specifically theological point of view (2009). He develops Homi Bhabha's idea of hybridity (1994) and draws on the work of Sandercock and others to talk of the 'third space' within the city and within the church. Baker has a strong emphasis on praxis and particularly the way churches and other religious bodies can engage with hybridity in order to align themselves with the marginal and the excluded. He presents a number of examples of this from both Manchester, where he is based, and the US, including the classic context of Chicago. He also engages with the work of Peter Ward (2002), John Reader (2005) and others to explore what a 'third space church', a church suited to the hybrid city, might look like (2009, 111–36). Despite beginning his book with an account of the bombings in London in July 2005 and the concerns that he believes this raises for the place of Muslims in the UK (2009, 1–2), and despite a constant focus on the 'other' throughout the text, there is little or no recognition that this 'other' may be of a different faith, no account of how different faith groups may work together within the third space, and no sense that other faith positions may provide a challenge to his theology. This absence of other faiths is equally true for Ward and Reader and many others attempting to engage critically and radically with the contemporary urban scene within the Christian churches (although Owain Bell (2009) does provide an interesting comment on relations with Bangladeshi Muslims in Kidderminster in a book edited by Baker and Reader).

The second set of theories I wish to explore within this quadrant can all be linked through the idea of 'flow'. The idea of flow came into the sociological imagination most explicitly through the work of Zygmunt Bauman in his work on *Liquid Modernity* (2000). Using the image of the World Wide Web, Castells began to re-envision the global economic context in terms of nodes and flows, seeing the focus of the economy in the production of knowledge rather than the production of goods (1996). Building on Bauman's and Castells' work the idea of 'flow' has been used in many different ways within urban studies. At the widest level we have the flow of people between cities and between rural and urban contexts as suggested in the work of Park and Redfield within the Chicago School and later by theorists such as Sassen with her emphasis on the role of migration and immigration to all major global cities (1991, 299–317). This is exemplified, with specific reference to religion, in the work of Thomas Tweed, although he draws more on the hydraulic tropes of Deleuze and Guattari rather than the liquid metaphors of Baumann or the network imagery of Castells (2006, 59, Deleuze and Guattari 1987). However, there are other kinds of flow, within the city and even over relatively short periods of time, that have been captured by other theorists although not yet fully applied to religion.

An interesting perspective on the idea of flow is picked up through a study of Manchester and Sheffield undertaken in the 1990s (Taylor, Evans and Fraser 1996). This work used focus groups to identify categories of people who used the city and the different perspectives of the city that they developed. The first two groups identified by the study were commuters and shoppers and the different trajectories that these populations traced led to different perspectives on the city (1996, 91–160). Later study focussed on categories of people who were more or less absent from the wider surveys and looked at the trajectories through the city taken by ethnic minorities, women, older people and the youth of the city. Each group were seen to have a different understanding of the city as a whole because of the places they visited, the places where they felt safe and places that were perceived as no-go areas. This whole analysis builds up into a very complex and multi-layered understanding of the city as a whole when seen through the eyes of the many people who travel through it each and every day. I will pick this up again on a number of occasions through this text as the issue of movement through space and the methodologies developed by Taylor and his colleagues have been very influential in this study.

Many of the arguments in this quadrant are focussed on the idea of public space and as such relate back to the debates about the 'public sphere' that were raised in the previous section. The focus of these studies, however, is much more on the idea of physical space. The city is made up of many different kinds of spaces, the vast majority of which exist in private, whether individual houses, corporate spaces or spaces that are public, in the sense of being owned by the city or national authorities, but from which many people are excluded, or need to have a specific reason to enter (Low and Smith 2006). There are also public spaces, spaces that any member of the public feels that they have a right to access. These could be roads and pavements, open squares, or perhaps even privately owned spaces such as shopping malls that people assume are public. The divide between public and private spaces is always ambiguous and contested and it is not easy to recognise in all cases where one kind of space ends and the other starts. Mitchell and Staeheli even talk of 'pseudo public space' and 'pseudo private property' to capture the way the public and the private intermingle within specific city spaces (2006, 152–3). It has often been argued that in recent years space has become increasingly privatised, both in the sense of private ownership (with malls replacing high streets) and in the sense of physical exclusion from what might in the past be considered as public space (roads in gated communities for example) (Low and Smith 2006, 3–5). The idea of exclusion is, of course, central to these discussions and links back to the ideas of Sibley and Sandercock. Who is allowed to use the public space and who is excluded (and how) are central questions. The idea of flow is also embedded in discussions of public space as it is within the public space that the flow often takes place, rather than through the exclusionary private spaces.

From the perspective of this book the concept of public space is also important as all the conversations and narratives that form the basis for the evidence of this text have occurred within public spaces. This is obvious when I come to look at street festivals in chapters 5 and 6, where the concept of the public space will be picked up again in more detail, but even when I am looking at communities like Highgate and Handsworth in Birmingham (in chapters 3 and 4) the information I am collecting has been heard and observed within public spaces, on the high street or in local parks. This means that the discourses that I am describing here are 'public discourses' in a very real sense. Again this is an issue that I will pick up in the discussion of methodology in Chapter 2 and in my conclusions in Chapter 8.

Bottom Up–Micro

The last quadrant is clearly where I would place much of the research that underpins this work. This is the arena of bottom up–micro studies, focussing on the specific experience of particular social groups and individual neighbourhoods within the city. Most of my previous work (Stringer 1999, 2008), and the work of my students, falls into this quadrant. All ethnographic work on the city, from the Chicago School onwards, also fits into this category in some shape or form. I will begin therefore by focussing on the range of ethnographic work on the city, including that which takes religion and religious communities as its primary subject. I will then conclude by looking at two texts that have had a significant impact on my own thinking for this book, and that clearly fit into the bottom up–micro quadrant, but that do not really fit into any other theoretical frame.

The earliest of the strictly ethnographic material probably comes from the Chicago School. This was set out in Park's original agenda for the study of the city with the comment that: 'in the course of time every section and quarter of the city takes on something of the character and qualities of its inhabitants. Each separate part of the city is inevitably stained with the peculiar sentiment of its population. The effect of this is to convert what was at first a mere geographical expression into a neighbourhood, that is to say, a locality with sentiments, traditions, and a history of its own' (1952, 17). Zorbaugh's *The Gold Coast and the Slum* was among the first text to aim at a specifically ethnographic study of the city (Zorbaugh 1929). There are interesting elements here, not least the close, almost symbiotic relationship between the two neighbourhoods despite their great differences in terms of socio-economic position, but little specifically on religion. In the introduction to his book on the work of the Religion in Urban America Project, Livezey provides an outline of the development of ethnographic studies within Chicago over the twentieth century (2000a, 15–18). These include Nels Anderson's *The Hobo* (1923), Louis Wirth's *The Ghetto* (1928), Gerald Suttles' *The Social Order of the Slum* (1968) and Alan Anderson and George Pickering's *Confronting the Color Line* (1986). These form a strong tradition into which Livezey places the work of his own Project. The vast majority of these studies, however, only touched on issues of religion in passing and, as the titles suggest, the primary focus is on poverty and ethnicity. Setha Low's summary of anthropological studies of the city, primarily in America, devotes only half a page to studies of religion out of 16 pages of examples, and all the examples she offers of 'the sacred city' are studies of Hindu and Muslim cities in India and the Middle East (1999, 20).

Within the UK the most well known examples of ethnography as applied to urban areas probably comes from the work of the Institute of Community Studies who wrote about *Family and Kinship in East London* (Young and Willmott 1957) and then followed the community out to Dagenham (Willmott 1963). The close knit nature of this community is important, and the way in which the construction of the working class follows the Chicago version of the ideal community and questions the idea of alienation within the city as presented by Wirth and Simmel. There are no significant references to religion in many of these studies, with rites of passage and tables of churchgoing statistics being the only religious activities that are discussed. One interesting, early and notable exception is Madeline Kerr's study of *Ship Street* in Liverpool (1958). The vast majority of the families who live on this street are Roman Catholics, but only the children appear to attend mass on a regular basis. For Kerr it is not the official religion that is of interest but rather the concepts of luck, fatalism, dreams, talismans and fear (1958, 129–37). As she says, 'it is to be expected that this group, coming from a poverty-stricken area, would be prolific in the production of superstition and this has proved to be the case' (1958, 129). We might not accept the prejudicial undertones of this statement, but it is clearly based on close ethnographic study of the community itself and also links in to the work of Sarah Williams in her historical study of Southwark (1999).

The number of specific studies of urban communities in the UK within anthropology- and ethnographically-based sociology are actually very few. As Frankenberg commented in the 1960s the tendency has always been to focus ethnographic studies on smaller, more rural and marginal communities (1965). Delamont notes that by the mid 1990s, across the whole of Europe, this situation had hardly changed (1995, 107). This is not surprising given the tradition and values of ethnographic study, especially as it has developed within anthropology. It is much more difficult to define a specific community or to gain a holistic understanding of that community within an urban context than it is within a small rural village. It is only in the last 20 years or so, therefore, that the practice of urban ethnography in Europe and America has really been developed and expanded (Rapport 2002).

Recognising that the ethnographic study of cities is in many ways totally different from the more traditional studies of small scale, relatively isolated, village communities, Delamont identifies three possible approaches to ethnography in the city. The focus could be on a specific neighbourhood, on a specific population or on an organisation such as a hospital or a factory for example (1995, 111). Of these, some studies of neighbourhoods have mentioned religion in passing as we have seen, but few have actually focussed on religion as their topic (but see the studies of neighbourhoods in Hull by Forster 1995, and Bristol by Jenkins 1999). Studies of religious institutions from an ethnographic perspective are few and far between and very rarely focussed on the city. It is studies of specific populations, therefore, that have generated the most material and these have tended to be studies of specific religious communities. The work of the Community Religions Project in Leeds provides a significant early British example of this, as does Pnina Werbner's study of Islamic groups in Manchester (2002). In recent years these kinds of studies have been growing significantly. There are also a number of examples of studies of different religious communities in the States (Warner and Wittner 1998). These are very interesting and relevant in terms of the role of religion within the city but seldom have any comments to make about the way in which that religion is understood outside the community that is being studied and less about the concept of religious diversity per se.

One very interesting study that in some ways combines the neighbourhood and the religious community approaches, while also trying to say something about religious diversity and attitudes towards religion is the work of Lowell Livezey and his colleagues in Chicago (2000a). I have already mentioned this book a couple of times in this introduction. Under top down–macro the focus was on the wider conclusions of the book, situating religion in the wider context of Chicago as a whole. The Religion in Urban American Project, however, is rooted in the ethnographic study of specific neighbourhoods and these individual studies clearly fit within the bottom up–micro quadrant of my scheme. A clear decision was made within the project to focus very specifically on congregations. This in part reflects an American approach to religion, but it also reflected the specific questions that Livezey and his colleagues wished to address around agency and involvement. The vast majority of the studies, however, are of Christian congregations and only serve to reinforce what Livezey refers to as the 'religiously based, ethnoracial enclaves' that exist throughout the city (2000a, 16). Religious diversity, therefore, is seen in most cases as Christian diversity, but more specifically as congregational diversity. Suttles noted the same principle in his study of a Chicago slum in the 1960s when he states that 'differences of faith alone seem relatively unimportant because they are seldom raised in conversation. Churches are another matter' (1968, 42).

Two papers within Livezey's book pick up the wider interreligious context and focus on issues of religious diversity. Both of these papers emphasise the religiously based, ethnoracial enclaves that Livezey highlights and stress that this is the primary form in which religious diversity is understood within American cities. Paul Numrich's paper focuses on a number of congregations (Hindu, Muslim and Sikh) of south Asian origin across the greater Chicago area (2000) while Livezey's own paper picks up the significant religious diversity present within one neighbourhood in the north of the city (2000b). I will come back to the latter paper when I discuss a similarly diverse neighbourhood in Birmingham in Chapter 4. Neither paper, however, really asks how those who do not belong to the congregations being studied understand religious diversity within the neighbourhood or the city as a whole.

Finally, in this section, therefore I need to make reference to a couple of ideas that become central to my own analysis. The first is derived largely from Gerd Baumann's work on Southall on the outskirts of London (1996). This work will take a central role within my argument throughout this text and I will be discussing it, and the theories that it contains, at a number of points throughout the book. For now I simply need to note that the work fits into the tradition of the ethnography of urban communities, as it is rooted in a detailed long-term study of the specific neighbourhood, and it raises the concept of discourse which is central to my own discussions. I will explore this in far more detail in Chapter 2. The other set of ideas develop around the concepts of memory and narrative. Mark Crinson and his colleagues at Salford University have developed an interesting approach to what he calls 'urban memory' that is also rooted in detailed studies of specific sites within Manchester and Salford that are being, or have been, redeveloped (2005). The approach used by Crinson is not ethnographic as such, but the focus on particular places and the people who use these spaces clearly fits within the bottom up micro section of my own grid. I will be exploring these ideas in much more detail in Chapter 7.

Outline of the Text

In some ways what follows is a series of specific examples of bottom up–micro studies rather than a carefully worked through argument, although I would expect the whole to come together to form a bottom up–macro understanding of the role of discourses on religious diversity within the city by the end of the book. The examples that I have chosen are guided by a set of principles that I outline more fully in Chapter 2 where I explain my methodology and suggest a loose classification of everyday discourses about religion and religious diversity. These focus on clothing, buildings, festivals and items in the news. The discourses on clothing and religion were, in my experience, fairly limited and relatively easy to express. I have not, therefore, explored these further within the book. Chapter 3, however, picks up the specific discussion of buildings and focuses on work that I have undertaken in the Highgate area of Birmingham, an area that is dominated by two towers; the minaret of the Central Mosque and the tower of the nineteenth century Anglican church of St Alban's. This will lead on to an exploration of the discourses in the area around religious buildings and space.

Chapter 4 moves on to my other specific field site, that of Handsworth in the north of the city. This is distinctive in Birmingham, and perhaps in many other cities, simply because of the very wide range of ethnic and religious groups that are present within the neighbourhood. The area is dominated visually by a relatively new Gudwara but the community itself is made up of what can be called a 'super diversity' of peoples (Vertovec 2007). Any bus trip down the Soho Road from one end of Handsworth to the other will involve the traveller in a whole range of different and exciting religious discourses or discourses on religion. This chapter, therefore, sets out to try and understand the way in which these discourses work when they are brought together in such close proximity with a specific focus on the concept of boundaries.

The next two Chapters, 5 and 6, shift the focus to the street festivals that have become a regular part of the cultural calendar of a city such as Birmingham. Chapter 5 will focus on the history and development of the festivals within Birmingham exploring the relationship between what Baumann (1996) would describe as the 'dominant discourse' of the City Council, and how this has changed over the years, and the 'demotic discourses' associated with those who attend the festivals as spectators. Chapter 6 will then focus on one specific festival, that of the Chinese New Year, beginning with my experience in London in 2007, but developing the various discourses surrounding the festival and asking what we can see as 'religious' within this range of concepts and ideas.

To end the book I want to widen the scope slightly and pick up two ideas that I have already touched on in this chapter, the idea of memory from the fourth quadrant, the bottom up–micro, and the idea of management from the first quadrant, the top down–macro. Both of these in their different ways also address the final area of discourse surrounding religion, that of items in the news. In Chapter 7 I will pick up theories of memory; individual, collective and Crinson's idea of 'urban memory' (Crinson 2005). These will allow me to try and link the various discourses I have been looking at throughout the book into a wider theoretical frame. Finally, therefore, Chapter 8 will focus on the management of religious diversity and ask what, if the position taken by this book is correct, should city leaders be doing. By focussing on English Defence League graffiti on an inner urban estate, the troubles surrounding a controversial play set in a Gudwara that caused small scale violent protests from elements of the Sikh community, and some of the consequences of the riots that rampaged through certain English cities, including Birmingham, as this book was being written, I will look at the possibility of the management of religious diversity throughout the city as a whole.

Chapter 2
Discourses of Diversity

If we want to explore the nature of everyday discourses on religious diversity within the city we are immediately struck by all kinds of methodological questions. Not only do we have to define what is meant by 'everyday discourses', we then have to identify where we might find these discourses and how we might record them in order to undertake the kind of analysis assumed by this book. This chapter, therefore, sets out to explore some of these methodological questions and begins to set out a basic classification of such discourses that forms the basis for the analysis in the subsequent chapters.

Looking at the Literature

There are two bodies of literature that could throw a possible light on this discussion and a brief look at both will indicate where my own approach differs. There is now a whole library of work dealing with the popular understandings of forms of classification within society, most notably and most relevant for this study, the literature on popular understandings of 'race' (Mason 2000, Millington 2011). Race, or ethnicity, and religion are clearly related in many people's minds, but the recent move away from ethnicity as the primary focus of the classification of immigrants within a country such as Britain, to the use of religious labels for such classification has shown that race or ethnicity may be too limited for our present purposes (Mason 2000). Questions of stereotyping and the wider colonial and post-colonial discourses have also become far more subtle and far more complex in recent years building on the work of Homi Bhabha among others (Bhabha 1994). For all the work on race and ethnicity that has been developed at a theoretical level over the last 50 years or so there has been very few serious follow ups to the kind of study of race in popular discourse undertaken by Ann Dummett in the early 1970s (1973). Having said that, many of the texts about the nature of racial and racist discourses, and about ethnic identities etc., can be a very useful starting point for a discussion about the popular understandings of religious diversity and I will come back to this below.

The second body of work relates more to questions of 'identity' than of classification. This includes the very wide range of ethnographic material that has been undertaken within British cities, and elsewhere, in an attempt to understand the ways in which specific religious communities express their own identities to the wider world (e.g. Werbner 2002). Some of this material has been discussed in the previous chapter and, following traditional ethnographic principles, tends to concentrate on the specific context of a particular community and to look at the question of identity from the perspective of that community. Very little of this material is interested in the way in which the community constructs the identity of other religious communities within the wider society, or with the way in which religious diversity per se is understood. What is more, it is those with a strong religious identity of their own who tend to be studied in this way, rather than those, who arguably make up the majority in British cities, who have little or no personal religious identity but maintain more or less clear views about other religions within society (but see Day 2011).

Two works that bring these two bodies of literature together within the context of Birmingham are the classic studies of race and racism in Handsworth and Sparkbrook, neighbourhoods to the north and south of the city centre respectively. John Rex and Robert More wrote their study of Sparkbrook, *Race Community and Conflict* in 1967 and Peter Ratcliffe wrote *Racism and Reaction, a Profile of Handsworth*, in 1981. Both of these are typical British 'community studies' (Frankenberg 1965), undertaken through a combination of survey work and participant observation. The authors were interested in the social structure of the neighbourhoods, local politics and the role of racism in the functioning of the different communities. Ratcliffe has a chapter on 'Images of Contemporary Handsworth' that deals with questions of racial harmony, racial prejudice and racial disharmony, and draws to some extent on popular discourses of race within the community (1981, 97–138). In Rex and Moore's book the question of discourses and identity tends to be implicit rather than explicit, although they do have a chapter on 'Religion in Sparkbrook' (1967, 173–90) an issue that is discussed in relation to 'identity' and 'community' in Ratcliffe's text (1981, 75–92).

Neither of these books, however, are really interested in the questions of discourse that began to interest scholars in the late 1980s and 1990s. One book that does pick this up, however, and which is central to my own understandings of this issue, is Gerd Baumann's study of the London suburb of Southall in *Contesting Culture* (1996). Baumann is explicitly interested in discourse (and it is his definitions of discourse that I will be following in this text). He was also interested in the whole neighbourhood and not just one particular religious or ethnic group within that neighbourhood. *Contesting Culture* deals primarily with the way in which the different social groups in Southall deal with the concepts of 'community' and 'culture'. Baumann distinguishes between a 'dominant discourse', that tends to equate community, culture and ethnicity as relating to specific social groups, and various 'demotic discourses', which are used by the people themselves and in which these terms were used much more loosely and with far greater local nuances (1996, 30–31). Baumann is explicit about the fact that 'religion' as a category of classification actually complicates his overall picture, especially of the dominant discourse, as Muslims, for example, cannot be classified as an ethnicity or a culture (1996, 81–6), and the Irish or the West Indians did not share a common religion, even if it was possible to talk about an Irish culture or a West Indian community (1996, 86–98).

While Baumann's work raises all kinds of very interesting questions, it does not, ultimately, begin to address the kind of questions that I wish to raise in this project. Baumann was concerned with the ways in which different social groupings used the concepts of 'culture', 'community', and to a lesser extent, 'ethnicity' and 'religion', of themselves, rather than how they used these terms of the other social groupings within the neighbourhood. It is only the dominant discourse, as used by the local authority, which appears to provide a means to discuss the neighbourhood as a whole. Baumann makes it clear, therefore, that any social group that wishes to engage with the whole has to use the dominant discourse of the authorities (this is what makes it a 'dominant' discourse) and abandon their own demotic discourses. This, however, does not ring true for my own research. There must, I would suggest, be another kind of discourse, or even a series of discourses, that sit between Baumann's dominant discourse of the authorities and the different group's own demotic discourses about their own identities as 'cultures', 'communities', 'ethnicities' or 'religions'. It is some of these other discourses that I want to begin to uncover within this book.

Methodological Starting Point

As an anthropologist my primary research methodology is ethnographic, that is living and working within a community over a long period of time. There are two neighbourhoods within Birmingham that I have close associations with and have been studying for six to nine years. The first is Highgate, just south of the city centre. This is a clearly defined area bordering on to Sparkbrook, which was the site of Rex and Moore's study. However, while Sparkbrook is predominantly Muslim, Highgate, despite having the Birmingham Central Mosque within its boundaries, is very mixed with large Afro-Caribbean and local white populations. The second neighbourhood I have worked within is Perry Hall and Perry Beeches, another self-contained area nestling under the M6 in the north of the city. This area borders onto the Handsworth of Ratcliffe's study but could not be more different. While Handsworth is ethnically diverse, Perry Beeches and Perry Hall is a predominantly white neighbourhood with a very stable and gradually aging population (Stringer 2004).

Both of these long-term studies have provided a wealth of circumstantial evidence but in neither case was the question of religious diversity the primary purpose of the study. In both cases the focus of my work in both areas has been on Christian churches, the Baptists in Highgate and the Methodists in Perry Beeches and Perry Hall. This long-term work, therefore, has had to be supplemented by more detailed and more focussed studies looking at the specific issues raised by this project. More recently, therefore, and specifically for the purposes of this study, I have undertaken a period of 'fieldwork' in Handsworth itself, the results of which are seen primarily in Chapter 4, I have revisited Highgate, and I have attended a number of the street festivals that are the subject of chapters 5 and 6.

As well as my own studies I have had postgraduate students and research fellows who have worked in different neighbourhoods of Birmingham, also involved in ethnographic work, and also with their own particular agendas. These have focussed on Small Heath, Newtown, Bearwood, Mosely, Handsworth and Bromford, among others, all of which are inner urban neighbourhoods with more or less multi-faith communities. Ethnography has enabled my students to listen carefully to the language and stories people tell on the streets and within the different religious communities; stories about each other and about their neighbourhoods in general. While none of this work focussed specifically on the question of religious diversity (the interests of my students have been far wider than this) it is clear that this has to be a central theme in any study within the neighbourhoods that make up a city such as Birmingham.

In each of these studies the ethnographers, whether my students or myself, have been able to listen to people at many different levels and in a wide range of differing contexts and, as with much ethnographic work, it is often the surprising and the unexpected that has generated the most interest, rather than the set piece interviews or discussion groups (Stringer 2008, 19–20). What people say in unguarded moments reveals far more about their real thoughts and understandings than what they say when confronted with an interviewer and a tape recorder. This has also enabled us, over time, to go back and to test, again and again in some cases, the kind of material that we are generating.

It is this experience that has led me to explore a new kind of methodology in my more recent studies. I have investigated a range of methodologies from the anthropological and sociological literature that might offer a way into gaining the kind of information that I am interested in. A typical sociological example would be Taylor, Evans and Fraser's work on the experience of living in Manchester and Sheffield in the early 1990s (1996). This is an interesting study from my point of view partly because of its theoretical stance, which emphasised the importance of locality (1996, 9–15) and the possibility of difference, both between Manchester and Sheffield as two distinct northern towns, but also within each city as between different populations (1996, 23–33). Secondly it aimed to begin with the people who were actually using the cities at the time of the study. The methodology, therefore, began with a simple survey of people using specific public spaces in each city and from this initial, and very simple data, individuals were contacted and invited to a series of focus groups constructed around the researcher's understanding of the different groups of users within the cities (1996, 91–4). Having identified who was using the city some attempts were also made to generate focus groups made up of those categories of people who were underrepresented such as the elderly or certain categories of young people.

The emphasis on focus groups and the attempt to draw on the ordinary people of the city led to a perspective that the authors describe as 'local knowledge' or 'folk belief' and make it clear that they have not set out to 'test this "local knowledge" or folk belief against "the facts", so much as to listen carefully to the local play of stories and speculation, rumour and gossip, and perhaps contribute in this way to the understanding of urban folklore in the North of England, as well as interrogating these modalities of local knowledge as an expression of the "local structure of feeling"' (1996, 94). I am certainly very much in sympathy with a methodology that focuses on stories, speculation, rumour, gossip and the local structure of feeling and can see how that used by Taylor, Evans and Fraser begins to get close to uncovering this. The evidence they provide in their book certainly bears witness to a great deal of local expressions of difference. This book, however, does not engage with religion and while the attempt to generate uniform or homogenous focus groups, emphasising older people, women, school children or whatever, is important, it would be difficult to construct focus groups from the areas I have been working where I could guarantee that there was a common view, a lack of possible offence, and an atmosphere where truly open conversations could take place. Focus groups were not going to provide the kind of spontaneous information that I required.

It might also be obvious to turn to Baumann's own work as a model for the methodology that could be used in a study such as this, as many of his conclusions and the discussion of different levels of discourses that he draws from these, are central to many of the discussions in this book. In many ways Baumann's study follows traditional anthropological methods (1996, 1–8). He identified Southall as a possible site for his fieldwork and deliberately moved into the neighbourhood. He began with a focus on young people and made his home into a space where young people would feel comfortable and engage in conversations (1996, 2–4). It was these deep and unstructured conversations that led him to question the common assumptions around culture and community in the discourses of these young people and so to develop the methodology more broadly. The second phase of the research worked through conversations with adults in the area (1996, 5–6). These were encountered in many different environments and by this time Baumann himself had become a regular and accepted member of many of the sites where the conversations took place. Finally, Baumann, like myself, drew on the experience of students who were engaged in their own studies within the neighbourhood and this allowed him access to sections of the community that he might not otherwise have engaged with (1996, 8).

Throughout all this fieldwork the most important element was that Baumann was actually living within the community and engaging with members of the community on many different levels, socially, as a friend, and also politically as an activist in different arenas. It is this traditional deep engagement over many years, that is the hallmark of ethnographic methods, which led Baumann to challenge his own, and wider societal, assumptions about the meaning of culture and community, and also to listen carefully to wide range of different discourses in many different contexts where these terms were used, engaged with or challenged. Unfortunately this kind of long-term, deep embeddedness with specific communities was not open to me due to personal factors and other commitments in my job at the University. I did not have the luxury of being able to move into the communities I wished to study.

Having recognised that, the process of critically listening to the people of a neighbourhood and the challenging of specific discourses, was something that I was able to learn from Baumann's study. What I needed, however, was to find opportunities where I could listen to and identify the different kinds of discourse about religion that were present in the neighbourhoods and at the events that I had chosen to focus on.

One study that I found particularly thought provoking when I was thinking about this project was Setha Low's work *On the Plaza* (2000). Low undertook a detailed ethnographic study of two specific plazas in San José, the capital of Costa Rica, and while she does not present a detailed methodology in her book she does begin the text with quite extensive extracts from her fieldnotes relating to almost 25 years of study (2000, 3–30). From these notes it is clear that Low knew what it was, in principle, that she wished to discover, but had little real sense of how that might be achieved. The plaza is an accidental community, a group of individuals who pass through, or who choose to stay within the plaza for one of many different purposes, but who do not, on the whole, form a natural community with strong ties or bonds between them. Low chose simply to follow the pattern of the many other users of the park and simply to be present, to observe and to engage in conversations on an informal and ad hoc basis as the opportunity arose. The extracts from the fieldnotes give a strong sense of place with beautiful, detailed and evocative descriptions of the plaza at different times of day or year, of the people who use the plaza, and of snippets from conversations with the people she meets. In a later chapter Low presents a number of the conversations in greater detail (2000, 216–37), and it is from these conversations, along with an investigation of the history of the plaza, and literary accounts of the plazas she studied, that Low draws her own conclusions.

Low does undertake some detailed quantitative analysis of the numbers and categories of people entering and leaving the plazas, as well as the activities that they undertake while they are there (2000, 160–61). This leads to interesting maps of movement and behaviour (2000, 162–78), and I will come back to these in Chapter 3. The majority of her work, however, was simply involved in being present, observing activities and listening to conversations. It is worth noting that Low refers to these engagements with other users of the plazas, even in the chapter where they are transcribed more fully, as 'conversations' as opposed to 'interviews' (2000, 219–20). In some cases it is clear that Low did interview relevant people about their engagement with, and understanding of, the plazas, but it is the conversations about many other issues, that occurred as part of being in the plaza, which form much of the relevant data for Low's own analysis.

A similar pattern is seen in the comments Sharon Zukin makes in relation to her study of shopping in New York (1995, 187–257). On a number of occasions she refers to the activity of her research assistant Danny Kessler whose role appears to have been to walk up and down the streets being studied, to mingle with the crowds, get into conversations with buyers, sellers, shop owners and other users of the street as appropriate and to follow through with a few carefully chosen interviews (see e.g. 233).

It is this aspect of Low's and Zukin's work, therefore, as a means of undertaking ethnographic work in public spaces within the urban environment that I have developed within this particular project. I have aimed to be present, through walking and riding on public transport, in two specific neighbourhoods and I have taken the opportunity to listen and to fall into conversation with the people who pass through those spaces. The work on festivals develops this method within the specific context of the festival being celebrated. Once again, however, I have simply been present. I have mingled with the crowds, observed behaviour, listened to comments and, at times, engaged in conversations with others who are also present at the event. The data, therefore, consists of observations, conversations or comments that have been overheard, and conversations that I have personally engaged in.

It may be thought that there are ethical issues raised by this kind of activity. Is it right to listen in on other people's conversations and to re-present them as part of the data for a study such as this? Obviously it would have been impossible for me to ask for, or to gain, written consent to use the material collected. Do I have any right, therefore, to use material that, on the whole, has been part of a private conversation (albeit in a public space) for which, in many cases, I was not the direct recipient, as the basis for academic study? Part of my defence for this practice comes from the public space in which the observations took place and the fact that no attempt was made to hide the conversation whether on a bus, sitting in a park or as part of a wider crowd watching a festival or procession go past. Many people could have, and probably did, listen in to these conversations and so there is, clearly, a public element to this data.

I would also claim the use of 'anonymity' as a defence for the ethical nature of the study. I do not, at any point, wish to attribute comments to specific individuals, and could not do so even if I wished to, as I have no personal data on the people concerned. These are public statements, unattributable to specific people. That is not to say that issues of gender, age, ethnicity and where possible class or religion, are not important factors and these have been noted. Overall, however, the texts that I have collected form the common discourse on religion as expressed in unguarded moments, rather than the detailed, thought through and carefully considered views of specific players within the discourse. Before beginning to outline some of my initial conclusions, therefore, I do need to say a little more about the kind of conversations and comments that form the basis for the data underpinning the various analyses within this book.

The Nature of the Data

What I am primarily interested in is the way people talk about religious diversity when they are not forced to think about it consciously. This means that interviewing, whether formally or informally, individually or in focus groups, was not an option. It may be possible to undertake interviews to explore the meaning or significance of the kind of data I have collected for this study, but it could not have been the means of collection as it lacks the kind of spontaneity that is central to my own concerns. I am working on the principle, suggested in Baumann's work and experienced in our more formal ethnographies, that people will say different things at different times and that conversations about other topics will initiate comments on religious diversity that are unthought and more fundamental than the kind of thought out positions that could be generated through interviews. What I needed to do, therefore, was to place myself in situations where I could either overhear or otherwise initiate such conversations.

Given the current legal framework within Britain today there are many 'public' spaces where people are forced to engage with diversity. This can be presented as a positive thing, a result of specific equality and diversity regulations initiated by the government, or as something that adds to the uncertainty or fluidity of contemporary 'post-modern' life. Beck and Beck-Gernsheim note that despite the rise of individualism and the complaints about the decline of 'community' (or perhaps because of these factors) 'tolerance for other types of people and marginal groups, whether foreigners, homosexuals, handicapped people or the socially disadvantaged, has steadily increased as values have changed' (2002, 162). These 'public' spaces are typically schools, hospitals and other public sector institutions. Not only are people thrown together in these contexts and individuals from a wide range of religious backgrounds have to meet and interact in order to fulfil the task in hand, but the recent equality and diversity laws encourage all public institutions to positively promote religious diversity and equality alongside a range of other capabilities, including disability, gender and sexuality. These, however, are not the contexts that I am dealing with. As with interviews there is a sense in which, within these contexts, individuals are forced to think about the issues, and more importantly they are under some kind of obligation to make positive statements, or at the very least, suppress the negative. As one middle-aged woman on a bus said to her neighbour, while watching a young woman in a head scarf struggle off the bus with her buggy; 'of course, at the hospital we have to be nice to these people'. This was not said in any malicious way, and I have no reason to believe that the woman would not be nice to Muslim women at all times, it was a statement of fact that emphasised the 'we have to' rather than the 'being nice'. It is the woman's comment on the bus that really interests me, not what she may or not say when she has to be nice to people different from herself at work.

What, therefore, is the nature or status of the data that I collected and how does it differ from that which could have been collected through interviews? More importantly, how does the nature of the data lead to the particular kinds of conclusions that can be drawn from it, and hence to the nature of the arguments presented within this book? The first point to make is that I am not interested in this analysis with the way in which people describe their own religion or what might be identified as 'religious' within their own self narrative. There has been a great deal of work in recent years that has tried to get beyond the simple arguments of secularisation and the 'decline of religion'. Much of this has set out to find religion in places where we may not normally look. Kim Knott's work, for example, asks about the 'location of religion' and specifically about the location of religion in so called 'secular spaces' (2005a). I will come back to Knott's work in more detail in Chapter 3. Other scholars have looked towards spirituality as an alternative to religion and here the emphasis has generally been on the individual and the individual's own engagement with the religious or the spiritual (Heelas et al. 2005). Abby Day, for example, has aimed, very specifically, to engage in conversations about 'belief' with people who would not normally identify themselves as religious, and so, like Knott, she has aimed to find the religious where we would not expect to find it (Day 2011). In very recent literature this has developed through a rediscovery of Durkheim's concept of the 'sacred' to explore the place of the 'sacred' in everyday life, in secular spaces, in unlooked for and often unnoticed contexts. Some of what I am trying to do within this text can be seen in the light of the same trend, although I would not personally wish to use the term 'sacred' in this sense (Day and Cotter 2013). The important point to note, however, is that I am not looking at how individuals may, or may not, understand the religious, the spiritual or the sacred in relation to their own lives. What concerns me, and what the data that I have collected focuses on, is the way in which these people conceive of, use, and value 'religion' (whatever they mean by that) within everyday conversations and within society at large.

This raises the question of the nature of everyday conversation within public arenas. There has been a great deal of analysis over the last 50 or more years on the nature of everyday speech (Fairclough 2003). At a more philosophical level we can trace a genealogy through the work of Austin (1969) and even Wittgenstein (1976). Some of this developed into discourse analysis and what came to be known as pragmatics, the analysis of everyday speaking (Cameron 2001). The ethnography of speaking, with its roots in the sociolinguistic work of Dell Hymes can also be included here as offering a particularly anthropological approach to this methodology (Hymes 1972, Bauman and Sherzer 1974). If we bring this tradition into conjunction with that of Foucault and others on discourse, and some elements of late Freudian analysis, then the writing of de Certeau on *The Practice of Everyday Life* can also be included in this tradition (1984), although de Certeau is more interested in the correlations between speaking and other everyday practices such as walking and cooking rather than in the specifics of everyday conversations in themselves.

Of all these traditions, however, it is probably that of conversational analysis that gets closest to what I am looking at in the analysis of everyday speech (Cameron 2001, Fairclough 2003, 83–6). These approaches have focussed on the formal structural and grammatical nature of everyday conversations and have highlighted certain important points. Everyday conversations, for example, rarely follow strict laws of grammar. Many conversations are made up more of silences and spaces between comments than of clearly semantic statements. Sentences can be unfinished, or finished by the others involved in the conversation. Meanings can be left hanging, and the attempt to reach a clear consensus seldom occurs. The purpose of the conversation is not always clear. Secondary functions, such as initiating or renewing a relationship, or even filling silence, often subsume the desire to communicate meaningful information, and the tone of voice, emotional content and force of the comment can often say far more than the actual words used. Such conversations, therefore, are very different from the material transcribed in interviews, or even in the increasingly popular approach of life-story or other narrative based analysis.

To some extent there is a relationship here to Taylor et al.'s stories, speculation, rumour and gossip (1996, 94), although even this has more structure and form to it than most of the comments that make up the content of my own data. Whether what I am looking at can be classed as 'urban folklore' or 'local knowledge' is difficult to determine. I am choosing to use the word 'discourse' to cover the totality of the data, rather than folklore or knowledge, and it is, as I have indicated, Baumann's definition of 'discourse' that I am using within this study. Drawing on the work of Lutz and Abu-Lughood (1990), Baumann identifies two uses of the word 'discourse' that relate to his own study. The first emphasises pragmatics as opposed to semantics and the second relates to what Baumann describes as 'the efficacy of power relations' (1996, 10). Both pragmatics and power are essential to my own understanding, and I will pick up the power elements specifically in Chapter 8. However, it is the way in which Baumann, pragmatically, uses the term 'discourse' throughout his work to refer to the ordinary conversations of everyday people, as well as the more specific assumptions of those in power, that I have found most helpful. It is this pragmatic definition that I will be following within this text.

If I were to capture the most important elements that I took away from the conversations I listened to, or engaged in, therefore, then three things stand out. The first is that religion generally had a very traditional meaning. When people spoke about 'religion' then what they had in mind was one or more of the mainstream religions, primarily Christianity or Islam. Associated with this were a number of assumptions that Kirsten von Brömssen also found in a study of Swedish teenagers (2003). The view of religion being presented by these teenagers was generally something for other people and literalist in its assumptions. There was no general discussion of spirituality and no real subtlety in the understanding of religion itself. Second, the data consists primarily of short comments or turns of phrase that capture a particular idea or attitude. Occasionally this is expanded into an anecdote, but it is more normally a one off comment that encapsulates a whole argument and approach that forms the basis for the discussion that follows. The third element is the emotional content of the comments, the sense of positive or negative feelings towards that which is being commented on. This emotional content is, of course, much more difficult to register and is inevitably subjective, both in itself and in the reading of the situation by myself as observer. However, I would argue that the emotional register of the comments was usually clear and would have been obvious to any observer. Where there was significant ambiguity then that, of course, is clearly interesting in and of itself. It is important, therefore, before looking at some of the detail in subsequent chapters, to outline the basic principles that have come out of these conversations and my own initial reading of them.

Listening to Religious Diversity

Even before undertaking the detailed observation and analysis, drawing on the long-term studies I have undertaken and the work of my students, I was able to arrive at some simple conclusions and these have been used to provide the basis for further study and to structure the chapters that make up this book. There are, for example, four topics through which religious diversity tends to be discussed in ordinary, uninitiated conversations. The first relates to dress, the second to buildings and the built environment, the third relates to street festivals and the fourth to recent events in the media. I will look at each of these briefly within this chapter and explore some of them further in the chapters that follow. There are also three levels of analysis in relation to these discourses that I was able to identify and that I want to draw specific attention to within the following discussion. The first relates simply to the content of the discourses themselves, the second to the way in which different kinds of discourses interact, and the third to the way in which the use of these discourses lead to what I have referred to as the 'management' of religious diversity. I will begin, therefore, with the language itself.

There are perhaps two visual markers that appear to lead people to begin a conversation about religious diversity in Birmingham. The first is dress and the second is buildings. The question of dress is extremely complex and inevitably leads the speakers into a range of related discourses, not all of which have a specifically religious referent. Dress, as we have seen with my example of the plumber at the opening of this book, is probably the most confusing area of discourse and, without question, the one where ethnicity and religious affiliation become most clearly confused. It is also that area of discourse that leads to the most clearly negative comments on religious diversity, often tinged with overtly racist remarks. This has been true in the past with discourses around the Sikh turban and is currently the case for the Islamic hijab or veil. I could also add the traditional dress of some male Pakistani Muslims to this discussion, which has become associated in some people's minds with the idea of radical Islam and terrorism. There would have been a time when the question of dress was treated as a specifically ethnic or cultural discourse. This, however, has changed and the issues raised by the hijab and by radical Islam have been very influential in doing this. The hijab also introduces a discourse about gender and the way in which Muslims are supposed to 'treat their women' that adds another layer of complexity, and ignorance, to the whole debate.

It is clearly in this area where much of the previous work on attitudes to other religions and religious diversity already exists (Dreher and Ho 2009). There is a growing literature on Islamophobia, for example, that among other things identifies the question of dress, and the assumed treatment of women that derives from this, as central to these discourses (Allen 2010). The question of the generalised other, and fear of the other, as raised by Sandercock among others (2003), also comes into discussions about dress. Abby Day did a very interesting and detailed investigation of belief among ordinary (that is for these purposes, 'non-religious') people in East Yorkshire. For these individuals, who mainly lived and worked in the Yorkshire Dales, one significant archetypal other originated in the Asian communities of Keighley and Leeds (2011, 137–42). Their construction of this other drew on a range of factors, including racist views of Asians in general, but also including the fact that they were understood to be Muslims, and that Muslims were thought to treat their women oppressively. As one respondent said 'I don't want to bring racism into it, but it's difficult not to in certain cases. But ... I think it's always been my belief that the women are trodden into the ground in the Muslim world, entirely' (58). As the same man went on to say 'I'm not saying that Muslims are bad, in every sense of the word, they're not all terrorists' (58). Obviously I heard many similar comments throughout my work in Birmingham.

What is interesting in this context, however, is that these discussions are not, on the whole, aimed at specific people who wear a particular kind of dress. In Handsworth, for example, where there is considerable diversity of ethnicity and dress among the population, a young black man getting on and off a bus in a home made purple 'Tuareg' outfit caused no interest or comment from the other passengers on the bus. In Highgate, or on the bus in and out of Birmingham from the University, things would have been very different. These discourses, therefore, are not always triggered by the visual images in themselves and often occur in areas where the sight of women in the veil, or men in turbans would be unusual (as is also the case in the Yorkshire Dales where Day undertook her fieldwork (2011, 35)). It is usually when white, or other non-Muslim individuals, are gathered in a 'safe' environment, away from anybody wearing the hijab that such conversations will begin. This again, associates the discourse with specifically negative overtones and it is almost always treated as a discourse that defines and condemns the other. It is at this level that such discourse relates back to the fear of the other as identified by Sandercock (2003).

Finally this discourse suggests that if people insist on wearing a specific dress because of their religion then religious diversity is, in and of itself, a bad thing. The comments I noted, especially in a number of conversations on the buses, once again following individuals who had got on or off with full veils or identifiably 'Islamic' dress, linked the question of dress to that of human rights or the freedom of expression. These were not detailed philosophical debates, simply a statement that this is one area where religion comes up against human rights/freedom of expression (the two were used interchangeably) and was found wanting. What is more, it was generally assumed that there was something very British (or English) about freedom of expression, and that the Islamic example was seen to be just one of many, usually unnamed, examples from other religions where this British value was flouted. The freedom to do and to wear what the individual chooses is seen as a more significant goal than the freedom of religion, and divisions over the dress it is stated, can only be overcome through the downplaying of religious difference. Religious diversity in this context therefore, is seen to be entirely negative.

Moving on from dress to other visual triggers, the most interesting popular discourse on the religious diversity of Birmingham as a city came in relation to the buildings that are increasingly being put up in many inner-urban areas. Most of these structures are obviously and self-referentially Islamic, Sikh, Hindu, Buddhist or whatever. It is ironic that it is only the new Christian buildings that are not instantly recognisable as 'religious' let alone 'Christian'. These new religious buildings are often on prime sites within the neighbourhood in question and are often visible from many of the main roads in or out of the city (Gale 2004). Buddhist and Hindu temples are generally less obvious to the general public but are present in a very visible fashion within the neighbourhoods in which they are situated. What interests me about the discourses relating to the buildings, however, is the clearly ambiguous stance to these buildings taken by the general public.

As with the discourses on dress, those on buildings have been changing over the years. When the Central Mosque was built in Highgate, on a prime site next to the inner ring road, it was the first purpose built Islamic building in the city and caused considerable opposition and controversy within the area itself (Gale 2005). Most of the people of Highgate have now learnt to live with it and for most non-Muslims it is, in fact, a non building, they turn their backs on it and hardly appear to notice that it is there. Newer buildings, however, elicit a very different reaction. At one level they represent regeneration, the sense that an area is improving. The big Mosques and Gudwaras in areas like Small Heath and Handsworth, with all their associated educational facilities, sheltered housing and other community buildings represent a significant investment within many of the run-down inner-urban area communities in which they are situated. In the case of the Gudwaras they are also flamboyant and ostentatious in their use of marble, elaborate gilding and bright, almost garish, colours. None of these buildings fit the traditional Birmingham vernacular, but all of them, in their own way, work well within the range of new 'post-modern' structures that are being built in areas such as Brindley Place (an area of canal-side redevelopment aimed at the entertainment industry where a variety of styles have been drawn together to form a new and exciting urban space). Having said all this, it is very clear, both for local residents and for those who pass by in cars, that these buildings are there for religious purposes and are not primarily economic or entertainment focused structures.

The nature of many recent discourses about buildings can be seen through one specific comment made in relation to the development of the Gudwara in Handsworth. An older lady, a member of a local Afro-Caribbean church, commented to one of my students that, as the Gudwara and its associated buildings took over adjoining sites, one relatively recent building housing a video shop or games arcade had been demolished. This woman remembered, long ago, that there had once been a chapel on that site and she commented to my student that 'God always claims his own'. What is important in this throw away remark is first of all that the new building was thought of as 'religious', although this particular part of the development was designed for education or community work and was not in itself a worship space. Secondly, the comment also implied that somehow the specific nature of the religion did not seem to matter. The site was going back to God despite the fact that it was now part of a Sikh complex and not a Christian chapel.

Other comments from other parts of the city have reflected the same kind of sentiment, that the growth in buildings represents a development for 'God', or perhaps even from God, a reclaiming of land for God, irrespective of the particular religion that is doing the building. Of course there are those who still object to the building of Mosques or Gudwaras but these now appear to be the minority within the neighbourhoods themselves (the recent dispute over the building of a new Mosque in Dudley, however, does not follow this pattern). More important than the positive charge of these discourses, however, is the underlying universalism that is implicit in them, even from those who would claim no religious allegiance of their own. These structures are understood as being God's building and that is constructed as being a generally good thing within the wider materialism of the city.

A different, but in many ways similar view to the discourse on buildings is seen in relation to street festivals and processions. The main difference here, however, is that the specifically religious element is played down or even ignored entirely. If the Irish community celebrate St Patrick's Day in Digbeth, or the Sikhs celebrate Vaisakhi in Handsworth, or the Chinese celebrate their New Year in the city centre then they each come out onto the streets to take part in parades and festivals that are proclaimed by the City authorities as the biggest and best, outside of New York, Amritsar, Beijing or wherever. Each of these is a religious festival, and like the modern discourses on the buildings the overwhelming response of the people to these events is positive. As studies of festivals in other parts of the world have clearly shown, the exact nature of the sponsors or the defined purpose of the festival is largely irrelevant, everybody within the neighbourhood comes out to celebrate and the whole city is 'Irish' or 'Chinese' for the day (Marston 1989, Harris 2003). These festivals sit alongside the Afro-Caribbean Carnival and the Gay Pride marches, which also fill the streets and gather up all the passing crowds into their celebration, but neither of which is specifically 'religious'. Unlike the discourses on buildings, these discourses are generally not about religion, although they are, very clearly, about the celebration of diversity.

The discourses on news items and media events, for example that which followed the protests against the play set in a Sikh Gudwara at the Hippodrome Theatre in Birmingham, or those that followed the riots in many English cities, including Birmingham, in the summer of 2011, also raised serious questions about diversity, but these were far more complex and I want to look at these in more detail in Chapter 8.

Levels of Discourse

If the different contexts in which discourses on religious diversity come into play are explored in more detail then we can see something that is far more than the simple distinction between demotic and dominant discourses as outlined by Baumann. We can also see much more involved than the confusion between religion and ethnicity or culture. In the four areas of discourse that I have identified I would suggest that there are two features that are particularly important. As with the theories in the previous chapter, these features can best be understood as being two axis of a graph. On one axis there is the question of whether the discourse is essentially positive or essentially negative. It is not always easy to be clear-cut on this issue, hence the idea of a continuum set out on an axis. Taken as an overall attitude, however, we can draw some kind of distinction as we have seen in some of the examples I have already given. On the other axis we can look at the level of 'otherness' that is associated with the discourse, the way in which the discourse constructs those with other religions as 'others' in a wider sense.

If we take this pair of axes as a starting point then we could suggest that the discourse on dress represents those of other religions as being entirely 'other', that is, different from the speaker, while at the same time giving that otherness a negative value. For example, those who wear the hijab, or the religion that in the popular mind forces women to wear the hijab, are 'negatively other'. They represent something very different from the speaker and are generally to be opposed. On the other hand the discourses associated with festivities and street processions still maintain a strong element of otherness; that is the whole point of the festival, to celebrate the specificities of a different, other, culture. The value associated with that otherness, however, especially from those who are drawn into the festivities themselves, is entirely positive. Nobody is out there saying that these kinds of events should not be happening. They are seen as a positive thing for the city as a whole.

The discourses on buildings fall somewhere between these two extremes. These discourses are sometimes negative (and have generally been so in the past), but are often positive, especially when economic regeneration is brought into the equation. What is particularly interesting about these discourses, however, is the way in which the 'otherness' of these buildings, or the religions that they represent, is played down, especially when the discourse is positive. The buildings belong to 'God', they are religious symbols within the community, an entirely positive element within the landscape that can be equated with churches and other religious buildings and are not seen as entirely other to the speaker. The ability to maintain a shared value about a building, and the fact that many of these buildings house educational and community based projects mean that they are often seen as belonging to the wider community as a whole and not to one or other specific religious group. This is on first sight a very odd position to arrive at.

There is something in this discussion that links to a line of argument that has been developed by Grace Davie in relation to 'vicarious religion' (Davie 2002, 2007). Davie notes that for the European context the relationship to religion, by the majority of the population, cannot simply be categorised in the terms often presented in secularisation theories, as rejection. There is clearly a drift away from the institutions of religion, but the expectation that religion still plays an important part in society, and more specifically that somebody, somewhere is being religious on our behalf (vicariously to use Davie's terms) is part of the overall understanding of religion by European populations. There is a long history behind this particular position that I cannot explore in any detail at this point, but the essentially positive attitude to religious buildings, that they are a force for good within the community and people would prefer them to be there rather than not be there (irrespective of which religion owns and uses them) is essentially a development of Davie's proposal. Whether we are, in a city like Birmingham, moving to a position where a vicarious stance towards religion can be held irrespective of nature of the religion is one of the issues that this book will set out to explore.

What this range of discourses also shows, of course, is the central element that Baumann was keen to highlight in his own study of Southall. The important point for Baumann was that individuals can in fact move seamlessly between the different discourses he discussed without ever realising that they are doing so. This is what Baumann refers to as 'dual discursive competence' (1996, 195). The same, I would argue, is true of the various discourses that I have been discussing. As people move from discourse to discourse they are subtly and yet significantly changing both their understanding of the other, and the positive or negative value that they are placing on that otherness. They are fundamentally shifting their stance towards religious diversity.

This is not a new phenomenon. We are all aware, from the literature on racism and other forms of stereotyping within society, of what can be called the 'my best friend' phenomenon. In this situation it is perfectly possible for an individual to be a racist, a misogynist or a homophobe whilst at the same time claiming a close and positive relationship with one member of the group being despised. The 'best friend' is always seen as the exception that in some ways proves the rule. What I am suggesting here, however, is not entirely analogous to this, unless we wish to rethink the 'my best friend' analysis. It is not the case in relation to religious diversity, that most people have a standard background fear, mistrust or hatred for a particular religion, or religions in general while at the same time being positive towards some local manifestation (although there will be people out there for whom this is, of course, true). What I am proposing is that there is no one discourse that is pre-eminent for the individuals concerned. It is more the case that in different contexts, and in relation to different objects, then different values of otherness, and different conceptions of what is seen as other, come into play. People can, and do, shift between these different discourses with ease, primarily, I would suggest, because none of them impinge too fully on any one individual's perceptions.

It is at this point, therefore, that I wish to turn to the more detailed analysis of the different kinds of discourse involved, beginning with reflections on religious buildings in the Highgate area of Birmingham, and I will return to this wider discussion towards the end of the book.

Chapter 3

The Two Towers

When J.R.R. Tolkien lived in Kings Heath in south Birmingham as a child at the turn of the twentieth century, he would make his way every Sunday to attend mass at St Anne's Roman Catholic Church in Highgate. He would clearly have passed, and would therefore have known very well, one of the two towers that I wish to focus on in this chapter, that of St Alban's Anglican Church on Conybere Street. The other tower, the minaret of the Birmingham Central Mosque, was not to be completed until some 13 years after Tolkien's death. The image of the two towers, however, is an interesting one when the attitude to religious buildings in the Highgate area is explored. These two towers clearly dominate the landscape, and both were clearly designed to do so (Pollock 1890, Gale 2004), but the tensions between them, and the wariness of many in the population towards both of them, captures something of the image from Tolkien's most famous work.

In the previous chapter I outlined four kinds of discourse, or arenas of everyday conversation, where the question of religious diversity arose for ordinary people within the city. These discourses existed in relation to dress, in relation to buildings, in relation to festivals or street events and in relation to items in the media. I indicated that the discourses about these different aspects of religious diversity held differing values for 'religion' and for 'otherness' that could be set on a scale from the highly positive to the highly negative. I suggested that the relationships between the discourses involved are, in fact, extremely complex and at times even contradictory. This, however, should not really surprise us; it is true of much of everyday conversation. What I want to do in this chapter, therefore, is to pick up one of these areas of discourse, that on buildings and space, and to try and get inside that to explore this complexity even further.

In doing this I wish to draw on the work I have been doing in the Highgate area of Birmingham. Once again I need to stress that this did not start out as specific fieldwork dealing with the issue of religious diversity, rather it draws on over nine years of conversations with the people of the Highgate area and a trawl through the data that has been collected there over the years. This was followed up with more focussed research once the basic outlines of the argument had been developed, more in an attempt to test the ideas rather than to seek for anything new. I am, however, going to attempt to provide some kind of theoretical framework that makes some sense of the data that I have collected, and which has been confirmed through the more recent research.

Thinking about Space

It is only very recently that scholars in the sociology of religion have begun to explore the concepts of space in any detail and to draw on the wide range of exciting material that is currently being developed by social geographers and others. One of the most interesting and controversial contributions to this literature is Kim Knott's book on *The Location of Religion* (2005a). Knott draws on many different authors in her work but one of her primary inspirations is the work of the French geographer and social theorist Henri Lefebvre (1991). What I find most interesting about Lefebvre's work is the way in which it enables the researcher to link real lived space, the individual's perception of space and the ideological understanding of space as held within a particular social group.

Henri Lefebvre, who first published his classic text on *The Production of Space*, in 1974, aimed to revolutionise the way in which philosophy, and related disciplines, thought about space. In particular he was concerned with the social production of space, rather than space as an abstract concept or specific spaces in the world. All space, in Lefebvre's view, is socially constructed in that we cannot think about space without taking into account the way in which social relations determine the space and social interactions describe or understand the space. In talking of the social production of space Lefebvre also wants to place himself into a dialogue with Marx and others on the economic and particularly the political nature of space and our understandings of space. Much of the book deals with these economic and political ramifications, but he begins, in the introduction, by trying to classify what it is about space that he is specifically interested in (1991, 1–67).

Lefebvre begins by clarifying what kind of space (or discourses on space) he is going to discuss and specifies his own focus as being on social space (as opposed to physical or the mental space) (1991, 21). From here he identifies three levels of the understanding of social space as 'spatial practice', 'representations of space', and 'representational spaces' (1991, 33). Spatial practice is relatively straightforward as this relates to the everyday use of space and the individual or social interaction with that space. The words Lefebvre focuses on for spatial practice are 'competence' and 'performance'. The other two categories are much more difficult to distinguish conceptually but it is important to realise that in many cases Lefebvre is dealing with discourses about space, or ways of conceptualising space, rather than engagement with real spaces (which would be covered by spatial practice). So representations of space relate to knowledge, to signs, to codes and the way in which this knowledge, or the signs or codes associated with it, are ordered. In other words this is the way social groups think about space and conceptualise it. Representational spaces, on the other hand, are the consequences of this thinking and are best understood in relation to art. They are the images and understandings that we all carry around in our heads but seldom articulate, the ways of thinking about space that are embedded in our cultural discourses.

Over the years Lefebvre's basic concepts have been discussed, critiqued, and even translated into English in a number of different ways. Like many other scholars

I find Lefebvre's language, and the distinctions he is trying to make, somewhat complex and counterintuitive (Knott 2005b, 163). Knott, in her discussion of Lefebvre sets out to rethink this triad. 'Spatial practice', in Lefebvre's language, is what Knott refers to as 'perceived space' and 'representational spaces', or what Knott chooses to term 'spaces of representation', are what Knott goes on to refer to as 'lived space' (2005a, 36–7). This is not merely a problem of language. Knott's terminology of 'conceived or ideological space', 'lived space' and 'perceived space' certainly makes more sense as a way of categorising the way social groups engage with space. It is not at all clear, however, that these ideas map onto, and entirely correlate with, Lefebvre's own distinctions. Knott does not really capture the distinction that Lefebvre is trying to make, for example, between representations of space and spatial representations, but as I have indicated I am not sure that this is a distinction that has great theoretical value when we are focussed on actual practice (see Knott 2005b 158–66). On the whole I do find Knott's classification more helpful in this respect and it is this that I will follow in the rest of this chapter.

What sits under Lefebvre's analysis, and Knott's reworking of his terms, is a concern with issues of power and economy. Space, whether perceived, lived or ideological, is not produced in an ideological vacuum; it is produced by certain people within the society with specific purposes in mind. This is particularly true of Lefebvre's representations of space and representational spaces. These are to a greater or lesser extent imposed by those with the power to do so and they control, through their taken-for-granted nature, the way ordinary people perceive space or engage with space at the practical level. This kind of analysis is picked up by a number of radical geographers and, by analogy, by theorists in other fields, leading to what Tweed refers to as the spatial turn in theory (2006, 9). Within the context of geography Ed Soja's development of the idea of 'thirdspace', linked to Lefebvre's representational spaces, suggests the possible associations of these with political undergrounds or arenas of cultural resistance (1996). Homi Bhabha takes the idea further by transposing the debate into the context of literature and presenting the spaces of resistance within the context of post-colonial theory by talking about the 'location of culture' (1994). It is difficult to relate these debates directly to the understandings of space and religion within a specific inner urban neighbourhood in Birmingham, but following Knott's lead I will offer some reflections on this within this chapter.

Setha Low makes a slightly different distinction when drawing on and developing Lefebvre's ideas for her own purposes. Low distinguishes between the social 'production' of space and the social 'construction' of space. The 'social production' of space for Low includes 'all those factors – social, economic, ideological, and technological – that result, or seek to result, in the physical creation of the material setting' (2000, 127–8). The 'social construction' of space deals more with the symbolic and semantic issues raised by Lefebvre and Knott. This is important for this particular study as it is often very difficult to distinguish discourses that derive from the production of space, the actual construction of the buildings under discussion, from those that derive from the social construction of the space by later generations or even by subsequent users. This will play a very significant role in what follows.

What I wish to explore within this chapter, therefore, are the different ways in which the people of Highgate relate to the religious buildings in their neighbourhood, and other related sites that are recognised as having a religious element, and what this says about the way in which the people of this area think intuitively about religious diversity. I want to focus particularly on the final two of Knott's understandings of space, the lived and the perceived, but I will make some passing reference to the ideological, and to Lefebvre's representational spaces, towards the end of the chapter. Before embarking on the analysis, however, I need to outline something of the area of Highgate itself.

Highgate

The specific locality that I wish to focus on is Highgate in Birmingham. This is a very clearly defined neighbourhood and an area that, in terms of religious diversity, is relatively simple. The area is tucked into a corner of the central zone of the city, within the inner ring road, one of the few residential areas that are quite so close to the city centre itself. It is bordered on two sides by the inner ring road (A4540) and on the other two sides by two of the primary roads into the city, Bristol Street (A38) and Digbeth/Camp Hill (B4100). To the north west of Highgate is the old market area of the city that leads directly on to the new Bull Ring shopping centre, New Street Station and on into the city centre itself. The area has always been residential beginning as an area of affluent housing and then becoming, for much of the late nineteenth and early twentieth century, a classic slum. This was demolished in the 1970s and new tower blocks were erected. In between the towers there is some low-level housing but not a great deal for an area of this size. In recent years the blocks themselves have begun to be renovated, although not to the level of some further west around the city and only a few have actually been demolished. From the building of the blocks to the present day the population has been relatively stable, which is also unusual for an inner-urban area of this kind.

The census data on Highgate is difficult to isolate as the boundaries for Middle and Lower Layer Super Output Areas for the 2001 census tend to cut across the neighbourhood and all of them include some elements outside of what I, and many within Highgate, would think of as Highgate proper. This is important in terms of ethnic and religious distribution as just before the rebuilding in the 1970s Highgate had a significant Bangladeshi population, although many of these people were moved out during the renovation (Gale 2004, 32). Some of the Bangladeshi community returned, but Highgate today is an area with a relatively high white and black, Caribbean, population surrounded by neighbourhoods with strong Asian and Muslim populations. As no one census area includes the whole of Highgate and all of them, even at the lowest levels, include sections of adjacent neighbourhoods this tends to distort the figures. However, if Lower Layers Birmingham 068D, 071A and 071C are combined, which are probably the nearest fit, then the following figures for 2001 are generated:

Table 3.1   Ethnic breakdown of the population in Highgate according to the 2001 census

Population	**3,371**
White	41%
Mixed	8%
Asian or Asian British	28%
Black or Black British	19%
Other	4%

Table 3.2   Religious breakdown of the population in Highgate, compared to Birmingham and the national figures, according to the 2001 census

	Highgate	**Birmingham**	**National**
Christian	45%	59%	71%
Muslim	27%	14%	3%
Other	6%	7%	4%
None or not stated	22%	20%	22%

It is generally recognised that the number of people who self identify as Christian within the census as a whole is significantly higher than those who may claim such an identity in other circumstances and there are many reasons for this (Day 2011, 174–90). Having said that the number for Highgate is low when compared to the national average. It is fair to assume that many of the 27 per cent that self identify as Muslim live outside the inner ring road, but it should be noted that some of the original Bangladeshi community do still live within Highgate.

In terms of religious buildings the most important structure is the Central Mosque, which sits on the inner ring road. Behind the Mosque, sitting on a hill on the corner of Conybere Street and Stanhope Street, is St Alban's church, a Victorian Anglican church with a strong reputation for high-church worship. At the bottom of the hill, also on Conybere Street and on the edge of the shopping area is a small Baptist church in a purpose-built structure that was constructed at the same time as the flats and has suffered greatly from the 1970s' construction methods. St Anne's Roman Catholic Church is also technically within Highgate but is to the north of the community, on Alcester Street, just off Digbeth, and is not really within what most people locally think of as Highgate proper. The same is true for the Guru Nanak Gudwara on Moseley Road.

Back to Back

If I begin with the actual movement of individuals through space, I can focus specifically on the congregations of the three places of worship within the neighbourhood. Setha Low, in her study of two plazas in San José, Costa Rica, develops two distinct ways of mapping the movement and behaviour of people within the plazas (2000, 157–78). These maps work at the first of Lefebvre's understandings of space, what Knott refers to as the 'perceived space'. This is the level at which people actually move through the space itself. The first of Low's maps focuses simply on movement and generates a map of the primary movements of people over time, giving a thicker line on the map to identify a larger quantity of people. What this shows is that at different times of the day, within the same plaza, the movement of people and the parts of the plaza that are used varies considerably. This is what Low refers to as the rhythms of everyday life in the plaza (2000, 157–8). In my analysis of Highgate I am not specifically interested in movement over time, but I am interested in the movement of people in and out of the various religious buildings. In the first instance I am interested in the movement of the congregations as they travel to and from the buildings for worship.

If I were to draw a scatter diagram on a map showing where the members of the three religious congregations come from, with the particular building at the centre, then we would get three very distinct patterns. The congregation at St Alban's is well known for the fact that the individuals tend to commute in from a great distance to attend the church. There was even one member of the congregation who came every week from Scunthorpe, a round trip each Sunday of just under three hundred miles. The rest of the congregation do not come quite so far but very few actually live within the area defined by Highgate and most travel some considerable distance to attend this church. Beyond the length of the lines linking the congregant's homes and the church there would be no other discernible pattern of any real significance.

The congregation at the Baptist church, on the other hand, is almost the opposite of that of St Alban's. While a certain section of the congregation, like that of St Alban's, is made up of members who used to live in the area and have now moved out, many members of this congregation continue to walk to church and live within a 15-minute walking distance of the church. As the church is situated close to the southern edge of the residential area, just behind the shopping centre close to the inner ring road, then the pattern of lines from the local residents would form a fan from the front door of the church looking north and west into the residential area of Highgate itself, while that of those who have moved out would probably stretch down the Alcester Road through Moseley and Kings Heath.

The pattern for the Central Mosque would also form something of a fan, although with over two thousand individuals attending Friday prayers each week the overall scatter would be very broad. As with the Baptists and St Alban's there would be some members of the congregation on a Friday who come to the Central Mosque because of what it is and where it is, or who had been members of the congregation since it opened, or since their own childhood. These would travel some distance from different parts of the city to attend. A very large section of the congregation, however, comes from the neighbourhoods of Balsall Heath, Sparkbrook and Small Heath just the other side of the inner ring road from the Mosque itself. The fan from the Mosque, therefore, would spread out to the south and the east, from the Mosque's front entrance on the inner ring road, out of the neighbourhood of Highgate itself.

If we are talking about spatial practices in real time, therefore, the relationship between the Baptist Church and Mosque is by far the most interesting. The land they each occupy does not quite touch but they are in reality very close. If an individual wished to travel, however, from the front door of the Baptists to the front gate of the Mosque, then they would have to travel some distance via the pedestrianised shopping centre, and even further by road. It would not be easy to provide directions. These two buildings are effectively back-to-back. Neither, however, really recognises the presence of the other and the main entrances face out in opposite directions. What is more their congregations, the fans of lines linking congregant's homes with their place of worship, also spread in opposite directions. In practice the two communities represented by these buildings are functionally invisible to each other, that is to say that each, despite the physical proximity of the other building, can continue their work and worshipping life without ever recognising, or even noticing that the other exists. Given that the congregation at St Alban's does not live in, or significantly engage with, the neighbourhood surrounding it then this also is functionally invisible to both the Mosque and the Baptists, as they are invisible to the congregation at St Alban's. This is an important point when we come to see what the members of these three congregations and others think and say about religious diversity in Highgate.

The Two Towers

All that I have been talking about so far are the congregations who worship at the different religious buildings. These, as I have suggested in the previous section, are only a very small minority of the population of the neighbourhood of Highgate. Highgate is primarily a poor white community with significant minority populations of Bangladeshi and Afro-Caribbean descent. The majority of the Baptist congregation come from the black population. Others in the neighbourhood will attend St Anne's Catholic Church, local house churches, or churches outside the neighbourhood. The majority of the Bangladeshi population within Highgate would identify themselves as Muslim and there are a small number of residents from other religions. The majority of the population see themselves as nominally Christian, as having no real religion, or not being prepared to state a religion. In fact, at 11 per cent, the percentage not stating their religion is somewhat higher than Birmingham, the West Midlands or the UK as a whole, all of which are around 8 per cent. For the purposes of this study we can probably claim that over a third of the population is 'non-religious', and, if we accept that most of the Muslim population lives in the areas of the three Lower Layer Super Output districts that are outside of Highgate proper, then the overall proportion of 'non-religious' within Highgate might well be higher than 50 per cent.

These 'non-religious' people watch others go to the two churches and the Mosque but this does not really register with them and nobody would be able to give an accurate account of how many people attended the various religious institutions. Given the fact that a significant proportion of those who do attend these institutions also come from outside of the Highgate area then it is fair to argue that it is not as communities, or as congregations, that most people within the neighbourhood come into contact with the religious on a day-to-day basis; it is as buildings. If we go back to the main theme of my argument then it is clear that it is the buildings that are the primary triggers for those conversations where the people of Highgate raise the issue of religion and this is borne out in the evidence that I have collected.

The building of the Mosque was, of course, very controversial, but this is now in the past. Others have explored this history in some depth and undertaken surveys of what the people of the area thought and think about the building and what it represents (Gale 2004, 2005). This again is not really what interests me at this point. As Low points out, there is a clear distinction between the social production of space, and the social construction of space (2000, 127–8). It is the social construction that concerns me here. It is also the spontaneous reference to the building and/or the religion that it represents that I am keen to hear and identify, not what people say when asked a specific question. This spontaneous conversation is in fact very different from a detailed discussion of the history, and I would argue, of considerable interest, especially within the context of religious diversity. To some extent we could relate this spontaneous conversation to the third of Knott's understandings of space, 'the perceived space' of the people (2005, 39). This does not necessarily relate to the lived spaces through which people walk, it refers more to the way in which the people actually see spaces and the buildings that inhabit them.

What is interesting here is that it is only two of the religious buildings of Highgate that are seen and identified as being 'religious' by the people. These are St Alban's and the Mosque. In some senses this relates to the fact that these are the two buildings that are most visible. Each has a tower that is visible and obvious from most places within the neighbourhood. What is interesting, however, is that the spontaneous conversation within the community on both these buildings is almost identical. Each is seen as in some senses a foreign presence within Highgate.

Each also has a superficially negative value for many of the 'non-religious' people who are talking.

The two most common comments that I heard about the Mosque were first that 'it's not really part of Highgate is it?' or words to that effect. Secondly a number of people in conversations about the Mosque simply stated 'I guess we're used to it' with a kind of resigned shrug. Only very occasionally have I heard a directly negative comment about Muslims or the Mosque from the local people in a public space, which is not to say that negative views are not held, and many of these were expressed within the planning disputes surrounding the building of the Mosque, its minaret and the use of the minaret for the call to prayer (Gale 2005). The Mosque, therefore, although the people are used to it as a building and would claim to have nothing against Muslims as such, is seen as being for others, particularly for the people of Sparkbrook. It is not 'for us'. It is not a community building. The authorities at the Mosque itself have done a great deal in recent years to try to change this perception by providing a range of community facilities, but it is still largely the Muslim community from beyond the inner-ring road who use these, not the people of Highgate.

St Alban's is also seen as being not 'for us'. This, however, has more to do with the eclectic nature of the congregation and the kind of activities that are offered by the church; concerts of classical music and the like. The kind of comment that I overheard was that 'they are all stuck up, up there' and the directional or spatial language was significant as we shall see. The intensive security and the locked and barred doors do nothing to help this perception. In fact one of the most common comments I got in conversations about the church over the last nine years was that it was about to be demolished: 'I didn't know they still met there, thought it was due to be pulled down soon.' Interestingly the Church of England secondary school, now an Academy, that once stood almost opposite St Alban's church is seen by the local people as a community space and has done a great deal over the years to integrate itself into the neighbourhood and to open its space up for people to use. The Academy prides itself on its multi-faith stance and notes a member of the Central Mosque on its Board of Governors, although no member from St Alban's congregation (the Anglican Diocese is, however, represented). The school and the church, however, are not seen, in the everyday conversation of the people of Highgate, as connected and nor, I would have to say from my own experience, are they seen in this way by most of the congregation at St Alban's.

Finally, therefore, I need to look briefly at the Baptists. This is a very open church, with a very large number of activities happening every day and with many members of the neighbourhood going through the building for one reason or another. This is an available space and is recognised by many within the neighbourhood as being very clearly 'for us'. What is very interesting, however, is that in the everyday conversations of the people, the Baptist building is not understood primarily as a religious building, it is a building of and for the community. Even Google Maps has the building labelled as the Highgate Family Support Centre and not as a religious building, unlike St Alban's and the Mosque. Many people commented on the different activities that took place within the Baptist Chapel, and these changed over time, but never in my experience was it referred to as 'Baptist' except by those who attended or by members of other churches. It was 'the centre' or even, and most commonly, 'that place over there'. The Baptists therefore are not seen in relation to the two towers, St Alban's and the Mosque, slightly apart from and unrelated to the neighbourhood, but as an integral part of the community and as essentially non-religious.

Uniquely Highgate

In the previous chapter I placed the perception of religion as expressed in everyday discussions about religious buildings towards the 'positive' end of the continuum. In relation to Highgate, however, where buildings are associated with religion, the discourse appears to be generally negative. It is only by separating the building from the perception of religion, as with the Baptist Chapel, that the space can be seen in a positive light at all. Did I therefore get my data wrong in the previous chapter?

I am not so sure. In that chapter I was drawing on data from Handsworth, which is a very different context to Highgate despite being another inner-urban area of Birmingham. In Handsworth there have been a number of new religious buildings built in recent years, most notably an impressive extension to an already significant Sikh Gudwara on the Soho Road. What is more the Sikhs who built the centre have gone out of their way to incorporate the community into the planning and use of the new buildings. I mentioned in the previous chapter the story told to me by one of my research students of an Afro-Caribbean lady who, on seeing the Gudwara expanding onto a site that had been a games arcade of some kind, remembered the chapel that had originally been on the same site and claimed that God always comes back to claim his own. The Sikhs in this case, and Muslims or Hindus in other parts of the city, have gone out of their way to court the community and to include them in the building and so the buildings are seen by many in those communities in a positive light. The Dar ul-Uloom Islamia complex in Small Heath for example was built, like the Gudwara in Handsworth, with a wide range of facilities for community use and has been received much more favourably by all elements of the local community (Gale 2004, 40–42). These new buildings, however, are still understood as being essentially religious. I also stressed, from the comment of the Afro-Caribbean lady, that the specific nature of the religion did not, in itself matter, it was the religious nature of the building that was stressed in conversations, they were 'of God', and this was given a positive value.

So why is Highgate so different? One reason may be that the builders of new Mosques and Gudwaras in other parts of Birmingham have actually learnt from the experience of the Central Mosque in Highgate and have aimed to include the community from the start. The Central Mosque only started to develop its community outreach at a later date – and probably as part of an attempt to build bridges that have already been seriously damaged. It is also not entirely clear that bridge building with the community was the real reason for recent proposals to develop community space within the Central Mosque. One insider suggested to me that the development of community space was the only way in which the Mosque could gain planning permission for further development and if that is what was needed then that, on the plans at least, is what the expanded space would be used for. Others in the Mosque are less cynical and have a very clear desire to provide real facilities not just for their own congregation but also for others who wish to use them.

The original plans for the Mosque did, in fact, include space for commercial and community activity (Gale 2004, 33). This was not designed primarily to engage with the neighbourhood, it was designed to provide revenue to cover the costs of running the building. The planning office in the City, however, in the light of a new shopping centre that was part of the same process of redevelopment being built close by, decided that commercial premises at the Mosque would be inappropriate. When the idea of a Mosque on this site was first proposed in the 1950s the area still had a significant number of Bangladeshi residents. It was, therefore, designed to be part of a Muslim neighbourhood. It was only with the subsequent redevelopment, however, leading to many of the Bangladeshi households moving elsewhere in the city and new, non-Muslim, populations moving into the area, that the land for the new Mosque became available. The Council was still interested in supporting the development of the Mosque on this site, not primarily because it served a local community, but because it could act as a significant landmark building for the city, sitting as it does in a prominent position on the inner-ring road (Gale 2004, 33). In the first round of planning permission, however, a minaret was not included and the city planners insisted that the Mosque was built in brick to 'blend into the surrounding aesthetic' rather than the white marble that was proposed. The minaret was built in 1986 and the request for a call to prayer being broadcast from it only came in 1992, although there had been a previous request in 1989 that was withdrawn at the last minute because the Mosque authorities did not think it was going to be successful (Gale 2005). In each of these planning rounds, especially those related to the call to prayer, there was considerable opposition from local residents, primarily on the grounds either that Muslims did not live in the area, or that the Mosque was seen to be 'un-English' (Gale 2004, 2005).

The fact that the Mosque does not actually face the community, and that it is not easy for the community to reach the Mosque without venturing out on to the inner ring road, is also an issue in the relationship between the Mosque and the neighbourhood. However hard the Mosque has tried to include the community and welcome them into its space, the community would find it difficult to respond. Although it would be interesting to see what might happen if they made more of the entrance to the community facilities at the back of their own property opening out onto Highgate. The people of the neighbourhood, however, as we have seen in the comments I have noted, tended to exclude the Mosque itself, as a building, from what they consider to be Highgate proper, and so recognise its continued 'otherness' without specifically rejecting the religion it represents. However, it is the 'othering' of the Mosque that is most significant in the comments, even if many people have actually got used to its presence and the call to prayer.

The history of St Alban's and the community's prior response to that building and its congregation could also have had some impact on the response to the Mosque. Both were lumped together by the people as being not 'of us' and this was not related to the fact that one is Muslim and the other Christian. In the later nineteenth century St Alban's was a typical Anglo-Catholic slum church with a large staff and a real sense of mission to the community and its people (Pollock 1890). At the funeral of the first parish priest there were hundreds of people lining the streets and a real sense of loss throughout the neighbourhood. Many of those who currently attend were also born and brought up in Highgate and retain a considerable affection for what the area used to be. It is their long-term family loyalties that keep them coming back to the church despite the fact that they have long since left the neighbourhood and, in relative terms, done very well for themselves.

The general perception of the church today, however, from among the people of Highgate, is of a community that is distant, snooty and alienated from the people. It is not a place for the people to venture into, even for weddings and funerals. More recent clergy at the church have attempted to break down many of these barriers and a recent edition of the church magazine even had an article devoted to 'Living with people of other faiths' (Sultan 2012). The spatial language used by local people, however, referring to the church as being 'up there' is quite significant. The church is seen as being above the people, not just at the top of the hill, but probably in a social sense as well. This reputation is widespread and has nothing really to do with the fact that the church is Anglican or even Christian. It is the attitude, or the perceived attitude, of the particular congregation that appears to matter. Once again, as with the Mosque, there is a process of 'othering' in the language that is used, the setting of a distance or difference between the people of St Alban's and the people of Highgate. In the case of St Alban's, however, the boundary that is being established, or highlighted, is constructed as one of class, rather than one of ethnicity or religion as with the Mosque. This must imply some element of power relations and/or ideology, but that is notably absent from the language I was listening to. People do not feel oppressed by the Church, despite its sometimes brooding presence over the neighbourhood, it is merely irrelevant.

There could, in theory at least, have been some kind of causal relationship between the local people's attitude towards St Alban's and their attitude towards the Mosque, but once again the particular history and the conflicts that surrounded the two buildings probably have more impact on these similarities than any specific attitude towards religion as such. In fact there is no real sense in which the people of the area see the buildings as representatives of 'religion' in terms of the 'spatial representations' or 'ideological spaces' following Lefebvre or Knott, rather they are spaces of 'otherness' and it is this otherness of the spaces that is transferred to the understanding of religion and not the other way around.

Having said all this, it remains to be true that for the people of Highgate, in their everyday conversation, the word 'religion' is closely associated with two specific buildings that dominate the visual landscape and cannot easily be avoided. When talking about these buildings, or referring to them in conversation, then their negative, dismissive, or othering, responses to these buildings matches their negative attitudes to the word 'religion', or the other way around. The lack of association between the Baptist's building and 'religion' only serves to reinforce this view. Given the kind of boundaries that are constructed between the people of the neighbourhood and the two other religious buildings, and given the way in which Chris Baker, for example, draws on Homi Bhabha and others to analyse the potential of 'hybrid spaces' that sit across such boundaries, then we might want to think of the Baptists in Highgate as an ideal example of what Baker calls the 'hybrid church' (2009). Theoretically this is possible, and works within the frameworks that Baker and others like him are constructing (Beaumont and Baker 2011). It is a position that I am sure the people of the Baptist Chapel would welcome. However, given the very absence of any religious language used by non-religious people from the neighbourhood of the building and the activities that it contains, I am not sure that this is really a valid conclusion to be drawn.

Space, Buildings and Religious Diversity

This then brings me to some conclusions, however provisional at this stage. In drawing my conclusions I want to come back to the main question, which is that of attitudes to religious diversity, rather than to questions about space or buildings. As I suggested at the beginning of this chapter my aim is basically to see whether some aspect of the theoretical material on the understanding of space could provide a way into exploring ordinary people's attitudes to religious diversity, and the case study of Highgate is just one small example that attempts to do this. What conclusions, therefore, can be drawn?

Let me begin with the two towers. It was noteworthy that when the Mosque was looking around for justifications to broadcast the call to prayer from its minaret it looked across Highgate to the tower of St Alban's and argued that if the latter could ring bells as a call to prayer, the Mosque could play the traditional Muslim *azan*. This is a convincing argument and was only really countered, from within the community's responses, by those who said that bells were 'musical' or 'English' while the call to prayer was 'like a strangled cat' or 'foreign' (Gale 2005, 1168). The response of the City Council, however, was very telling, although probably the result of a political ploy. They recognised the similarities and then went on to say 'although church bells are part of this country's heritage, they produce a high noise level and have given rise to complaints' (Gale 2005, 1169), so linking the two towers and setting both against the neighbourhood in which they are situated.

I think that the first conclusion, therefore, is a fairly obvious one, but one which is very often overlooked. This is the realisation, which is central to all ethnography, that the specifics of the particular locality matter. One of the main points that Taylor et al. wished to make in their study of Sheffield and Manchester was that we should not treat all Northern cities as a unified block; 'the industrial north' (1996, 19). Rather, by using ethnographic methods and listening carefully to local stories they attempt to show not only that Manchester and Sheffield were very different places, with different stories and different cultural identities, what following Raymond Williams they referred to as different 'structures of feeling' (1996, 5, Williams 1965), but that within the cities there were also different publics who responded to these cities in different ways (1996, 23). In relation to my work in Birmingham I could also add the difference of neighbourhoods within the city, which like the northern cities, might each have their own stories, their distinctive cultural identities, and their own individual structures of feeling.

In other words, therefore, from the perspective of this study, it is not possible to generalise from the situation in Highgate to the whole of Birmingham, let alone to all British cities or any general understanding of religious diversity in modern cities throughout the world. While this may be obvious, and in some senses goes without saying, it is a conclusion that I do really want to stress. The comparison that I have drawn attention to within this chapter between the situation in Highgate, with a generally negative reaction to religious buildings and their communities, as opposed to that in Handsworth where the response is far more positive, is one that has to be noted. As I emphasised in the previous chapter, people without a clear religious identity of their own within the context of British cities do not have an in-built intuitive reaction to religion as either positive or negative, nor is their view strictly neutral; the context matters. In the previous chapter it was the context of the type of discourse that I stressed, in this chapter it is the geographical context, and the specific history of the relationship between that which is perceived as being 'religion' and the people speaking, which provides the interpretive frame for the negative or positive values. These local histories matter and are essential to any attempt to understand, and ultimately to manage religious diversity in the city. I will come back to this in my discussion of memory in Chapter 7.

My other conclusion is perhaps less obvious and, I would hope, more general. Where Highgate and Handsworth differ is in positive or negative value placed on 'religion'. Where they reflect the same general conclusion, is that in both cases the specific nature of the 'religion' is largely (although never entirely) irrelevant. In Highgate, St Alban's and the Mosque, Christians and Muslims, are both categorised as being 'religious' and both are rejected. It is certainly true that a more detailed conversation with any ordinary member of the public would soon begin to generate a very different discourse on Christians to that on Muslims, drawing on stereotypes, images from the media and so on, that is not the point that I am making here. When people, in casual conversation, use the word 'religion' in passing, and make negative comments about the communities associated with St Alban's and the Mosque, they instinctively link the two together and use the same kind of language about both. Neither community, neither building, neither religion is 'of us', and that is the central factor. Something similar can be seen in the positive responses and reactions to the Gudwara and other new religious buildings in Handsworth and other parts of the city.

It is in this context that the failure to see the Baptist building as 'religious' is important. It is the word 'religion' that, for the people of Highgate, carries the negative associations, as confirmed for them by their own experiences of St Alban's and the Mosque, and it is the negative associations of the word that makes it inappropriate for their generally positive relationship with the space of the Baptist building and the community activities that take place there. Religious diversity, therefore, as such, is not fully recognised in the language of the people of Highgate. What is recognised is 'religion' (negatively charged and with no distinction between Christian and Muslim) and 'non-religion', or perhaps in this particular case 'community'. This is an important point and one that we would do well not to ignore when we talk about religious diversity or interreligious relations. The whole debate about religious diversity only really makes sense from a position within one or other of the religions, from the perspective of somebody who has a religious identity. For the vast majority of people on the ground in many of the inner-urban areas of Britain (especially those that are majority white, but this may also be true of many areas of non-white or mixed communities as well) then the question of 'religious diversity' is of little or no real relevance. It is the relationship between the 'religious' and the 'non-religious' that is, in fact, of far more practical value.

Finally, therefore, I want to come back to Lefebvre, his three understandings of space, and Knott's refashioning of this. I think this is important as this provided a way into my understanding of the reactions to religious buildings and communities within Highgate, but I also think that it relates directly to the conclusions that I have just drawn out.

Lefebvre's concept of 'spatial practices' led me to look at the positioning of buildings on the ground and on the journeys congregations and members of the community had to make in and out of these buildings. It was this that led, at a purely geographic level (that is before we actually have to talk to anybody), to a realisation that the Baptist building faces onto the community, draws from the community and is generally open to the community, while the Mosque faces away from the community, draws from outside the community and has its back turned to the community, and St Alban's stands aloof from the community, draws from outside the community and is locked and barred against the community. This same understanding was then reflected in the narratives of the histories of the relationships between these spaces, their congregations, and the community. This 'spatial practice', therefore, emphasises the specifics of Highgate and reflects, or perhaps underpins, the reasons why 'religion' as a word has a particularly negative charge within this community.

It is, however, by looking at Lefebvre's other two layers of the understanding of space that have led to my other conclusion about the lack of distinction between religions and the prioritising of the distinction between 'religion' and 'not religion' over that of religious diversity as such. It is 'representations of space', the general conversations about the specific buildings and what they mean, rather than the movement in and out of these buildings, which is the generator of these kinds of ideas. It is the sense of the two towers brooding ominously over the community as opposed to the low-rise, almost domestic, 1970s community centre occupied by the Baptists that fuels an understanding of a space as being 'religious' and the values that are associated with it. It may also be some sense of 'representational space' that also underpins these kinds of discussions in that some kind of preconceived ideological understanding of religion leads the community to see certain types of building as religious and therefore to have a negative attitude to 'religion', although the general drift of my analysis has actually been away from this conclusion. In my view this ideological space is the product of a specific history in Highgate and not a preconceived pattern that is imposed upon the landscape.

It as this point, therefore, that I want to move from Highgate to Handsworth, from an area of relatively low religious diversity and relatively low religious identity, to one where both are significantly higher, what I am referring to, following Steve Vertovec, as super-diversity (2007). In the study of super-diversity in Handsworth, however, we will see many of the same principles coming through: the importance of locality; the importance of the distinction between 'religion' and 'non-religion'; and, despite the much higher visibility of religious images, a lack of real interest in the idea of religious diversity as a concept.

Chapter 4
Religion in a Context of Super-diversity

Lowell Livezey opens his account of Roger's Park, a neighbourhood on the northern most fringe of Chicago, by taking the reader on a walk down Devon Avenue, the main street of the neighbourhood (2000b, 133). This begins inland, walking towards Lake Michigan, and moves through a series of areas each defined by its own ethnic and religious community; Jewish, Indian, 'Indo-Pakistani', and Mexican (134–5). In each section of the road Livezey outlines the religious buildings associated with the community; synagogues, community centres, temples, mosques and churches. This leads Livezey to articulate the nature of religious diversity within this neighbourhood, and by implication throughout the city of Chicago, in terms of 'ethnoracial enclaves', a concept he takes back to the study of Jewish ghettos, the Catholic national parishes and many Protestant, primarily German, neighbourhoods in the classic Chicago School analyses (139). Only one of the congregations in Roger's Park either is, or even aims to be, diverse in terms of its ethnic and racial make up. Practically all the others, through positive development or simple inaction, reinforce the ethnoracial differences (156–60). It is difficult to see, therefore, Roger's Park as a whole, or how religious diversity as such is envisioned or discussed within the neighbourhood.

In 2010 the photographer Liz Hingley spent a year in the Handsworth neighbourhood of Birmingham taking photographs of the religious diversity of the area that were subsequently put together into an exhibition in Walsall and London. In a paper associated with the exhibition, given at Birmingham University, Hingley talked about taking a bus down the Soho Road through the centre of Handsworth in a manner very similar to Livezey's walk down Devon Avenue (see Hingley 2011). She commented that it is impossible from the vantage point of the top of the 75 bus not to be struck by the religious diversity of the area, not just because of the view of many different religious buildings, images and shops, but also because of the conversations of the fellow travellers on the bus. She notes a comment from a local voice in a paper related to the project saying that: 'On Soho Road people are conscious of their faith rather than where they came from. People used to say "Oh I am from Bangladesh, Pakistan, West Indies, Poland". Now people say "I am a Muslim, I am a Sikh, I am a Baptist, I am a Catholic; this is my identity"' (Hingley 2011). It is also in Handsworth that I have heard the widest range of discourses on, or about, religion and the most intensive conversations that could relate to religious diversity. In this chapter I want to set out to make some sense of the range of discourses that exist within this area of the city.

Livezey treats Roger's Park as one of the most religiously diverse neighbourhoods in his wider study of the greater Chicago region. However, his view of a series of distinct communities along Devon Avenue, and the idea of ethnoracial enclaves that derives from it, do not really reflect the situation in Handsworth. It is true that the Sikh Gudwara and its related buildings dominate one end of the Soho Road. There is, however, no obvious series of communities, defined by specific shops, businesses or places of worship, associated with specific sections of the road, or of the community. The central part of the road is dominated by a series of small shops that are reminiscent of the discussions in Zukin's nostalgic view of shopping streets in New York and Philadelphia (1995, 187–257). The shops themselves reflect a wide range of different ethnic and religious allegiances. At each end of the Soho Road are a cluster of religious and community spaces reflecting considerable diversity. Towards the Birmingham end is the Rastafarian Juice Bar, a Romanian Community Centre, the Anglican Parish Church, the International Christian Fellowship and a couple of large Gudwaras. At the West Bromwich end is a Slovak general store, the Union Baptist Church, an Asian Funeral Parlour, the Chinese and Vietnamese Buddhist Centre and a couple more Gudwaras. It is probable, therefore, that Livezey's ethnoracial enclaves are not a helpful way of analysing or envisioning religious diversity within a neighbourhood such as Handsworth. It is through searching for another model for this analysis, therefore, that I turned to some recent debates about super-diversity.

There are certain neighbourhoods within the contemporary British city, such as Brick Lane in London or Handsworth in Birmingham, where the range of national, religious or other identities present stretches the possibilities of multi-culturalism to the limit. Where the different groups have lived alongside and amongst each other for some time, with the inevitable intermixing and mingling of ideas and people, then we are entering the context of super-diversity (Vertovec 2007). Within Handsworth, and other areas of super-diversity, there are many different religious communities and individuals present within a very small neighbourhood. One aspect of this super-diversity is the wide range of languages that are heard either on the 75 bus or along the road. There are a range of Eastern European languages spoken, as reflected in the Romanian and Slovak centres already mentioned, alongside a very diverse series of south Asian languages. Even the young people who ostensibly speak English do so with a strong street style that often makes listening in to conversations almost impossible. The process of simply hearing and listening to conversations, therefore, as I have done over the years in Highgate and Perry Beeches or Perry Hall, is much more difficult and at times practically impossible. The material for this chapter, therefore, derives from more substantial work in the area among my students and through my own local contacts. As Hingley suggests, however, considerable insight can be gained simply by being, by looking and by observing the details of the street (2011).

Having explored the concept of super-diversity a little further, my focus within this chapter, picking up a couple of the concerns that were raised at the end of the previous chapter, will be primarily with boundaries and the question of indifference. The traditional theories of boundaries, for example those of Anthony Cohen (1985), which presuppose clearly defined and distinct social groups, simply do not work in such areas of super-diversity. Nor can we really apply the theories of Wirth and Simmel in their discussion of radical alienation where each individual is a unique case (Wirth 1938, Simmel 1950). Through a close study of the discourses used within, between and about religion in the neighbourhood, therefore, I wish to outline a much more fluid, transient and limited understanding of religious boundaries within the community and how these can be used to express ideas of religious diversity in such a neighbourhood. Issues of indifference come back because previous studies of neighbourhoods that can be thought of as 'super-diverse', Greenwich in New York and Tooting in London for example (Sennett 1994, Albrow 1997), have highlighted the way in which individuals respond to that diversity, primarily through an indifference to difference. This gives a slightly different perspective to the overall discussion on religious diversity to the kinds of indifference identified in the context of Highgate.

Super-diversity

The concept of super-diversity was coined by Paul Vertovec in a paper published in 2007, although there have been some previous uses of the term (Green 2002, 191). The aim of this paper was to try and capture some of the changes that had occurred within the nation as a whole, specifically the question of where we go once the idea of multi-culturalism is no longer valid. More specifically Vertovec notes a change from a discussion of diversity based on large well-organised Afro-Carribean and south Asian communities to one 'distinguished by a dynamic interplay of variables among an increased number of new, small and scattered, multiple-origin, transnationally connected, socio-economically differentiated and legally stratified immigrants who have arrived over the last decade' (2007, 1024). Within the paper he highlights a number of cross cutting characteristics that both subdivide existing communities and neighbourhoods, but also provide new links across the ethnic divide but based more on gender, language, socio-economic status, sexuality, religion, locality or any number of other sources of personal or social identity.

Vertovec's concern is primarily a policy one; how can the local and national authorities adapt their service delivery and other policy issues to meet the increasingly complex needs of this growing 'super-diverse' society (2007, 1047–9). It is as part of a national debate, therefore, or a discourse about the national condition, that super-diversity has been most clearly developed. In recent years the concept has been applied to a number of different fields such as migrant businesses (Ram et al. 2010), the delivery of health care (Phillimore 2011), or community cohesion (Cantle 2010). My purpose, however, is to apply this concept to a specific neighbourhood where the ethnic and religious diversity, at the micro level, is so much greater than in most neighbouring areas. Contemporary Handsworth is an ideal example of this situation.

It is interesting to note, therefore, that a number of the classic areas of super-diversity in the UK, Handsworth being one, but also Brick Lane in London, are associated with thriving shopping centres. This is significant given Sharon Zukin's discussion of the role of shopping streets of this kind in giving a sense of identity to a neighbourhood and the community who live there (1995, 187–257). Zukin makes the point that many recent studies of shopping tend to focus either on city centres or on outer city shopping malls. However, it was her experience in Philadelphia that it was the local street with its mix of small ethnically-focussed shops that established the identity of the area. Her analysis goes on to look at sites in Harlem and Brooklyn where the liveliness and enthusiasm of the shopping street, often spilling out onto the sidewalk and onto vacant plots, provides a strong sense of local identity. In this sense Handsworth can clearly be seen to have an identity all of its own that is focused on the Soho Road. Unlike many parts of the city, practically all the local shops are in use and there are no significant branded supermarkets and no charity shops. This is a street of small local businesses catering to the many different ethnic and cultural groups of the locality. What is also clear is that the clientele of the shops is mixed; there are not specific parts of the street for particular types of shop or particular groups. Sari dealers sit next to Caribbean food outlets, next to Asian sweet shops, next to urban music stores, next to east European grocers and so on. Super-diversity is obvious and celebrated through the stores of the Soho Road.

Handsworth

Leonie Sandercock, an Australian city planner, who has also worked in the States and Canada among other places, offers a story of the rise of diversity within Birmingham through recounting her own experience as an advisor to the city council in the early years of the new millennium (2003, 14–20). She begins by providing an account of the history of urban planning within the city from the 1950s to the early 2000s. She describes Birmingham in the 1950s as 'a "city of everyman", an honest, hardworking, unpretentious, unglamorous city. The city of a thousand trades, the city of metal bashing, of cars and assembly lines, of pubs and football. A masculine city of sweat and swearing' (2003, 14–15). The 1960s, and then the 1970s, saw two very dramatic changes to this situation. The first was the rise of immigration, primarily to fill the jobs created by Birmingham's heavy industry, and then the collapse of that industry as manufacturing moved to cheaper parts of the world. This led to serious social problems, not just in Birmingham but in many British cities, around race and around unemployment (2003, 15–16). The response of the city government in Birmingham was to invest in new 'post-industrial' sectors and to transform the city centre with conference centres, theatres and concert halls, canal side apartments and the Bull Ring shopping centre making Birmingham the 'meeting place of Europe' (Henry, McEwan and Pollard 2000, 4). This however did little to address the underlying social problems and meant that the city had less funds to spend on social and educational budgets in the 1990s (Sandercock 2003, 17–18). Sandercock became involved with the city in the early years of the twenty-first century in an attempt to reposition the city in relation to its citizens (2003, 19–20).

Handsworth shared much of this city-wide history, especially the growth of ethnic diversity and unemployment in the 1960s and 1970s. In fact Handsworth, as a neighbourhood, has become the area within Birmingham that is most clearly identified with ethnic and religious diversity. In a classic study of the neighbourhood published in 1981 Peter Ratcliffe emphasises the associations that the area came to have in the 1960s and 1970s with the Afro-Caribbean population, even when this was a relatively small proportion of the local population. He notes in particular the change that occurred between 1961 and 1971. In 1961 the Afro-Caribbean population outnumbered the Asian population by three to one. However over the 1960s the Asian population grew sixfold and by 1971 the Afro-Caribbean community was in the minority (1981, 60). Ratcliffe also notes how this growing ethnic diversity led to a similarly growing religious diversity. The majority of the Asian community were Sikhs, and even in the 1970s there were a number of Sikh Gudwaras in the area (1981, 84), Hindus, Muslims and other minority religions were also represented (1981, 75–8). Many of the Afro-Caribbean community also belonged to a range of Pentecostal and other churches (1981, 78–82). Ratcliffe sums up the situation in the 1970s with the following observation:

> At the street level the "community" appears to contain a myriad of very distinct social groupings which rarely have significant points of common contact. Only at a superficial visual level do the startlingly beautiful saris mingle with the brightly coloured hats of young Rastas, or the turbans with the trilby hats of the middle-aged West Indians. Only in the same sense do greengrocers selling Caribbean fruit blend in with the Muslim butcher and Indian sweet centres and sari stores. (1981, 91)

The most significant public marker of ethnic diversity within the neighbourhood, and the events that most people in Birmingham will always associate with Handsworth, were the various riots. The first riots occurred in July 1981, following similar disturbances in Brixton (London) and Toxteth (Liverpool). These were described at the time as 'copycat riots' but they were also labelled nationally as 'race riots' despite the fact that they had more to do with unemployment than racial tensions as such (Southgate 1982). The 'Handsworth riots', or those most closely associated with the neighbourhood, occurred in 1985. The riots began following an incident at the Acapulco Café in Lozells Road and lasted for two days from 9–11 September. Two brothers were killed and over 45 shops were looted. Further disturbances followed on 2 September 1991, alongside similar events in Oxford, Dudley, Tyneside and Cardiff. The riots of 22 and 23 October, 1995, were the most clearly racial in origin although the majority of the disturbances took place within Lozells, an adjoining neighbourhood. These riots occurred primarily between young Black and young Asian men following the rumour of a rape by Black youths on an Asian girl. Finally there were some disturbances in the area during the general riots of August 2011 that affected a large number of cities across the country.

Following the various riots many of the more affluent White, Black and Asian families have moved out of the area and new arrivals from Eastern Europe, Africa and elsewhere have moved in. The ethnic diversity, therefore, has changed again in recent years and is part of a constantly changing environment. Even the 2001 census data may not offer a clear picture of the current situation, but this is the most recent material currently available. In some ways Handsworth is more difficult to identify on the ground than Highgate as there are no clear boundaries and different people see either Soho to the east or Handsworth Wood to the north as part of Handsworth or not depending on the purposes of the conversation. On the other hand this ambiguity does make it easier to use the census data to draw arbitrary lines that make dealing with the data itself much easier. For the purposes of this study I am focussing on the two wards of 'Lozells and East Handsworth' and 'Soho' as my area of investigation (the Soho Road where much of the fieldwork was done fits well within these two wards) with the proviso that this provides only illustrative statistics.

Taking these two wards we can look at two sets of statistics to get a sense of the diversity that I am talking about. First we can look at the country of birth (as percentage of population):

Table 4.1   Breakdown according to place of birth for Handsworth, compared to Birmingham and the national figures, according to the 2001 census

	Hansdworth	Birmingham	England
People born in the UK	65%	84%	91%
People born in other EU	2%	3%	2%
People born elsewhere	35%	13%	7%

Given the number of second- and third-generation immigrants, that would not be apparent from these numbers, the level of potential diversity is already apparent. If we look at the figures for ethnicity then we will see that those who identify themselves as 'White British' only make up around 20 per cent of the population as compared to 65 per cent of Birmingham and 87 per cent of England as a whole. Those who identify themselves as 'Asian or Asian British, Indian' make up 24 per cent of the population, 'Asian or Asian British, Pakistani' 21 per cent, 'Asian or Asian British, Bangladeshi' 9 per cent, 'Black or Black British, Caribbean' 18 per cent. If we then look at religion (as percentage of population) we see a similar element of diversity:

Table 4.2   Religious breakdown of the population in Handsworth,
             compared to Birmingham and the national figures,
             according to the 2001 census

	Handsworth	**Birmingham**	**England**
Christian	31.71%	59.13%	71.74%
Buddhist	1.03%	0.30%	0.28%
Hindu	7.82%	1.98%	1.11%
Jewish	0.04%	0.24%	0.52%
Muslim	29.71%	14.33%	3.10%
Sikh	11.79%	2.93%	0.67%
Other	0.66%	0.26%	0.29%
None	7.45%	12.44%	14.59%
Not Stated	9.79%	8.39%	7.69%

In recent years there has been a great deal of work within Handsworth, through various different agencies, to try and deal with the issues of racism and multiple deprivation that are seen to exist in this area. In some ways Handsworth has become the archetypal deprived inner-city neighbourhood, the place where all the different agencies choose to go and the measure for success across the city as a whole.

Sandercock mentions the Community Fire Station and the work that is being undertaken there as illustrative of the kind of community cohesion work encouraged by the city in the early years of this century (2003, 172–7). The work Sandercock refers to was focussed primarily on the black youth of the neighbourhood and the issues surrounding gangs and knife crime which were major issues at that time, and for much of the following decade. The work from the Fire Station involved black men, who had themselves been caught up in drug culture and gang activities, been to prison and since chosen to help others avoid the same path. These local men worked with the support of local business to contact and get alongside the current generation of young black men, to mentor them and to bring them away from gangs to develop more legitimate issues. Sandercock notes this scheme as a significant arena for overcoming fear and difference, but also notes that the city council, while supporting the scheme itself, did little to direct economic development into the neighbourhood in a way that would offer broader support for the young men who were going through the scheme by way of employment or business opportunities (175). In 2003 this was still, in Sandercock's words, 'work in progress' (176), and today the Fire Station is noted more for its fire safety work than for this kind of community outreach.

Boundaries

One way of trying to think about the nature of religious diversity in an area such as Handsworth is to focus on boundaries. If we follow Gerd Baumann's dominant discourse and assume that an area such as this is made up of a series of communities that each have their own ethnicity and/or culture, and their own religious identity (1996) then the most significant discussions could be assumed to take place at the boundaries between these different communities. One of the most interesting works on boundaries and communities from within the anthropological literature is Anthony Cohen's little book on the *Symbolic Construction of Community* (1985). In this work Cohen argues that communities are constructed through their interactions with others. By drawing on a wide range of examples from the ethnographic literature Cohen confirms the observation by James Boon that cultures 'only need to formulate a sense of themselves as coherent and distinctive because they confront others' (1985, 115, Boon 1981). What is more this context of engagement with others leads communities to concentrate on those things that distinguish themselves, in their own eyes, from others and what makes them 'different'. 'Since the boundaries are inherently oppositional', Cohen argues, 'almost any matter of perceived difference between the community and the outside world can be rendered symbolically as a resource of its boundary' (1985, 117). Cohen's conclusion, therefore, is that communities are often symbolised by their boundaries. It is those things that mark the specific community out from other social groups in the same, or similar, geographical space that come to define the identity of that group. Sometimes very small distinguishing markers can come to have very large symbolic value as the objects around which communities cluster and develop their own particular identities. This is exactly what I expected to occur between the different religious communities within Handsworth.

Other authors have developed similar sets of ideas around boundaries and borders in different kinds of directions. David Sibley, for example, draws on a very wide range of theoretical material, mostly rooted in the work of Julia Kristiva and Mary Douglas (Douglas 1966, Kristiva 1982, Sibley 1995), to look at the concept of exclusion in relation to boundaries. While Cohen sees the boundary essentially in terms of its symbolic element, Sibley makes the point that 'spatial boundaries are in part moral boundaries' (1995, 39) and that the relationship between the self and the other is given moral weight. This is supported by reference to Sennett's work on American suburbs (1970), but also on many other explorations of stereotyping, race relations, pollution and demonisation. Such a view would suggest that the discourse on religious diversity within an area of super-diversity would be entirely negative, with each group distinguishing itself from its close neighbours both through symbolic markers and through moral judgements.

A slightly different take on this is developed by Michel de Certeau in a discussion of space (1984, 115–25). Here de Certeau also recognises the moral element of boundaries, but by linking his discussion to law, and especially the practice of law courts in relation to boundary disputes, de Certeau suggests that the boundary is set through the telling of stories (1984, 123). In fact, he goes slightly further than this in suggesting that the telling of stories, in all contexts, is in part a setting of boundaries. Boundaries in this sense are talked into existence and are expressed in the telling of narratives about the self and the other. In some ways this takes us back to Cohen and the symbolic construction of the boundary, although de Certeau is probably exploring this in a more abstract sense than that offered by Cohen. What this suggests in practice, however, is that it was probably in the stories people told about their own religious group, and about others, that I was most likely to find information about religious diversity within Handsworth.

If I wished to find the nature of the boundaries between the different religious communities in Handsworth, therefore, how these were formed in the discourses of the area and how they were understood both by those who work within them and by those who observe their existence, then I needed to listen to the stories, the narratives and the discourse of the people of the area. This is what I aimed to do within my fieldwork in the area. What I discovered, however, did not support the view of boundary marking that I had assumed from the literature and theory.

Difference and Diversity

I have already noted the difficulties I faced in simply being around the Soho Road and overhearing conversations, a method that worked well in Highgate and at the various festivals. In order to elicit conversations about religion and religious diversity, therefore, I need to engage more directly in conversation. Some of these occurred naturally in the streets and on a couple of occasions on the bus as we drove along the Soho Road. Other times I needed to open a conversation. My most common tactic was simply to ask about whichever religious building I happened to be standing in front of in an open, naïve tourist, kind of way. These openings led to some interesting conversations and much of the data that I have drawn on here come from these, often short, but informative narratives. The first thing to say is that 'story' did form a strong element of many of the conversations as individuals told me either what they knew about the history of the building in question or something that related them to the building, be it a neighbour who was of the faith in question, an event that they had attended, or some more general fact about the faith community. In almost all the conversations, at some point, I was told something along the lines of 'of course, there are lots of religions (religious buildings) in Handsworth'.

One of the things that struck me particularly, however, was that I did not get the kind of boundary talk that might be assumed from the work of Cohen or Sibley. Even if the person, or people (I often tried to make sure the query was directed to a group of passers-by) I was talking to was clearly of a specific religious group, or offered that information as part of the conversation, there was no real sense of the religion represented by the building, or other religions in general, being other or apart from them. This may, of course, have been simple politeness and that is an important element of the public discourse in such situations, but more often than not the attempt to find some kind of connection ('I don't know a lot about the Sikhs, but there is a family down the road and we get on very well, our kids attend the same nursery, and they are really good people, always very generous') or the sense of pride that was expressed about the other community ('I'm not a Hindu myself, but this was the first Hindu temple in Birmingham you know, established in the 1960s I think' or 'I am told that the Sikh community here paid for all the gold on the dome of the Golden Temple in Amritsar, they are very keen on charity work') meant that it was clear that some kind of attempt was being made to provide a positive image of the other rather than to try and distinguish them from the self.

What I also found interesting was the number of times that 'we', or related markers of inclusivity, were used in conversation. The building we were discussing was often 'our church', 'our Buddhist temple' or 'our Gudwara' despite their being other temples, churches and Gudwaras on the same road. The 'our' in this case referred to Handsworth as a whole and that was the focus of identity for many of the people I spoke to. So I was often told that 'we like the colour and variety of this street, all the different shops and cultures and all that', or even 'we take a pride in the different religions round here, we all get on together, it's a great place to be'. The sense of distinguishing the different religious groups, or setting one community/religion against another simply was not part of these conversations. Once again, I do need to stress that I, as enquirer, was clearly an outsider, and the fact of the riots and the assumed reputation of Handsworth, could easily have led to an over-emphasis on unity and togetherness, but this, in itself, is an important observation.

In a paper on women's groups and their use of the internet Sarah Green makes an interesting distinction between 'difference' and 'diversity'. Green noticed a change among politically active women's groups in London in the 1980s and 1990s as the range of possible identities grew due to new responses to gender and sexuality. This led, she suggests, to a move away from a focus on difference as a political position to an increasing focus on diversity. 'The concept of difference always implied a stable difference between one kind of person and another kind of person: you either are or are not a woman; are or are not black; are or are not gay' (2002, 187). On the other hand 'the concept of diversity ... focused more on the continual process through which categories are constructed, and argued that these apparently stable categories were in fact constantly having to be constructed and maintained in order to continue to exist' (2002, 187). There is much here that relates to Bhabha's concept of hybridity (1994) and ideas of the third space that come out of post-colonial writing. What is interesting in this analysis, however, is the specific use of the terms 'difference' and 'diversity'. It is this that I think relates clearly to the situation I was observing within the conversations about religion in Handsworth.

I had expected to hear more about difference, that is about the importance of boundaries and the maintenance of identities. This was suggested, perhaps, by Baumann's dominant discourse. Baumann himself, of course, found that the demotic discourses within Southall were themselves much more fluid (1996). However, if in Baumann's analysis there was still a focus on difference, albeit with moving boundaries, within the comments I was listening to in Handsworth the focus on 'we' suggested that it was diversity and not difference that was important. It is not that there were no distinctions, these were clear, it is just that the distinctions, the differences, were subsumed into a larger sense of what it was to live in Handsworth, the overriding diversity that could encompass and contain the differences. Religious diversity was, in this sense, a fact of life. It was, however, also something that was also very positive, something to be proud of, at least when speaking to an outsider. It was, in part, a counter discourse to the assumed discourse of riots and negative differences, but it was a discourse that many within Handsworth that I met and talked to felt very comfortable with.

The other point that Green makes, looking forward into the 1990s, was the way in which the increasing connectedness made possible by the internet, especially within a women's internet support group in Manchester, led to an increasing disconnectedness among the women themselves. This Green also links to the idea of difference and diversity, although in a more negative fashion. She notes how the internet has become a metaphor for connection and for disconnection, a powerful set of imaginings that made the net 'represent, and actually produce, something like concentrated super-diversity within apparently limitless connection potential' (2002, 191). The outcome, she suggests, is little more than a cardboard cut-out, or stereotype of what it is supposed to represent. Does that suggest, therefore, that all the positive talk about diversity, made to impress the inquisitive outsider, was something of an illusion, giving me what they thought I wanted to hear?

Boundaries, Identity and Religion in Handsworth

In the previous section I have suggested that the fact of diversity, rather than the difference between the religions as represented in boundaries, was the most important element of the comments and stories that I was told on the Soho Road. At one level this may be true. However, I cannot ignore the fact that the people I listened to, and others who spoke of these things on the street or on the bus, always used 'religions' in the plural. The very emphasis on diversity recognises that in Handsworth there was more than one religion involved and it was the sheer multiplicity of religions that led to many of the comments. Within the wider discourse on diversity, therefore, there was recognition of difference, or at least of differences, even if these were not the element that was stressed. Some understanding of boundaries, therefore, was present within these conversations. One interesting development of the academic discussion of boundaries picks up the relationship between the exclusion of the other, with all the moral horror that is associated with that, and level of structure within the society itself. Sibley, for example, draws on Bernstein's classic work on educational processes to suggest that open organisations or societies celebrate participation and cooperation, blur boundary relationships and mix categories, while more closed systems do the opposite (Bernstein 1967, Sibley 1995, 79). The Handsworth of popular discourse within Birmingham as a whole (and often beyond) is characterised by its reputation for the level of racism and the riots that were associated with the area in the 1980s. If this were still true today then such discourse might reflect highly structured, or at least high density, communities clearly separated from each other looking suspiciously at other communities and offering moral condemnations of their lifestyles.

Whether there ever was any evidence for this, and I will come back to that question below, what is clear today, from the kind of evidence that I have been collecting about religion, is that this is not the case today, except perhaps in a few very small minority groups. Or rather, to pick up the point made at the end of the last section, in the presentation that people wished to offer to outsiders, diversity is prioritised over difference. What struck me, however, even in the overheard comments on the street or on the buses, was the almost complete lack of language relating to boundaries and borders, or to conflict and antagonism within the conversations that I was listening to. At first sight this might suggest that Cohen is wrong, that these people were not symbolising their boundaries, but if we link this with Sibley's references to Bernstein then it is possible to suggest that the society is so open, especially in relation to religion, that the boundaries themselves have been blurred almost to the point of non-existence. This is a society, in its casual conversations at least, that is open, that does celebrate participation and cooperation and that clearly does, on many different occasions, mix categories.

Lefebvre has an interesting view on a similar situation, except that he is talking about space in a more abstract sense, rather than about communities or social groups as such (1991). Lefebvre is arguing that we must be careful not to see space in terms of the kind of classifications and boundaries that we normally place on it. These boundaries, he argues, are part of the social construction that we need to be investigating and are not a given in and of themselves. In practice spaces, or ideas of space, overlap and interact with each other. They are relative, and how a single theorist may classify them will depend on where that theorist stands. The image he uses is of millefeuille pastry where the different layers overlap and intersect in such a way that it is impossible really to distinguish them and to pull the whole apart without destroying what it is that we are looking at. There is clearly something similar going on in relation to discourses about religion and religious communities within an area such as Handsworth. This kind of image, and the language Lefebvre is using, relates back to Green's suggestion that diversity demands the continual construction and maintenance of categories rather than the acceptance of the pre-existing boundaries of difference.

There is some connection here with Baumann's analysis of Southall, another area that could potentially be described as 'super-diverse' but which does not represent quite the same level of diversity as Handsworth (1996). As I have already suggested the kind of model assumed by Cohen, and perhaps by Sibley and even de Certeau at the point in his argument when he is talking about boundaries, can be linked quite closely to Baumann's dominant discourse. This is the model where distinct, and definable, communities exist that match culture, ethnicity and religion and have clear boundaries that enable the authorities both to define the groups and to work with them. The differences occur, however, when we come to consider Baumann's demotic discourses. Here the view from the social groups on the ground is that the boundaries are not so clear cut or that they do not always exist in the places that the dominant discourse, or even other demotic discourses suggest that they do. One of the examples that Baumann uses relates to the Sikhs and Hindus within Southall (1996, 116–22). Here it was not always clear, when talking to ordinary Sikhs or Hindus on the ground, whether certain groups and their temples, were to be classified as Sikh or Hindu or even whether this distinction was important or not (1996, 118). The answer to the question largely depended on where the observer was positioned.

No doubt there is the same kind of blurring of boundaries and re-envisioning of groups going on in Handsworth as there is in Southall. The significant presence of the Sikh community in both neighbourhoods would make this a distinct possibility. What I have been observing, however, is not this kind of playing with boundaries. In the conversations I have observed I am noting something very different. There is a recognition of a variety of different religious groups. However, there is, at the same time, an almost complete denial of boundaries in the sense assumed by Cohen and Baumann's dominant discourse. There is an almost deliberate avoiding of the boundary issues in the everyday conversation. In some cases this is expressed as an overlapping and intersecting of social groups, and even of discourses, that is much closer to Lefebvre's pastry, and therefore something that is much more difficult to grasp than Baumann's dominant discourse. However, for all that there is not the apparent need to constantly construct and maintain identities, Sikhs are Sikhs, Muslims are Muslims and Catholics are Catholics. These categories remain, are widely known, and are widely used; it is just the boundary between them that is hidden by the conversations.

Difference and Indifference

Following the riots in British cities in 2001 the then-Labour government commissioned a study to investigate the causes and to offer possible policies that might mitigate against, and hopefully prevent, subsequent repeat events. This report was delivered in 2001 and had a significant impact on government policy for the next decade (Home Office 2001). I will come to look at the policy itself in Chapter 8, for now it is the analysis of the problem that interests me. Here the problem was seen to lie in a wide range of different causes, both macro and micro. Poverty, deprivation, bad housing etc. were clearly identified. However, alongside this was the tendency for ethno-religious communities to separate themselves into different neighbourhoods within the cities establishing ghettos of people who ceased to associate with one another (Home Office 2001, 8). This picks up exactly

Livezey's analysis of Roger's Park, and other narratives about Chicago and other American cities, and is understood to be a bad thing and something that, at its worst, can lead to riots. Underpinning this, as we shall see in Chapter 8, is the kind of dominant discourse that is presented by Baumann with its emphasis on the merging of culture and community (and ethnicity and religion, Baumann 1996) and there has been a great deal of criticism of the report and its assumptions, both at the time and more recently (e.g. Amin 2002). However, we have to ask whether studies of neighbourhoods that could be described as super-diverse, where there is no sense of ghettoisation, have the same kind of dynamic.

Robert Sennett, in a reflection on living in Greenwich Village in New York, suggests that the level of diversity within that neighbourhood is encapsulated only in the gaze, in other words people see diversity but do not specifically engage with it (1994). He offers a description of Second Avenue that mirrors that of Livesey's description of Devon Avenue in Roger's Park. To observe how 'Hispanics, Jews, and Koreans interweave along Second Avenue' Sennett suggests, 'is to pass through an ethnic palimpsest in which each group keeps neatly to its own turf' (1994, 357). Living within this neighbourhood, that is characterised by a very high level of diversity, is facilitated, so this analysis concludes, by the fact that the people who live there choose to ignore the diversity around them, to remain indifferent to difference; 'the sheer fact of diversity does not prompt people to interact' (1994, 357). J. Donald almost turns this into an ethical prescription suggesting that for the urban dweller in super-diverse neighbourhoods, what is of most importance is 'reading the signs of the street; adapting to different ways of life right on your doorstep; learning tolerance and responsibility – or at least, as Simmel taught us, indifference – towards others and otherness' (1999, 167). Work that has been undertaken in other areas of extensive diversity has reached a similar kind of conclusion, although with some subtle differences.

Martin Albrow, for example, in a study of Tooting in South London emphasises the fact that the level of cultural and ethnic diversity does not lead to greater integration, in fact just the opposite (1997). Here the people almost deliberately reinforce their own identities and avoid any engagement with other populations, even in an area of considerable mixing. Above all Albrow wants to stress that anything approaching a community with shared values simply does not exist in this neighbourhood, and is not desired by a significant proportion of the population. What is important for Albrow and his respondents is the way in which 'these people inhabit co-existing social spheres, coeval and overlapping in space, but with fundamentally different horizons and time-spans. The reality of Tooting', he goes on to say, 'is constituted by the intermeshing and interrelating of these spheres' (1997, 48). This is not quite the indifference of Sennett's study but does reflect something of how a locally super-diverse area can lead to a rejection of the need for a local community.

Behind this kind of analysis, as Donald suggests, and Albrow implies, lies the work of Wirth, Simmel and others who understand the city primarily in terms of alienation, that it is a space that allows the individual to shed something of their communal identity and to develop a new, unique and essentially individual identity. Albrow relates his analysis of Tooting to Anthony Giddens' idea of disembedding, the process of creating social connections, and even communities, beyond the local, geographical neighbourhood (1997, 54, Giddens 1991). Post-modernism with its emphasis on play and the breaking up of old grand narratives reinforces this perspective, as we saw in Chapter 1, leading to individual understandings of identity built out of the ruins of the past (Beck and Beck-Gernsheim 2002). This initial phase of post-modernity, with its nihilistic view of the future has, perhaps, passed, but the post-colonial notion of hybridity has come to denote a very similar approach (Bhabha 1994).

This picks up again Green's discussion of diversity and difference, although with an emphasis on her more negative position (2002). Even the positive view talked about the need, in a situation of diversity, or super-diversity, to constantly construct and maintain categories through which to understand identity. Vertovec implies something very similar when he suggests that contexts of super-diversity are defined by the ability of the observer, and by implication of those who are part of the context, to cut across the community through any one of a number of different identity markers (gender, socio-economic position, ethnicity or whatever) (2007). In real life, therefore, people can choose to make connections and mark differences along any axis they choose. The woman who told me outside the Gudwara on Soho Road that a Sikh family who lived down the road took their children to the same nursery is choosing to focus on the connection of age and family position rather than the difference of religion, for example. But does this imply, as Green's statements about stereotypes and the implied assumptions of indifference to difference in the works we have just been looking at suggest, that the religious difference is irrelevant?

Given what I said earlier, I would say that the answer to this question is 'no'. However, if I go back to the comments and stories that I collected on the Soho Road then I could suggest that what many of those I listened to are indifferent to is not so much religious difference as religion itself, even in an area of such high religious visibility as Handsworth. More than once I got the response, when asking about a specific building, of 'I dunno' or something similar. A little more informative were the comments of 'its religious, innit?' Even when the building inspired a story or further conversation I was struck by the fact that what I was being told about was the community or even the local group and not really about the religion at all. So to comment that a particular building was the first Hindu temple in Birmingham, or to say that a respondent thought that the Sikhs now owned most of the bottom end of the Soho Road, says nothing about what it is to be Hindu or Sikh and shows no knowledge of this on the part of the individual concerned. Overall there was a significant lack of 'religious literacy' among those I talked to (although I have to admit to not pressing on this to discover how much people actually did know), and more importantly a clear sense of general disinterest. The tone was almost universally neutral. Where this did change, however, was in the tone of pride in

Handsworth itself, as a place of diversity and, we might almost say, harmony, that
was conveyed by a significant number of those I talked to.

Belonging, Identity and Hybridity

In a study of non-religious people from the towns and villages of North Yorkshire,
Abby Day identifies the issue of 'belonging' as central to an understanding of
belief (2011). This is not the place to engage with her specific ideas about belief
and their relationship to a discussion of religion, but a number of her informants
have interesting things to say about religious diversity and Day's own analysis
of belonging puts this into a context that has important things to say with regard
to the discussions in this chapter. The first thing to note is that none of Day's
informants come from neighbourhoods that could remotely be described as 'super-
diverse'. This is a point that Day herself glosses over, but which is important
when comparing her data with that which I found within Handsworth. All Day's
informants come from small-scale communities, often from villages and towns
on the edge of the Yorkshire Dales (2011, 35). Day makes a big point of the
development of the 'other' in relation to the beliefs of her informants, and one
of those 'others' is clearly, and physically, situated in the multi-ethnic and multi-
religious towns of Leeds, Burnley, Bradford and Keighley to the south of the
region under consideration (2011, 137–42). Other religions, therefore, exist within
the urban context and are 'other' to the essentially rural informants Day chooses
to interview.

However, even to talk of 'other religions' actually raises an important point
that is central to Day's own analysis. Why is it that Islam, in particular, and the
south Asian communities associated with it, are seen as 'other'? Or to turn the
question around into the form that Day herself asked it, why do these white rural
(or small town) individuals see themselves as 'Christian'? It is the fact that so
many people self identified as Christian in the 2001 census that set Day off in her
investigations in the first place. Her answer to this question comes back to the
question of belonging. Day suggests three different kinds of identities that are
associated with Christian nominalism (2011, 182–8). The first, natal nominalist
identities, is related directly to the family and underpins all other forms of
belonging. The third is aspirational and is in essence personal and individual.
The second is what Day describes as 'ethnic nominal identities', the idea that to
be English is to be Christian and that the 'other' is therefore not Christian. It is
this essential association of Christianity with Englishness, Day argues, that can
account for most of the decisions to identify as Christian on the census.

The situation in Handsworth is very different from that of North Yorkshire;
although I have no doubt that there are areas within the city of Birmingham that
have exactly the same kind of construction of belonging as Day's informants.
What is interesting and significant from Day's work, however, is the association
between belief and belonging and I am sure the same kind of association is

identifiable from my own data. It is much more difficult to identify the relation between belonging and family from the kind of data that I was collecting as I was not looking to these kinds of conversations, although the 'othering' of women and young people is obvious from any bus ride through the city (Day 2011, 142–50). The sense of belonging to the neighbourhood, however, was very clear and came through in many different conversations as I have already suggested. Handsworth was a place to be proud of, and to come from Handsworth was an important part of belonging and identity for a significant number of the people I listened to. The language about adjacent areas was exactly what would have been expected from Cohen's analysis of boundaries and Day's relating of this to belief and belonging. However, what is significant is the way in which this belonging to Handsworth as a neighbourhood in itself undermined and contracted the second of Day's kinds of nominalist identity.

Part of belonging to Handsworth was an acceptance of the diversity of the neighbourhood and hence of religious diversity as a fact of life. In many ways the kinds of conversation that I overheard on the street and on the bus, and that Hingley also identified through bus rides along the Soho Road, makes this point. The fact that there was much more overt religious language and religious reference within conversations in this neighbourhood than in an area such as Highgate, for example, indicates that this can be seen as an area where religious diversity is common and accepted. It was the cross religious conversations that were actually most prominent, not individuals talking to others of the same faith, but religion arising, without embarrassment or conflict, in conversations between people of different faiths, that was most striking and this suggests that belonging to this neighbourhood meant an acceptance of the super-diversity of the area. It is almost a belief statement in itself, a part of the construction of belonging, to say that religious diversity is normative (Stringer 2008).

If we go back to Sennett's Greenwich Village or Albrow's Tooting and other studies of a similar nature, we see the centrality of the concept of indifference. In these studies the term relates to the way in which people relate to difference, although understood here as indifference to that which is different. What we have seen in the analysis of conversations from Handsworth, however, is a different understanding of indifference, not to that which is different, but to difference itself. This is especially clear in relation to religion. This understanding of indifference is essential to my own argument as it appears that the many different approaches to, understandings of, and values given to religion and religious diversity is in part due to the fact that religious diversity is not a topic that is of direct personal concern, even to those who are religious. It is known, and assumed, and it is essentially seen as positive (or at best neutral) based in part on the individual's own assessment of religion, but also on their sense of belonging to Handsworth and their understanding of Handsworth as an area of considerable religious diversity. In itself, however, religion, or religious diversity is not a matter to get seriously worked up about.

Conclusion

In a study of the mixed Black and Latino area of 'Adams-Vermont' on the south
side of Los Angeles in the 1990s, Alisdair Rogers offers 'four models or ideals of
the multi-ethnic metropolis; the assimilated city, the city of division, the multi-
cultural city and the city of difference' (1995, 135). The assimilated city and the
city of division are seen primarily as older models, the first an unachievable ideal
based on the idea of the melting pot, the second an assumed and bemoaned reality
in many American cities. The last two reflect some elements of contemporary
policy in a city such as Los Angeles. The distinction is not that different from
the distinction I have developed in this chapter based on Green's discussion
of difference and diversity. The multi-cultural city is that epitomised by
Roger's Park, Greenwich, and perhaps Tooting, where the different 'ethnoracial
enclaves', to use Livezey's terminology (2000b), have some level of equal status
but remain very much distinct and clearly identifiable units. I have associated
this with Baumann's dominant discourse where community, culture, ethnicity
and perhaps religion are seen to be coterminous (1996). The city of difference,
in Rogers' analysis, is based on the writings of Iris Marion Young who talks of
an as yet unrealised ideal of 'openness to unassimilated others' (1990, 227). The
work of Leonnie Sandercock also points in the same general direction and she
saw the work of the Community Fire Station in Handsworth as one of a number
of beacons on the road towards such an ideal (2003). My emphasis within this
chapter on discourses of diversity in relation to religion within Handsworth may
also indicate that in some ways at least, within this neighbourhood of super-
diversity, such an ideal may already exist.

It may, but I would also want to add a number of warnings. The first is the point
that I made towards the end of this chapter, when I emphasised the underlying
indifference to religion that was expressed within the discourses of diversity that
I was listening to. Religion is an area where we can, perhaps, talk of the ideal
'city of difference' or 'openness to unassimilated others' as it really does not
matter all that much to us anyway. Clarifying this slightly, I think I do need to
note that it is not specifically 'religion' that carries this level of indifference. For
those who are religious I have no doubt that their own religion, their spirituality,
their faith, or however they wish to describe it, is of utmost importance. More
generally, religion, spirituality, belief (again the terminology is difficult to nail
down) is of vital importance even to those individuals who are not openly, or
specifically, religious. The work of Abby Day and my own previous studies have
shown this to be the case (Stringer 2008, Day 2011). What I am drawing from the
field work I carried out in Handsworth is that it is religious diversity, the presence
of other religions and their overt expression within the neighbourhood in terms of
dress, buildings and other visual images, that is seen to be irrelevant, or we could
say, accepted and normal. This does demonstrate a marked shift among many,
from many different religious backgrounds, but specifically from the Christian
perspective, from an insistence on the rightness of our own religion as the only

path to God, to the acceptance, at least in public discourse, of many different possibilities each of which is positive in its own terms. This is an important finding and one I will come back to in the final chapter.

The second warning I will offer as a conclusion to the discussions in this chapter, takes us back to the multi-cultural city and more specifically to the quote that I offered from Hingley's informant at the start of the chapter. Hingley was told that 'people are conscious of their faith rather than where they came from' (2011). It is probably worth noting at this stage that her informant was an Anglican priest. However, this is a common position to take in viewing ethnicity and difference in the post-9/11 city. The language has moved, we are told, from an emphasis on ethnic identities (where people come from) to one of religious identities (their faith). This ignores the fact that the only real religious identity that most people are interested in is Islam and that this is identified as a communal identity primarily because, as Baumann rightly reminds us, there is no single ethnic community that encompasses it (1996, 123). On the ground, and even in an area of super-diversity such as Handsworth, it does not take long to realise that the underlying divisions of 'White', 'Asian' and 'Black' are still of central importance. As with Albrow's study of Tooting most people draw their closest friends and acquaintances from their own 'community' (1997) and it is obvious, watching the shops along the Soho Road, that Asian shops attract primarily Asian customers, Caribbean shops Black customers, and so on. Certainly there is a level of mixing and integration, but as the riots of 2005 showed this 'diversity' may not be all that deep within the neighbourhood and when the crunch comes it is 'difference' that matters. In this the people of Handsworth may not, after all, be all that different from Day's informants in the Yorkshire Dales. The fundamental difference, however, remains ethnic and we should never confuse this with the level of openness to discourses of religious diversity that is apparent on places like the Soho Road.

Chapter 5
Taking to the Streets

With this chapter I wish to move away from the study of specific communities into a wider context. The third area I suggested that it would be possible to hear discourses on religious diversity is in and around street festivals, especially those that have, or are supposed to have, a religious content. There has been a great deal written about festivals of this kind, their organisation and their proposed functions. Nothing that I have found, however, asks the question of the kinds of conversations such events generate among those who attend them, or how the festivals are talked about by individuals going about their daily business away from the festivals themselves. This is going to be my focus in this and the following chapter.

In this chapter, therefore, I am not going to look directly at what the people say in relation to the festivals. Rather I want to explore the festivals themselves and the range of discourses that surround the festivals, or the everyday discourses about the festivals in the conversations that I have been listening to in Highgate and Handsworth. In particular I want to look at the City Council's policy in terms of arranging and supporting public festivals and the role discourses about culture, religion and inclusivity play within this context. Behind this analysis is once again the work of Gerd Baumann in *Contesting Culture* (1996). On this occasion, however, I want to look specifically his discussion of the 'dominant discourse'. I am particularly interested in the way in which a city, such as Birmingham, has used this dominant discourse over time in its management of street festivals and how the organisers of the festivals have responded to this. In particular I am interested in the subtle changes in this discourse over the last 50 years or so, especially as that has related to the Council's policy on street festivals.

According to Baumann the content of the dominant discourse is built around three concepts; culture, community and ethnicity (1996). The process begins with the 'reification of culture'. Within this process what begins as a conceptual tool for anthropological analysis becomes something that is claimed to exist and associated with specific 'cultural' groups. As Baumann states, 'outside anthropology, ... the word was borrowed and assigned a new, and far more concrete, meaning the discourse of what Rothschild has described as "ethnopolitics"' (Baumann 1996, 11, Rothschild 1981, 2). This ethnopolitics also draws on the use of 'community' in public rhetoric. Again a term that is treated with a great deal of suspicion within the academic literature is used to give respectability to a discourse about other peoples; 'to make general statements about "the Asians", "the Jews" or "the Irish" reeks of disrespect, ignorance and even prejudice. Yet the same statements can be made to sound respectful and even solidary when uttered about the Asian, Jewish or Irish "community"' (Baumann 1996, 15). It is for this reason that within the 'dominant discourse, "community" can act as the conceptual bridge that connects culture with ethnos' (1996, 16).

As Baumann makes very clear within his discussion this all works moderately well until the question of religion is introduced. In particular complex issues start to emerge once authorities choose to talk about the 'Muslim community' with the same assumptions about culture and ethnicity as they might use of the 'Pakistani community', or even the 'Jewish community'. Baumann quotes Michael Ignatieff talking about the Salman Rushdie affair in the early 1990s: 'One of the ironies of the Salman Rushdie affair was that the only thing on which anti-Islamic liberals and their fundamentalist opposite numbers agreed was that there was such a thing as a "Muslim community". Having outlined some of the consequences of this Ignatieff concludes by saying "at the height of the affair, Muslims in Britain could be forgiven for wishing no one had ever thought them a community at all"' (1992, Baumann 1996, 15). Such concerns, however, did not prevent the dominant discourse from accommodating the 'Muslim community' within its more general discussions on culture and community. In recent years it could well be argued that the dominant discourse has actually gone further in preferring to talk of 'religious' communities as opposed to 'ethnic' communities, as we saw in the previous chapter. That is one of the elements that I wish to explore, with specific reference to the street festivals within Birmingham and the discourses surrounding them.

For now, therefore, I am happy to accept Baumann's assertion that the dominant discourse is one that equates 'culture', 'community', 'ethnicity' and perhaps 'religion' as a working model, and to see how that is played out in the development of street festivals within the city of Birmingham. Before looking at the specific details, however, it is worth standing back and looking at the way street festivals and other public events have been studied within the wider anthropological, geographical and sociological literature in the last 50 years or so.

The Study of Public Events

There is no one single source from which the contemporary study of carnivals, street theatre, festivals and parades emerged. There are various strands that have come together over time from different sources and which coalesce or merge within any one contemporary study. There are two clusters of sources that I think are useful for my purposes within this text and which I will come back to in the more detailed analyses of this, and the following, chapters.

The first of these, and the earliest in time, is the folkloric study of popular festivals across Europe. Again this did not emerge in one place at one time but in itself consists of a number of different strands. It is perhaps strongest in Spain, where the profusion of local festivals and street parades is still more prevalent than many other parts of Europe, and from here it moved very quickly to the study of carnivals, festivals and other public events across the Caribbean and Latin America. One of the founding figures in this tradition is Julio Caro Baroja, the Basque anthropologist and historian of Basque culture (1965). His work identifies a number of the themes of this kind of analysis. The first emphasis is on the 'popular' nature of such events. These are viewed as 'folk' events; public outbursts of popular creativity that often run counter to the official, or the dominant narratives of the society. There is a strong oppositional nature to many carnivals and other popular feasts. This, according to Caro Baroja is rooted in the medieval traditions of Europe where oppositional festivals, such as the feast of fools, and carnival itself, were seen to provide a safety valve for the rigid social structures of society.

Peter Burke's analysis of the religious festivals in early modern Europe is one of many works to pick up this kind of analysis and to situate festivals and carnivals in a wider philosophical and political movement (1994, first published 1978). A wider range of historical studies has subsequently built on the work of Burke and his colleagues, along with that of Emmanuel Le Roy Ladurie on the massacre during the carnival at Romans-sur-Isère in France (1979), and often referencing Mikhail Bhaktin's work on the carnivalesque in the literature of the late renaissance (1984, first published 1965), to offer a wider historical perspective on popular or oppositional festivals.

Not all street parades and public performances, however, are counter-cultural in the way that carnival is often portrayed. There are many parades and other events to mark days of national importance that are very formal and that firmly reinforce the dominant discourse and the structures of society. Don Handelman, for example, distinguishes between three kinds of public event; 'models', which do not concern us here, 'events-that-present' and 'events-that-re-present' (1998). The distinction between the last two relate to the way the event engages with Baumann's dominant discourse, or other significant narratives within the society. In other words events-that-present are those that reinforce the dominant discourse of the society: 'statements, mirror-images, reflections – these are the hallmarks of events-that-present. The pivots of such occasions often are the very visibility of symbols throughout. Their relative plenitude of orderliness is the product of the over-signification of exactness, replication, and uniformity of detail' (1998, 41). The examples that Handelman offers are the Nuremburg rallies of the Third Rich or the old Soviet Red Square march pasts. Events-that-re-present, on the other hand, offer an alternative view of the society. Such events are also aimed at reinforcing the dominant discourse according to Handelman, but they do this through engagement with more complex and often counter-social discourses. 'This kind of event re-presents lived-in worlds by offering propositions and counter-propositions, within itself, about the nature of these realities. Whether through the juxtaposition and conflict of contraries, through the neutralization of accepted distinctions, or through their inversion, the more hidden or controversial implications of the propositional character of the world are exposed' (1998, 49). The classic medieval carnival, that turns all the accepted morals and hierarchies of the society upside down for a short and clearly defined period, is a good example of an event of re-presentation.

The second cluster of sources for the study of public events derives much more specifically from the anthropological literature and focuses on the way in which a specific public event can be used to form the basis for an analysis of the wider society and the issues that underpin it. This approach was developed particularly within the Rhodes-Livingston Institute in Zambia in the 1950s and 1960s and the classic study in this field is Max Gluckman's paper on the opening of a bridge in Zululand (1958). This essay has become something of a classic in anthropological studies of public events. The event itself was very simple and relatively straightforward; it consisted of the opening of a bridge by the district governor and the driving of the first car across the bridge. Gluckman, however, chose to use it to make a number of different points, focusing particularly on the role of both African and European players within the event. At one level the essay is an example of a style of anthropological method developed by Gluckman and his colleagues within the Rhodes-Livingstone Institute and the anthropology department of the University of Manchester. These studies aimed to begin with a specific event, often a dispute, and to use that as the focus of an ever-widening analysis of the various people, relationships, structures and discourses that coalesce around the event itself (Rogers and Vertovec 1995). At another level, however, Gluckman was also trying to demonstrate that we cannot study any public event without recognising the wider political and colonial context. What this essay does is show how, within the single event, both the native Africans and the colonial authorities came together in a single activity and how each had different messages and meanings that were rooted in their own interpretations of the event.

J. Clyde Mitchell developed the same technique and used it to focus on an event that might be closer to the kind of street festivals that I am discussing in this chapter (1956). His analysis of the Kalela Dance in urban Zimbabwe focuses on a very specific public event to demonstrate the way in which migrant men within an urban environment use the context of dance to begin to negotiate and to construct ideas of identity and ethnicity. For Mitchell ethnicity itself is a fluid notion that needs to be constructed or negotiated within events such as the Kalela dance. It is not a concept that has meaning outside of the diverse social gatherings created by the socio-economic framework of migration. It is within the dance, therefore, within the public event, that the concept of ethnicity is negotiated, constructed and asserted within a very specific urban environment (Kapferer 1995).

A very specific take on this kind of analysis develops out of Victor Turner's rethinking of Arnold Van Gennep's work on rites of passage (1969). Van Gennep saw all rites of passage, which included rites that concerned the change in seasons or from one year to the next, as having three parts. There is a rite of disaggregation or removal from the previous year, a liminal or in-between state in the middle, and then a rite of aggregation into the new year (1960, first published 1908). It was the liminal phase that is picked up by Turner and explored in a wide range of differing contexts. For Turner this is a time of ambiguity, licence and radical togetherness, a state he describes as 'communitas' (1969, 82–3). It is also a time that is filled with monsters and half-human creatures, where gender barriers are broken down and the normal rules of society no longer hold. Turner distinguishes between 'structure', the normal state of society, and 'anti-structure', or the state of liminality. Edmund Leach takes this analysis one stage further (1961). By drawing on Turner's ideas of 'structure' and 'anti-structure', Leach argues that it is societies where the structure is strong that the need for periods of licensed anti-structure is greatest, so long as they can be brought to a clear sense of closure through the application of Van Gennep's ritual process and a clear rite of reintegration (1961). This is much the same argument as that developed by the folklorists and historians from my first cluster, and is often stated alongside the wider historical analysis in many contemporary analyses.

In more recent years the discussion and analysis of street festivals has moved from the folkloric, the historical and the anthropological to the geographical. It is as an event in public space that the festival is considered as a geographical issue. At one level the festival, or its route, can be seen to define the space itself, at least for the time of the festival (Smith 1995). At another it is the way in which public space is claimed by conflicting publics that is seen as the most significant element of the festival (Marston 1989). In very recent analysis the place of the visual elements and even the soundscape of the festival and/or procession are highlighted as having a specific role to play in claiming space or constructing identity (Kong 2005, Ingalls forthcoming). I will come back to some of these specific studies and the issues they raise in the following chapter.

Many of these different sources, and the kinds of analyses associated with them, come together in a classic study of the Notting Hill Carnival written in the 1990s. Abner Cohen, who wrote the book, came from the kind of anthropological tradition expressed in the work of Gluckman and Mitchell and he uses the Notting Hill Carnival as the basis for a wider analysis of the role of cultural movements in formal and informal political activity (1993). The book focuses on the history of the Notting Hill Carnival showing how the different historical contexts lead to differing understandings and expressions of the Carnival itself. Throughout the period covered, however, 1966–1992, the Carnival developed as one of the country's leading sites for the development of, and the expression of, Black Caribbean culture. Given the practical difficulties faced by the Afro-Caribbean population in meeting and organising in any formal sense, Cohen argues that the Carnival, through its informal networks and diffuse leadership, provided a context both for opposition to White majority rule, but also, where appropriate, for collaboration and integration with the wider society where that was possible and appropriate.

Cohen argues that any large-scale public event, such as the Carnival, needs to retain a balance between conflict and alliance: 'If the festival is made to express pure and naked hegemony, it becomes a massive political rally of the type staged in totalitarian regimes. If, on the other hand, it is made to express opposition, it becomes a political demonstration against the system' (1993, 128). These two types relate to what Handelman described as events-that-present and events-that-re-present (1998), but what Cohen offers beyond Handelman's analysis is the need to provide a balance between these two types within any one event, and the way in which this balance allows for a more subtle and complex set of political discourses. Through a process that Cohen describes as the 'aestheticisation of politics' (1993, 133–47) the Carnival is able to maintain this balance by focusing on issues of conflict surrounding the production of music and dance rather than taking a specific stance on more overtly political issues. The political issues, however, are always present and are obvious to both participants and observers alike. The Carnival, therefore, with its specific set of networks and its emphasis on art, music and movement, provides a context where the political issues can be addressed in a more complex and nuanced way without anybody really having to state a position, so retaining the balance between the rally and the protest.

One interesting point that Cohen makes in passing, while acknowledging that there is nothing specifically religious about the Carnival in Notting Hill, is the way in which ethnicity, when it becomes too difficult to handle politically, is often morphed into religion. He draws specifically on his previous work in West Africa to make this point, showing how the ethnic conflicts and identities among different groups at independence are transformed into religious identities when the language of ethnic diversity is repressed by the newly instated regimes (Cohen 1969). This develops Mitchell's arguments about the fluidity of ethnicity and identity but relates very specifically to a number of current debates around ethnicity and religion that I am raising in this book. I will come back to this point in my final chapter.

Birmingham Festivals

Having looked at some of the sources for the study of public events, carnivals and street festivals, I want to go on look at a series of public events within the city of Birmingham that illustrate, in a developing fashion, the way in which the dominant discourse of the city has both followed Baumann's original understanding of distinct cultures being equated with specific communities, but also how it has developed in recent years to include 'religion' as an important marker of such communities alongside, and even co-terminus with, 'culture'. I also want to keep an eye on the counter-cultural element of the study of public events that I have highlighted from the sources, but in doing this I want to emphasise how, within Birmingham at least, what may have begun as counter-cultural, or even representing the voices of a demotic discourse, has slowly been encompassed within the city's own dominant discourse and has, in many ways, become part of the establishment. I will pick up other elements of the analysis of public events in the next chapter when I will follow Gluckman and Mitchell and focus on one specific event to explore the role that discourses on religion play within that event.

The history of street festivals within Birmingham can be explored with reference to three kinds of event: protest events/demonstrations; cultural/community parades; and religious festivals. In very approximate terms these can be seen to form a process of historical development (protests originating in the 1970s and 1980s, cultural parades in the 1990s, and religious events being recognised more fully by the Council since the turn of the new millennia). However, the history of each event is, in fact, much more complex than this kind of division might suggest.

Protest Events/Demonstrations

There have been street festivals of one kind or another within a city such as Birmingham almost since its founding. Churches would have processed either on major Christian festivals, perhaps at May Day, or for evangelistic purposes. There would have been street markets in the centre of the town and through the nineteenth and early twentieth centuries trades unions and other campaigning bodies would have taken to the streets on a regular basis. The Christian use of the streets probably began to die out between the wars, and would have reduced considerably in the 1950s and 1960s leading to a sense in the 1970s that the only events on the streets were those of protest. The latest range of street festivals therefore, can be seen as something of a resurgence of a phenomena rather than something entirely new.

This resurgence of street festivals can be seen particularly in two very different events, both of which are essentially protests although not of the kind usually associated with trades unions or similar bodies. One of the oldest of the current group of street festivals are the Birmingham Pride marches. These have had a rather chequered history in Birmingham and have never reached the level of public awareness that is associated with such events in London or Manchester (Knowles 2009). The first march in 1972, from the Bull Ring and up New Street to the Town Hall, appears to have been spontaneous and consisted of about 20 to 30 individuals (Knowles 2009, 50). This occurred just one week after the first Gay Pride event in London although it was only repeated for a few years in the early 1970s. The idea of a gay event, organised by the commercial sector, was resurrected in 1983. However, as Knowles makes clear, this was an entirely non-political event, described as 'Five Days of Fun', and held behind closed doors in the pubs and clubs of the 'gay village' and their associated car parks (2009, 51). The first official Birmingham Pride event, recognised by the Council, took place in 1997 (2009, 56) with the first parade not taking place till 2000 (2009, 60). This was funded and supported entirely by gay businesses and the wider LGBT community and Knowles notes that the Birmingham City Council, unlike their compatriots in Manchester, never formally supported the gay cause or provided any funding for the Birmingham Pride event.

In recent years Birmingham Pride still continues, but it has been contested and very uncertain in some recent years. The official website describes the 2012 event, held over the Queen's Diamond Jubilee weekend as the 'largest LGBT two day festival in the UK'. The event also included what was specifically described as a 'carnival parade' so picking up the carnival imagery with its associations of licence and excess. However it is also clear from the internet chatter around the event that there is still some dispute over the protest element of the parade. Some groups, including union representatives and local university groups, wanted to use the event to protest about the government cuts in services and their impact particularly on organisations that support gay, lesbian, bisexual and transgender people. Others wanted to use the event primarily for commercial purposes, or simply as an opportunity to have fun. The people who have moved into flats recently built around the gay village also complained about the noise and the intrusion of so many people (over 50,000 in 2012) into 'their space'.

There is no specific religious discourse, or discourse about religion associated with Birmingham Pride, although it is clear that overtly religious symbols and references (almost universally to the Christian traditions, and most with Catholic overtones) were very visible, albeit in an ironic or subversive fashion. One placard read 'Jesus had two dads and so why can't I?' The official line, however, was one of inclusiveness (a free street party) and that would in theory include religious groups if they chose to support the cause.

The second festival, dating a little later than Birmingham Pride, is the Birmingham International Carnival based in Handsworth. This was consciously based on the Notting Hill Carnival in London. Carnival came to the UK from the Caribbean, and particularly from Trinidad. As Cohen demonstrates it has always been seen as a celebration of Caribbean culture, despite the fact that one version of the origins of the Notting Hill Carnival sees this founded by a white British woman on the model of traditional English fair (Cohen 1993, 10–11, Connor and Farrar 2004, 258). The Birmingham Carnival also grew out of a very traditionally British activity, the Handsworth Flower Festival, held in Handsworth Park on an annual basis. The Carnival was first held in 1984, building on the strong Afro-Caribbean community within the Handsworth area. The first Carnival consisted of a short street procession via Holyhead Road to the main event in Handsworth Park. In 1995 the Carnival moved out of the park onto the streets of Handsworth and in 1999 to Perry Barr Park, establishing itself as a biennial event. In 2011 the Carnival moved back to Handsworth Park, a move that was welcomed in much of the local press as a process of 'coming home'.

Like the Notting Hill Carnival, the Handsworth event is essentially a celebration of culture, but it has also been understood as a form of protest, a chance for the Afro-Caribbean community to make a number of important statements about race and racism (Connor and Farrar 2004). In this respect, although on nothing like the same scale, the same balance that Cohen saw in the Notting Hill Carnival, between political rally and political protest is clearly present within the Handsworth Carnival (1993, 128). The protest element is still present in the contemporary discourses surrounding the Carnival with internet sites asking specifically whether the Carnival is to be seen as a 'local Carnival or a political Carnival'. This tension will continue to be present because of the nature of the event and the presence of racism within our society. What is very clear, however, again like the Notting Hill Carnival, is that the cultural element is the primary focus and the event firmly remains a celebration of Afro-Caribbean culture in terms of the styles of dress, music, dance, and in most cases, of participation. The 2011 event attracted a number of trucks and mas bands and brought 25,000 people on to the streets of Handsworth, and to the party that followed in Handsworth Park. There is no overt religious language or imagery associated with the Carnival and no discourse on religion that I am aware of among those who attend.

Both of these events are seen as giving voice and visibility to otherwise oppressed groups. They both reflect Cohen's balance between political protest and political rally (1993). Both events are also originally organised by members of the representative group themselves and only in recent years were they given official approval and financial support from the city. Neither event happens within the city centre and both take place in the heartland, as it were, of the community they claim to represent; in Handsworth for Carnival, and within the gay village around Hurst Street for Birmingham Pride (although the carnival parade associated with Birmingham Pride did begin within the city centre).

What is also interesting is that both events have become increasingly commercialised over time with the organisation of Birmingham Pride in particular being taken over by limited companies and a far greater emphasis being placed on the role of commercial bands, the sponsorship of events, and overt advertising associated with many aspects of the event. This commercialisation has, in some senses, allowed the events to continue beyond the protests when, in many ways, the battles have been won. However, as we have seen the protest element has not gone away and the recent debates around government cuts, especially as they affect the communities who host these events, has brought a clear political agenda back into both Birmingham Pride and the Carnival. There is also a considerable debate as to whether the commercialisation is in some senses a 'selling out' of the original purpose of the events, or the communities that support them, and whether in emphasising sponsorship and other commercial activities the community element of the events has been lost. There are, of course, much wider issues at play here in relation to globalisation and localisation and I will come back to some of these in relation to the Chinese New Year in the following chapter.

During the period from 1970–90, therefore, there was no direct relationship with Baumann's official discourse in a formal sense. Neither event was really pushed by the Council as a celebration of a specific culture or ethnicity (that would have been difficult in relation to Birmingham Pride anyway). If anything these events, at least in their conception, were about an anti-racist or anti-homophobic discourse and while those discourses were clearly aimed at a wider society, far beyond those who actually attended the event, they were developed through a clear restatement of an in-group discourse on identity.

There is an interesting question here, however, in relation to Handelman's classification of public events (1998). If we look at the Carnival in Birmingham and the earlier Gay Pride marches then the question of whether these are events of presentation or re-presentation starts to become interesting and appears to depend on where you stand. In their early days, when the element of protest is clearly a strong part of the imagery and discourses associated with both these events then, from the perspective of the City as a whole, these are events-that-re-present; they are statements and expressions of an alternative model of society. However, even at this point, for the communities involved, Afro-Caribbean or LGBT, then the events themselves are events-that-present as they celebrate and reinforce the dominant discourses of these particular communities, albeit by claiming, perhaps even reinforcing, and only occasionally undermining, the stereotypes of the wider society. In both cases this process of 'presentation', as seen from within the population involved, could itself be seen as oppressive and marginalising for those from within the respective communities who did not conform to the cultural norm. There were few Afro-Caribbean faces at Birmingham Pride, despite the colonisation of carnival imagery and terminology within the parade. There is also no expression of LGBT identities from within the Afro-Caribbean community within the Handsworth Carnival (see Marston 2002).

Over time, however, as the dominant discourse (of the Council and of society more widely) became more accepting of difference and began to move towards a celebration of multi-culturalism, as represented by the different ethnic communities of the city (Baumann's presentation of the dominant discourse) then these events were recognised and claimed for the dominant discourse itself and inevitably lost a great deal of their critical edge. They became, in Handelman's terms, classic events-that-present, both for the community involved and for the wider society that wished to celebrate its own multi-cultural credentials. The message presented by the City Council, and clearly received by the casual observers at these events, is that of inclusivity, acceptance and diversity. This is an entirely positive, celebratory and upbeat message throughout the media, and it is this, I will argue below, that helps to provide the positive charge for discourses on religious, and other kinds of, diversity that are so clearly associated with similar events where religion plays a much greater role.

Cultural/Community Parades

Beginning with the Sikh community, other social and religious groups began to seek permission to hold street festivals through the 1990s. In some ways these go back to traditional 'Christian' events, the procession of a religious community through the streets on a special day as an act of worship and/or an act of witness. They also relate back to practices that Sikhs and members of other religious groups bought with them when they migrated to the UK. In India there would have been such street processions to celebrate Vaisakhi or similar religious festivals and there is no reason why that should not happen in the new homeland. In Birmingham in the 1990s, however, these events were often recast as 'cultural' activities. Sharon Lea, Director of Environment and Culture for Birmingham City Council, said of the 2012 parade that 'Birmingham's vibrant Vaisakhi festival shows how people come together in the city to celebrate their cultural identity and is part of a calendar of diverse community events in the city' (http://birminghamnewsroom. com/2012/04/vibrant-vaisakhi-2012/). 'Culture' and 'community' are clearly linked here as Baumann would predict for the dominant discourse (1996).

Vaisakhi is celebrated in Birmingham with two large-scale street parades, one from each of the Gudwaras in Smethwick and Hockley, which draw in devotees from across the Midlands. The event to celebrate the 300th anniversary of the founding of the Khalsa in 1999 was said to be the largest outside of the Punjab and was addressed by Tony Blair. The event in 2012 attracted over 90,000 people (four times the size of the International Carnival) and was proclaimed to be the largest outside India. The event, like Carnival, is based in Handsworth, and is sponsored by the Council of Sikh Gudwaras and Birmingham City Council. It ends with a mela, or festival, in Handsworth Park including the traditional Langar or free vegetarian feast. It is very important to the Sikh community that this is a public event and that people from the local neighbourhood, but also from across Birmingham, come to watch and to take part.

The Vaisakhi celebration is also very clearly a religious event and is understood as such both by those who participate and by those who come to watch. The association with the Sikh religion, the wearing of orange turbans and other religiously-identified clothing, the processions with religious artefacts and religious texts all make it clear that this is primarily 'religious'. The organising committee chairman was quoted on the *Birmingham Mail* website as saying 'the most important message is to recognise all religions as one because God lives inside us all' (http://www.birminghammail.net/news/top-stories/ 2012/04/23/in-pictures-90–000-people-attend-vaisakhi-2012-celebrations-in-handsworth-park-97319–30815653/). This was also reflected in many of the comments among non-Sikh spectators and observers. Stereotypes of Sikhs as open, tolerant and welcoming of all religions were stated on a number of occasions in conversations around the event and the general comment that it was 'good to see religious people affirming their faith in a positive fashion' seemed to be the main focus of these conversations. The boundary, however, between the designation of 'Sikh' as a 'religious' label and its use as an 'ethnic' marker was very blurred. There was also talk about the celebration of 'Sikh culture', and the idea of the 'Sikh community'. The evidence that I collected suggests that references to culture and community were, in fact, far more common than direct reference to the Sikh 'religion'.

A similar blurring of the boundary between culture (or community) and religion can be seen in the celebration of St Patrick's Day, although here the number of non-Irish spectators was much higher than the number of non-Sikhs in Handsworth, and any discourse on religion was all but absent among both the participants and the spectators. Celebrations of St Patrick's Day have taken the form of a small street festival for many years, beginning as early as 1952 in Digbeth, the traditional centre for Irish immigration within the city. However, following the pub bombings by the IRA in the early 1970s the Irish population in

Birmingham suffered considerable persecution and the celebration was kept very low-key. In the 1990s the parade began to grow as confidence in the Irish economy grew and confidence in Irish national identity also grew. The parade returned to its original home in Digbeth in 1996 and has grown steadily each year. The festival is now advertised and celebrated as one of the largest St Patrick Day parades outside of Dublin and New York with a turn out in 2012 of 85,000.

What has been particularly interesting in the presentation of the 2012 event was the way in which non-Irish elements have been incorporated into the event. The theme for the 2012 parade was sport, linking in with the national emphasis on the Olympics. Various sporting groups from around the city, most with some kind of Irish connection, were invited to be part of the parade. What is more significant, however, is that alongside Irish pipe bands and other recognisable forms of 'Irish music', drummers and other musicians with their origins in India, China and the Caribbean were all invited to be part of the celebration. The internet-based accounts of the event all stressed the international flavour of the parade and the way in which this event celebrates not just the Irish, but the diversity of cultures and communities within Birmingham. This is Baumann's dominant discourse made manifest, and is one of the reasons why the St Patrick's Day parade is seen by the City Council as the iconic festival for the city.

Finally, therefore we move to the Chinese New Year. The Chinese community moved the celebration of their New Year into the public sphere, following similar moves in other cities in the UK in the 1990s. This was in part a reflection of the growing confidence of the Chinese community itself, but in this case it also reflects something of a demand from the wider population of the city. The celebration of the Chinese New Year, like Carnival and the St Patrick's Day parade are seen as 'cultural' events that any self-respecting city should have, and while the Chinese community, and the Chinese quarter of Birmingham is relatively small compared to those of, say Manchester or London, it was felt to be important that the Chinese New Year was celebrated in Birmingham much as it was, although on a smaller scale, in other cities.

There is no procession as such associated with the Chinese New Year, but the Arcadian centre is turned into a kind of amphitheatre for a series of cultural performances including fire crackers, lion dancers and the entrance of the dragons. What is interesting is that if we look at the three festivals explored within this section the proportion of non-community members making up the crowd, the spectators as opposed to the performers, in each event rises to a point where the vast majority of people who came to celebrate the Chinese New Year were non-Chinese. It was only the very small number of performers and the local traders who were of Chinese origin. Jeffry Yap, the chair of the Birmingham Chinese Festival Committee, said 'each year we are thrilled to welcome people from all communities to join in the fun and enjoy celebrating one of the oldest celebrated festivals in the world'. This was an event for the city as much as, and perhaps even more than, the community itself, although all the sponsorship of the various events appeared to come from Chinese-owned businesses. It was also clear that in the

Birmingham celebration in 2012 (with a turnout of around 30,000 people) there was little or no discourse about religion and religious diversity among the crowds, although I will explore this in more detail in the following chapter.

Ostensibly each of the celebrations in this section is a 'religious' festival; the Sikh celebration of the Guru's birthday, the celebration of patron saint of Ireland, and New Year within the Chinese cosmology. However, the religious element of each event is played down (except perhaps with the Sikhs), particularly within the City Council's own presentation of the events. It is the cultural or community element that was stressed. Each event, therefore, expresses very clearly Baumann's dominant discourse emphasising the unity of culture, community and ethnicity and this is the way the Council presents the events and its own support of them. What we see is not only a link between 'community' and 'culture', but there is also a similar explicit linking to 'ethnicity' and 'religion'. So, each community has its own culture, is ethnically distinct and shares a common religion and this is what is celebrated within the various festivals.

To this extent we could also argue that in relation to Handelman's analysis these are events-that-present rather than events-that-re-present (1988). The balance that Cohen sees in the Notting Hill Carnival, and that is still present in Birmingham Pride and the Handsworth Carnival despite the increasing levels of commercialisation within these events, between political rally and political protest has fallen completely on the side of the rally (Cohen 1993). The Vaisakhi celebrations are clearly an event-that-presents for the Sikhs who take part in the event. They assert the unity of their 'community' and while there may be difficult political negotiations between different elements of that community in the build up to the event in terms of organisation, priority or even inclusion, the event itself proclaims very loudly a united front. This rite of presentation is, in many ways, commandeered by the Council, with the approval of the organisers who value the Council's support, as part of their dominant discourse of 'culture' and 'community'. The Chinese New Year, at the other end of the spectrum, almost appears to have been overtaken by the City Council's discourse, to be held for the enjoyment and reinforcement of the City's multi-cultural credentials, and is in a very real sense an event-that-presents, even perhaps a political rally in Cohen's sense of the word. St Patrick's Day sits somewhere between these two positions, but the way in which the performance of the parade itself, and the reporting that followed, claimed and celebrated the dominant discourse of multiple communities with distinctive cultures both allowed the 'Irish community' to reinforce its own position within that dominant discourse, so making the parade an event-that-presents in a real sense, but also reinforced the City Council's dominant discourse to the wider world.

At the demotic level, however, this is clearly far more complex as Baumann himself showed in the context of everyday conversations in Southall (1996). St Patrick's Day is clearly a Catholic festival, but the parade aims to unite all the Irish (and a number of other cultural/ethnic/community identities) and so the specifically religious element of the festival is seriously underplayed. This is not a festival that is claimed by either the Catholic or the Protestant sections of the Irish 'community' (in this it is very different from the New York parade as outlined by Marston, 2002). Listening to the conversations that occur among the crowd at this event then there is much talk of shamrocks and Guinness and other icons of Irish identity, but nobody is asking questions that suggest that there is anything religious going on here, and St Patrick himself is hardly ever mentioned at all. We might also want to ask what religion is being celebrated at the Chinese New Year? As I will show in the following chapter most of those present at the event would not be able to answer this question. New Year is not a religious festival in the UK; it is almost the antithesis of a religious event with the emphasis on excess in terms of partying and drinking (Leach's archetypal rite of anti-structure (1961)). There is no expectation that it would be any different for the Chinese, although things are not quite as straightforward as this, as we shall see.

What is more, if the City Council were following the principles of Baumann's dominant discourse then we might ask why the Pakistanis, the Bangladeshis and other south Asian communities are apparently excluded. Why is there not a street festival for each of the many communities/cultures of the city? Of course, at one level this is a meaningless question, and the City Council itself would say that if the 'Bangladeshi community', for example, wished to celebrate some event central to their 'culture', they would consider such an application favourably and include it in their calendar of events. It is simply that they have never been asked. What is most important, however, from the perspective of the wider discussion of this book, is that the City Council, in its policies and in its publicity, has done all it could to downplay the religious element of these festivals. They were presented as 'community' events, open to all, but celebrating the 'culture' of a particular community within the city, and this is clearly part of the dominant discourse as Baumann presents it.

Religious Events

There has, however, been a noticeable shift of emphasis since 2001, and the events of 9/11, from talking about ethnic diversity within the city, to talking about religious diversity as we saw in the previous chapter. This reflects a similar change in the language of what might be described as the 'dominant discourse', especially in the light of the Labour government's 'prevent' and 'community cohesion' agendas. 'Religion' has arguably become a more significant marker of the identity of the communities of the city than 'ethnicity' or 'culture'. This has not changed, however, the way in which the big events such as the International Carnival, the St Patrick's Day parade or the Chinese New Year have been portrayed in the Council's publicity. They are still advertised as cultural events, although they have been drawn into a wider discussion focused on cultural cohesion and celebrated not so much for their difference, but more for the way they can draw a wide range of people from across the city, from different cultures and communities, together.

There is, therefore, still a dominant discourse around the celebration of 'cultures', but 'religion' is also becoming a much more visible part of that dominant discourse.

Lying behind this change is a continuing history of specific religious events organised within local neighbourhoods and relating to particular religious institutions, be they specific mosques or churches or particular Sufi tariqas or Christian organisations. Some of these events, such as the Milad-Un-Nabi Jaloos and gathering in Aston Park have continued to attract considerable numbers (over 50,000 in 2012 according to the organiser's own estimates, and claimed to be one of Europe's biggest gatherings of Muslims) but they are seldom reported in the local press and do not attract City Council support. There are two annual processions to celebrate Ashura among the Shia community, one Khoja and one Iranian, and various Sufi traiqas such as the Ghamkol Sharif hold annual jaloos or processions attracting devotees from across the country and speakers from the international community. The annual Good Friday walk in the centre of Birmingham, led by the Catholic Archbishop and Anglican Bishop, attracted around 400 people in very bad weather in April 2012, and various local church processions are held for Palm Sunday, Corpus Christi and other Christian celebrations.

What is interesting, however, from the point of view of the 'dominant discourse' is what the City Council has chosen to sponsor and to highlight in its publicity. In more recent years this has not been focused so much on the big cultural events on the streets, but rather on the public parks and other public spaces and on more tightly focused, more specifically religious events that are taking place within these spaces. The 'family day' in Canon Hill Park for Eid Mela is a good example of these city-sponsored events. This is not a major street festival with lots of people processing together in an act of celebration or witness. In many ways it is much more private, held within the Park for those who choose to come to it. Physically the space is constructed as a kind of stockade with clear boundaries on the outer edge and all the events focused into the centre. Canon Hill Park, unlike Handsworth Park or even Aston Park, is not associated with a specific neighbourhood where there is a high level of ethnic diversity and is perhaps a more 'neutral' or 'safe' space, although it is difficult to understand exactly what that might mean in this case. Canon Hill Park is, however, a public space and the Eid Mela events are organised in close association with the Council. Earlier in 2012 there was a series of stories in the local press complaining that community leaders had been removed from the organising committee to be replaced by a panel of seven councillors. Former committee member, Safdar Mir, was reported as saying 'Maybe this is the council's new Labour administration's idea on how the Big Society should work'. The event receives £20,000 in council sponsorship and is specifically designed to promote 'Muslim culture and heritage'. It receives around 40,000 visitors each year and the new organising committee chairman Councillor Majid Mahmood said 'The Mela is for the whole city, to highlight and showcase the valuable contribution of Muslims to this city. We want to welcome all Muslim groups, Pakistanis, Indians, Bangladeshis, Yemenis, Somalis as well as non-Muslims and make it

a truly city-wide event' (http://www.birminghammail.net/news/birmingham-news/
2012/06/28/community-leaders-axed-from-birmingham-s-eid-mela-committee-973
19–31276567/#ixzz21d1Qasi5).

The Diwali celebrations within the Hindu community could also be included
in this category. These are organised by the Hindu Council of Birmingham and
supported by the City Council. Unlike other cities in the Midlands, with much
larger Hindu populations, Diwali is not celebrated on the streets in Birmingham
in the same way as Vaisakhi and St Patrick's Day. It is usually held in a large
indoor space that is, in some senses, 'public' and yet also 'private'. While a public
invitation is offered for all people, of whatever faith or none, to attend, the crowd
is primarily from within the Hindu community itself. Some sense of the Council's
approach to Diwali is, however, expressed in the comments from Councillor
Martin Mullaney, Birmingham City Council's Cabinet Member for Leisure, Sport
and Culture at the time, in advance of the 2011 event, 'Birmingham has a year
long programme of fantastic free community events of which Diwali is a great
example. Last year around 11,000 people enjoyed Birmingham's Diwali event.
This year's celebrations provide us with another wonderful opportunity to come
together in The New Bingley Hall and have a fantastic time'. Parat Hirani from
the Hindu Council of Birmingham added, 'The true spirit of Diwali is to bring
different communities together so that new relationships may be born, so everyone
is welcome to join our celebration' (http://birminghamnewsroom.com/2011/10/
birmingham-set-for-diwali-2011/).

One question to ask, therefore, is whether these new events, by rejecting the
explicit connection between religion and ethnicity, still reflect Baumann's dominant
discourse (1996)? The answer is probably 'yes', the dominant discourse lives on
although now 'religion' is clearly the organising feature rather than 'culture', and
the equation that is stated is that between 'religion' and 'community' rather than
that between 'culture' and 'community'. What is more, these new events indicate
an attempt by the Council to manage religion and religious diversity, particularly
stressing the openness of these religious festivals to all people from across the
city, irrespective of their religion or lack of it. They are imposing this dominant
discourse on the religions themselves through their sponsorship of the events,
especially in relation to Islam, and this is part of a wider process in British society
to establish a 'safe' Islam through the 'prevent' and the 'community cohesion'
agenda. I will come back to this discussion in my final Chapter.

It is also interesting to note, however, that what are being presented here are
'family' events, either in the park or within a venue often used for weddings
and other community activities. This is a domestication of Baumann's cultural
and community discourses. This is 'tea and cakes on the lawn', a reversion to
the flower show from which the Carnival originated, a celebration of different
cultures, but within a clearly defined 'safe' space (the Eid event in Canon Hill
Park for 2012 is being transferred, because of the Olympics, to a date in September
that coincides with the Birmingham Garden Show that will be held in another part
of the same park). These events are presented as something that are 'open' and

'fun' but they hide a very clear process of control. To this extent Handelman's categories of events-that-present or events-that-re-present (1998), or Cohen's distinction between political rally and political protest (1993) really do not work for these events. These are not 'public' events in the sense these kinds of analysis assume. Baumann's dominant discourse, however, clearly lives on albeit in different forms. It is still for the 'communities' to play the Council's games and to speak the Council's language if they want to have a presence within the (semi-) public spaces of the city and a slot on the Council's calendar of events. This is clearly part of a hegemonic process and can be analysed as such.

Conclusions: Religion in Public Spaces

In Chapter 1 I raised the concept of 'public space' within my discussion of bottom up–macro approaches to the city. I related this to ideas of exclusion through the work of David Sibley (1995) and to ideas of flow through the work of Thomas Tweed (2006) and others. At that point I also quoted the view of Low and Smith who, among others, had noted the increasing privatisation of space within the city (2006). I said that the idea of public space is important to this work primarily because almost all of the conversations that constitute the data relating to the discourses that I have listened to were held within public spaces of one kind or another. Within this chapter, however, by focusing on public events, I have engaged with the idea of public spaces in a very different way.

This first, and perhaps most obvious, point to make is that the kind of discourses that I have drawn on have been 'public' in a very different way. I have used internet sources and local newspaper reports to identify the comments of councillors and organising committees in order to identify a clear 'dominant discourse', or what could be claimed as the discourse that exists in the public arena. I have also listened to conversations within the context of many of these festivals and, apart from those with clear religious content, the 'public discourse' on religion at these events, especially among those who were not explicitly religious themselves, were negligible or non-existent. I will come back to some interesting approaches to discourses on religion within the Chinese New Year event in the following chapter, but it is not so much the discourses I heard within the events themselves that has specifically interested me within this chapter.

In my discussion of the various 'religious' events that have been supported by the City Council, I have stressed the fact that the Council, and the organisers, in their public statements stress their openness to all people within the city. This is true even for the Diwali event that is held within an enclosed, semi-private space. In emphasising this openness the Council is clearly designating these events as 'public' and the spaces that they inhabit, or pass through, are identified as public spaces. The condition that is placed on the use, or creation, of this public space, is inclusivity; they must be open to all, although in reality what we might be observing here is another example of Low and Smith's privatisation of public space which in practice restricts access while publically proclaiming openness and accessibility (2006). This is seen when we compare the language around the Eid Mala event in Canon Hill Park to that surrounding the Milad-Un-Nabi gathering in Aston Park. The first is announced as a 'family day' first and foremost and is clearly expected to attract people from across the city whether they are Muslim or not. The second is also held within a public space, a city park, but the discourses surrounding it (primarily provided by the organisers and participants) suggests that only those who share a specific Islamic faith should attend. It is not, in that sense, a fully 'public' event. Other events held by specific Tariqas are also constructed as being even more exclusive despite the fact that they take place in the 'public' streets and parks of the city. The access to the formally proclaimed 'open' events is, however, equally restricted. The very openness of the Eid Mala event, its sponsorship by the Council and the discourse around a 'safe' or 'moderate' Islam, will keep many Muslims within the city away while never fully offering a 'public' space where non-Muslims can comfortably celebrate with their Muslim neighbours. The designation of such events as 'public' therefore, or as being representative of 'public space', is part of the construction of the event.

What is important in this discussion, as it relates to the wider themes of this book, is the way in which the positive values of the dominant discourse surrounding these festivals feeds into the everyday discourses of people around the city about religious diversity in general. Even if individuals do not attend the various parades, processions and festivals, the information, images and reporting of them in the local media (television, radio, local press and on the internet) gives them a very high profile and, as I have hoped to show, is always accompanied by some reference to the dominant discourse, either through the comments of a representative of the City Council, a representative of the organising committees, or by the media themselves. This makes these festivals, and discussions about them, very prominent within everyday conversations that have no physically or temporal relation to the events. I have heard comments from individuals in Highgate and Handsworth about the Chinese New Year, about Vaisakhi (primarily in response to cars on the inner-ring road with orange banners fluttering from their windows at about the time of the Vaisakhi festival), and about St Patrick's Day. I also had one comment, from a young non-Muslim mother in Handsworth who told me that 'they celebrate the end of Ramadan with a big party in Canon Hill Park. I've never been, but my neighbour went last year and it sounds like fun'.

The dominant discourse that is being presented within the reporting, and re-presented within the everyday conversations, is to a very large extent that proposed by Baumann in the 1990s (1996). It assumes a match between 'community' (these festivals are presented and talked about as belonging to the Irish community, the Sikh community, the Chinese community and so on) and 'culture' (they are clearly presented as 'cultural festivals'). By implication this is also expanded to include 'religion' although this plays a much more limited role in many of the public representations of the events. Where this dominant discourse goes beyond Baumann, however, is in the insistence on the inclusivity and the openness of these events to all people from across Birmingham. That was seen very explicitly in relation to the St Patrick's Day parade in 2012, where other communities and their cultures were included within the parade, but has been a strong element of the discourses on all the events by both the Council and the organisers. This is also expressed within the everyday conversations where these festivals are mentioned. Even the comment from the young mother in Handsworth implies that it would be perfectly acceptable for her, as a non-Muslim, to attend the Eid family event and that she would enjoy it if she did. This very positive dominant discourse of inclusivity also underpins, and reinforces, the wider discourses that I have already identified about all religions being essentially the same, or rather that it does not appear to matter which religion an individual belongs to. This fundamental view of religion (not really religious diversity) is clearly reinforced by the dominant discourses on festivals and imbued with a very positive set of values.

Before exploring this further, however, with reference to memory, in Chapter 7, I want to look more closely at just one of the festivals I have been discussing, the Chinese New Year, and to ask further questions about the nature of the conversations and public discourses on religion that exist within the festival itself, and specifically among the crowd that attends it. This, I think, will offer a greater insight into what people might mean when they are talking about 'religion' (a question I have not really raised so far in this book) and how wider assumptions and stereotypes about a specific religion and culture might impact on this.

Chapter 6

The Year of the Golden Pig

Having looked at the wider context of public events and street festivals in the previous chapter, this chapter is going to explore one specific event, that of the Chinese New Year. In the introduction to the previous chapter I identified two possible 'public discourses' surrounding festivals and public events. The first, which I explored in more depth within that chapter, was the discourse of the City Council, what Baumann referred to as the 'dominant discourse' related to culture, community, ethnicity and religion (1996). The second relates back to my work in Handsworth and Highgate and consists of the discourses used by those who attend the event about religion and religious diversity. I suggested that the literature on festivals, carnivals and street parades tended to overlook both these discourses by focussing much more specifically on the participants themselves, what they were saying to themselves and what kinds of messages they wished to present to the wider public. Neither of these participant discourses concerns me within this analysis, although I will touch on both in what follows, as it is the question of 'religious diversity within everyday discourses' that is my primary interest. Overall, however, as we have seen from my survey of the various festivals in Birmingham in the previous chapter, overt discourses on religion and religious diversity among those who attend the festivals were rare. That does not mean, however, that religion was ignored entirely, and my study of the Chinese New Year aims to show how we may need to expand our understanding of 'religion', even when looking at local public discourses, if we are to get a full picture of the role of discourses on religion within, and around such events.

The Chinese New Year, therefore, is a particularly interesting example in relation to discourses of religious diversity because, as we have seen, the festival itself is often presented by City leaders as a purely 'cultural' event, while those who organise it, and many others from within the Chinese community, clearly see it as both 'cultural' and 'religious'. It is often very difficult, therefore, from a western secular perspective, to see how the religious element is expressed within the event itself and those who attend the event make very few, if any, direct references to 'religion' or 'religious diversity' as such. From my own experience of attending Chinese New Year celebrations in Birmingham and London, however, and in listening to the conversations of those who attend the events, then there is clearly a level of ambiguity over the religious nature of the event. Even if 'religious diversity' is not discussed in conversations surrounding the event, those who do attend do assume that there are some kinds of religious associations and they appear to reconstruct this through their own understanding of Chinese religion, most commonly associated with the idea of 'luck'. This is what I intend to explore in more detail within this chapter.

I will begin by looking more closely at a number of themes that come out of the literature on festivals and street events, particularly identity, space and syncretism. I will then present an account of the Chinese New Year celebrations in London in 2007, the year of the Golden Pig, highlighting some of the discourses that surrounded this event. In the analysis that follows I will focus on discourses of luck, issues of globalisation and commercialisation within the festival, and the way in which images of China and the Chinese are played out, both in the discourses of those who attend (especially as these surround the idea of 'luck') and within the event itself. I will then draw this together and relate the analysis back to the wider themes of the book on religious diversity within the everyday discourses of the city.

Street Parades; Identity, Space and Syncretism

Unlike the previous chapter, where I focussed on the sources of the study of festivals and public events, this section will focus on a number of theoretical approaches rather than the history of such studies and also on street parades rather than public events as a whole. There are three kinds of debate that can be identified within the literature that could inform our discussion of the Chinese New Year: those relating to identity, those relating to space and those relating to syncretism.

Theoretical issues relating to identity tend to relate primarily to the cultural group organising and presenting the event. In many ways Mitchell's seminal work on the Kalela dance, that I referred to in the previous chapter, is all about identity, although Mitchell tends to focus on the idea of ethnicity (1956). For Mitchell ethnicity is the form of discourse through which identity is negotiated and constructed for the rural migrants who come into the city to work and who express, or negotiate their identity/ethnicity within the dance (Rogers and Vertovec 1995, 21–6). Most of the recent analyses of street festivals, especially those with a strong ethnographic element, focus on the group who organise and take part in the event itself. For these theorists what is most important is the messages that these events deliver, both to the participants and to the wider population of the city. Such events are seen to be all about identity and the definition of the community. Sallie Marston for example, in her classic study of the St Patrick's Day Parade in nineteenth-century Lowell, Massachusetts, notes that the parade had two audiences, the Irish themselves and the wider public of the city. The parade was all about Irish identity, but it also engaged with that identity as it related to the wider Yankee-dominated identity of the city as a whole (1989). To this extent the parade both challenged the established order and at the same time reinforced it, the kind of balance that Cohen identified in the Notting Hill Carnival as we saw in the previous chapter (1993).

A slightly different approach, that builds on the same kind of ethnographic studies but which focuses on a more macro perspective, looks at the question of space and the use of space within the events. Some of the discussions that I engaged in towards the end of the previous chapter, about public and private space, come into this kind of analysis. Much of the work here, however, begins with the question of how the participants claim a right to certain spaces through the use of the parade. This is, once again, seen in Marston's account of the Irish in Lowell, where the parade was as much a claim to public space as it was an assertion of identity (1989). Susan Smith develops an interesting approach to this in her study of the Peebles Beltane Festival (1995). Here Smith focuses specifically on boundaries and borders. Peebles itself is a town in the 'Borders', an area of Scotland that sits just north of the English border, but also the Beltane Festival consists, in part, of a procession around the 'borders' of the parish, establishing in a symbolic sense, the extent of the town itself. Smith goes further than this, however, and shows how boundaries, borders and marginal spaces play an important place in the wider identity of the town and in the actual performance of the event. She concludes by commenting that 'while boundaries are constructions which celebrate difference, in doing so they often signal inequality. Boundaries define who belongs, and they set the terms for that belonging' (1995, 161).

Monique Ingalls approaches space from a very different perspective in a study of the Jesus in the City Parade in Toronto in 2010 (forthcoming). This parade draws in a very wide range of different national groups who, while all being 'Christian', represent a wide variety of cultural messages. As with some of the parades I mentioned in the previous chapter, the element of inclusiveness and openness, even multiculturalism is an important part of the construction of this event. Ingalls is particularly interested in the soundscape of the parade, how religious groups use musical performance in public spaces to constitute and represent themselves as a 'community'. In doing this she explores the ways in which the way music is performed relates to the different spaces that the parade passes through and the way in which the music delivers its own messages to the spectators that might, at times, be different from and perhaps even at odds with the stated messages of the organisers of the parade itself. There are two elements that are of particular note within the parade. The first is the ways in which the participants use music and songs to negotiate between competing ideas of the relationship between the religious community and the wider society. The second focuses on the specific ethnic, national and religious identifications of the participants. Ingalls draws these two strands together to talk about sound and space within the parade at a more abstract level.

In contrast to identity and space, the issue of syncretism may seem an unusual area for discussion when looking at parades and street festivals. There is something of an assumption in relation to many of the studies of identity and space that the participants speak with a common voice, or have a single identity, whether that is as the 'Irish' in Marston's work or as 'Christians' in Ingalls' analysis. Obviously, even these studies demonstrate differences and conflicts in the construction of identity, or the use of space, but 'syncretism' as such does not appear to be raised. Earlier work in this tradition, however, tended to see the popular festivals of Europe, following Tylor, as 'survivals' from a pagan past being played out within the context of a Christian present (Harris 2003, 7–9). Caro Baroja in his work on Basque festivals critiqued this position and wanted to stress the roots of the imagery within the Christian tradition itself (1965). The idea of syncretism, however, continued to remain as part of the analysis of these festivals and even Max Harris, writing in 2003, still felt the need to engage in a clear debate about whether the presence of dragons, devils, monsters and other characters in the festivals of Europe, the Caribbean or South America, had their origins in Christian mythology or in a pre-Christian pagan past (2003).

Even to suggest an element of syncretism, however, or the lack of it, is to make a political point. The Christian discourse and the official interpretation of these events, associated with specific saint's days, or the feast of Corpus Christi, is clear and well established. Much of the activity of the events themselves, however, with the celebration of devils, monsters and other fantastical creatures, has no obvious place within this official Christian discourse. These elements were often seen, within the official, dominant, discourse, as elements of a pagan past coming through. In doing this, however, the Church authorities are offering a critique of, and an attempt to control, those who are seen to introduce such elements into the festivities, that is the peasant communities themselves. By claiming that these elements are not syncretic is to suggest that the official discourse of the Church may not be as dominant as the church leaders would like to believe.

Modern post-colonial discourses clearly have interesting things to say about this, as they do about similar events within the context of India and other post-colonial societies (Stewart and Shaw 1994, Dempsey 2001). However, even the folkloric and historical traditions, while rejecting any historical link to pre-Christian pagan traditions, do recognise the challenge and the unsettling nature of the proposed syncretic narrative, including its potential to undermine the official, dominant discourse (Harris 2003, 8). Given that many of the 'interpretations' provided by these early scholars were often incorporated into the local accounts of the events themselves, however inaccurate or lacking in evidence the early interpretations may have been, it is not surprising that the anti-establishment, and even anti-Christian, nature of such events has been highlighted in many contemporary discourses (Harris 2003).

This leads us back to the questions which are raised by Baumann and others about the kinds of messages that are being presented by the event from the different perspectives of the organisers, the participants, the observers and the city or other authorities. There is also a question of the media representation of such events and the ways in which this can be managed by the different players. There is a clear analysis of power at play here, as I hinted in my discussion of the various festivals in Birmingham in the previous chapter, but this is also present within each and every event as I will hope to show in relation to the Chinese New Year below. This play of power, however, needs to be understood and explored as part of the wider analysis. Part of this is to ask about the nature of the conversations that occur around issues of culture, community and, from my perspective especially, religion as part of these events, and especially in relation to the conversations among those who attend the event but are not of the culture or religion being represented. I will come back to this in a number of different ways in the analysis that follows. First, however, let us look much more closely at what happened during the celebration of the New Year of the Golden Pig itself.

Three Parts of One Event

The event that I attended, and on which the analysis of this chapter is based, was held in London in 2007 as I had to be in London that year on the appropriate weekend. This was announced as the year of the Golden Pig and the celebrations in London had three parts. The celebrations began with a 'grand parade'. The route started on The Strand (near Savoy Court) at 11am. It continued along St Martin's Place and Charing Cross, before turning into Shaftesbury Avenue. The parade finished opposite Rupert Street at about 11:45am. The town crier went in front to announce the coming of the parade followed by a couple of figures dressed as pigs with their companions. The parade itself consisted of a number of groups. From the banners these appeared to be primarily martial arts groups, with one or two other Chinese cultural societies. The martial arts groups originated either in London, primarily it appeared south London, or, in at least one case, had come in from Kent. Some of each group were dressed in their martial arts outfits. Others were dressed as Chinese gods or in other Chinese outfits. Four or five of the groups also sported a dragon or a lion and danced in the traditional Chinese fashion. The Chinese cultural groups also provided dancers dressed in traditional costumes. There were a few gongs and drums and a truck playing Chinese music. Surprisingly few of the members of the parade were of Chinese origin and it was difficult to see in what way this was a specifically Chinese event, albeit a celebration of the Chinese New Year.

At the early stages of the procession, along the Strand, there were not large crowds and most of those who watched it pass appeared to be curious tourists who happened to be out that morning along with a few parents of participants who followed the parade along its route. As the procession approached Chinatown, and the second event of the day, then the size of the crowds grew to make seeing the procession, and following it all the way, very difficult. All the publicity made it clear that this procession was organised and funded by the City Council.

The second event took place in Chinatown on the edge of Soho. The streets just north of Leicester Square and east of Shaftesbury Avenue are known as London's Chinatown. Many Chinese businesses and restaurants are located here. Lots of street stalls were open for the Chinese New Year celebrations, and hundreds of red lanterns were hung up across the street. This street festival was made up of stalls related to the various restaurants and stores of the area that had spilled out onto the street. Where the parade was sparsely attended the street festival was packed. It was clear from some streets away that people were drifting towards the source of music. Due to the crowds it was often difficult to get close to individual stalls and their wares. What was also very difficult to determine from the conversations within the crowd was what proportion of the people who came had come specifically because it was the Chinese New Year and what proportion just happened to be there and were attracted by the crowds. Large banners over the street announced that this event was sponsored by the Bank of China and the crowd was ethnically mixed with a very large number of people of Chinese origin mixed in with those from European, Afro-Caribbean and south Asian origins. It was in this environment that the majority of the conversations that I report in the following section took place.

During the afternoon (from noon until 5pm) there were also Chinese cultural performances on a stage in Trafalgar Square. The timetable for stage performances included an opening ceremony with speeches and the dotting of the dragons' eyes, dragon/lion dances, cultural dance troupes from various parts of China, Shaolin Monks (martial arts), classical violin and string quartet performances, drums and the Nam Yang Pugilistic Association. There was a good crowd but they looked somewhat lost in the vastness of the square. Again this was a mixed crowd but probably with about three non-Chinese to every one of Chinese origin. Once again this event was organised and sponsored by the City Council. There was nothing overtly religious about this event, although the programme did announce to the arrival of the 'money god', and no conversations about religion or religious diversity took place within the crowd.

Conversations on Luck

As I have already indicated there were many representations of gods and other religious figures within the parade but nothing that was said by the few people who followed it or watched it pass suggested that they knew anything about these figures, related them to ideas of Chinese religion or that there was anything remotely religious about the event. The only comment that came close to a recognition that something 'religious', or at least out of the ordinary, was occurring here was a comment by a father to his son when a dragon came over and danced for a short spell in front of the crowd. The sight of the dragon obviously scared the youngster and his father reassured him with the comment that it is 'lucky' within Chinese traditions for a dragon to pick you out in this way. The man was not of Chinese origin and it was not clear where he got this information from, or even if he believed it, but this was the explanation he offered to his son.

This was my first observation of the use of 'luck' in relation to the event, and its specific association with Chinese traditions. Is the idea of 'luck' anything to do with religion? That is probably debateable and not really an issue that I would want to get into here. Nor am I particularly interested in the way the Chinese themselves use the concept of 'luck' within their own religious discourses. 'Luck' was, however, one of the most commonly stated words in the conversations that I overheard, especially within the street festival, and it is clear that for many British people there is a clear link between 'luck' and Chinese religious or cultural ideas. The reference to the dragon, however, was the only comment of any relevance from within the parade. For a more sophisticated analysis we need to turn from the sparseness of the Strand to Chinatown and the swirling crowds of the street festival.

Within the whole festival there was probably nothing that would have immediately struck those with little knowledge of Chinese traditions as obviously religious. There were statues and paintings of gods and other supernatural entities, but these were treated as cultural artefacts and I heard nobody ask about or comment on the representations themselves, what they illustrated or what they meant. There were also many Chinese texts but I was not, like I would guess the vast majority of non-Chinese attendees at this event, able to read the texts and had no knowledge about what these texts said. There were also many images of pigs, this being the year of the golden pig, and I heard a number of people comment that this was the year of the 'golden' pig because it was particularly 'auspicious' (a synonym for 'luck'?). This was clearly something they had read or heard in their preparations for the day, or had been told by somebody else at the event itself. All the publicity material, whether printed or on the web, reinforced this position, pointing out that such years only occur every 60 years and that children born within the year, or enterprises begun during the year, would benefit from particular good 'fortune' (another common synonym for 'luck' in this context). It was a common comment on an element of the festival that was seen to be specific to that year. The significance or relevance of the New Year festival itself, however, as a religious event was never raised in any of the conversations I heard.

It was various discussions of 'luck' (good fortune, the auspicious), therefore, that formed what I might call the 'religious discourse' of the day, or perhaps we ought to say the 'discourse on religion' as it was always difficult to determine whether this was a discourse that was supposed to be believed by those using it, or whether it was a comment on what others were supposed to believe. The evidence I was able to gather could not answer those kinds of question in any kind of detail.

If I try to analyse, and perhaps to classify, the various conversations that involved 'luck' within the street festival then I would probably want to put them into three categories. In no case was the idea of 'luck' itself either defined or problematised. These were not the kinds of conversations where people would ask what it means to be lucky or how luck should be understood or interpreted. The meaning given to the term has to come from the way in which it was used and it was the use of the term that forms the basis of the classification that follows, the implied meaning that derives from a specific context.

The first category of conversations almost seemed to associate 'luck' with some kind of magic. There were biscuits on sale, for example, that some within the crowd described as 'lucky biscuits'. It was suggested that if you bought and ate these biscuits then they would bring 'luck'; good things would happen to you.

These were not 'fortune cookies', which were also mentioned and discussed, although I am placing these conversations in my second category. In practice the biscuits described as 'lucky' may have been the same as those described as 'fortune cookies', it is two different discourses that I am distinguishing not two different foodstuffs. Nor am I able to say from my evidence whether the local Chinese community had a category of 'lucky biscuits', or whether it was always the same kind of biscuits that were always seen as 'lucky'. What I am identifying here is a linguistic construction where individuals within the crowd identified certain biscuits as 'lucky' and the luck was related directly to the process of purchasing and eating the biscuit. It was the automatic and instrumental characteristics associated with the acts of buying and eating that are usually associated with 'magic' (Cunningham 1999). The comment from the father to his son on the Strand about the approach of the dragon was very similar in construction, simply to be approached and picked out by the dancing dragon would bring luck, there was nothing more that the individual needed to do.

A second category, therefore, which I have already linked to 'fortune cookies', sees 'luck' as associated with 'fate'. An individual is either lucky or they are not and the text from the cookie identifies, or reveals, that luck, it does not of itself change the lucky status of the individual. Luck in this sense is something that can be revealed through various techniques, of which the fortune cookie is just one. Such luck can be ontological, a feature of a specific individual, or pertaining to a specific period of time. It is the next year that will be lucky for the individual concerned. There is a relationship with fortune telling here, a sense of revelation. However, this was also the context in which the framework of the Chinese calendar itself was understood and discussed within the crowd. The fact that this was the year of the 'golden' pig was commented on in many conversations as being particularly lucky. The BBC website states that 'the year of the pig is supposed to bring good luck and prosperity. But this time it is a golden pig year, which happens once in six decades' (news.bbc.co.uk). For some in the crowd this special luck was reserved for those who were born in the year of the pig. For others it was an auspicious year to begin an enterprise. For many it was simply noted as a 'lucky year' without any further elaboration.

The third way in which I observed 'luck' being used was in relation to luck that was earned. The most common context for this were the pots of sand outside many of the restaurants and shops where passers by were invited to light incense sticks and to place them into the sand. In many cases these were associated with small statues of the gods and it may have been the case that individuals felt that they were making an offering to the gods by lighting the incense. This, however, was not articulated. The comments or conversations associated with this activity again revolved around 'luck', sometimes 'fortune' and occasionally 'merit'. One person commented that 'It's a Buddhist thing, you gain merit from lighting the sticks'. In most cases, however, it was noted that luck could be earned through the process of lighting the incense and sticking the stick into the sand. This was not quite the same logic as the eating of lucky biscuits in the sense that it was not presented as being automatic, some kind of magic. The logic was one of a practice that if undertaken in the right spirit would earn luck for the individual. This was clearly the closest in practice to what might traditionally have been thought of as a 'religious' or perhaps 'devotional' practice and the presence of statues of gods associated with the practice may well have increased this religious element, although as I said, the gods themselves were very seldom commented on.

What we see in all these contexts, and others that followed the same kind of pattern, was considerable use of the term 'luck' or words associated with 'luck'. However, as I hope that I have also shown, the specific way in which 'luck' was used varied from context to context. It is also worth noting that in many contexts the nature of the conversations was such that a distinct use of the term was difficult to identify and that more than one logic may have been at work. This is not an area where we would expect to see perfect clarity.

There are two questions, therefore, that come out of these conversations for me, and they will both be picked up in subsequent sections of this chapter. The first is why 'luck' should be so closely associated with Chinese culture and whatever understanding the participants in the street festival had of Chinese religion and folk practices. The second is to ask whether any of this discussion of luck actually has any relationship with ideas of religion for the people talking, and hence whether I might be justified in exploring a discourse on luck in a text focussing on discourses about religious diversity.

The Global and the Local: Commercialisation

Before returning to the question of luck and religious diversity I want to address two further issues that pick up some of the discussions of identity, space and syncretism mentioned earlier. The material for this chapter was originally put together for a presentation in San Diego as part of the American Academy of Religion stream on religion and cities in 2007. Here the interest was much more on questions of 'the global and the local' and this particular case study offers a very interesting perspective on that discussion. The second issue relates to the specifically Chinese context for the event and more specifically to the ways in which China, Chinese culture and the Chinese themselves are understood by non-Chinese members of the crowd. This will raise issues of stereotypes, which are central to understandings of religion within British cities, and also the question of memory that will form the basis for the following chapter.

In investigating the question of the global and local as they relate to the Chinese New Year I am clearly building on the methodology, identified in the previous chapter, that was developed by Mitchell and his colleagues in relation to public events in Africa (1956, Rogers and Vertovec 1995). Mitchell, Gluckman, and others who followed their methods, began with a specific event and then widened the scope of their analysis to draw other, perhaps more significant, conclusions from it. The question of the global and the local also relates back to a number of the issues raised around space that I touched on at the beginning of this chapter. It is, I would argue, in relation to space, the use of space and the designation of space that we can see the local and global aspects of the New Year celebrations most clearly.

London is without question a global city (Sassen 1991) and the involvement of populations and sponsors from across the globe in this event, as well as many different social groups from across London and the south-east of England leads us to think this event has global associations. The wider questions, however, about the relationship between the global and local are focussed on those who took part and what they were actually doing. There are two specific spaces within which the New Year event took place and each of these spaces appeared to draw a different kind of crowd and certainly had a very different feel. Each also generates a different kind of discussions about the local and the global.

The first space is the Strand (and to a lesser extent Trafalgar Square) as the arena for the parade. This was sponsored by the City Council and it clearly intended to offer some kind of reference to China, including the involvement of individuals dressed in Chinese costume, or as gods, the dragon dancers, drummers and other musicians, all of which played on Chinese images and the stereotypical 'Chinese' procession. The dominant image of the parade itself was, however, groups in martial art outfits and banners proclaiming the origins of the different martial arts groups, whether from London or from Kent. Very few of the participants in this event were Chinese by origin, although a wide range of ethnic groups were represented within the martial arts groups and, I would guess, in the dressing up and the dragon dancing (although here masking made it difficult to confirm this). There was nothing really about China, or even the Chinese, in this event. It was a naturalised event, adapted to suit a very British audience, and even in most cases a very British involvement. The idea of China and the fact of the Chinese New Year sat somewhere behind the event but very few of those who took part really celebrated this as a significant cultural event, let alone a religious event, within their own personal calendar. It was not an important part of their 'ethnic' or 'religious' identity. This made the parade just another cultural show, a presentation of the Chinese culture of popular British imagination.

What we see within the parade, however, and in the celebrations that were put on in Trafalgar Square, was a very clear statement of the 'dominant discourse' that I identified in many of the parades and festivals in Birmingham in the previous chapter. These events were sponsored by the City Council and they proclaimed Baumann's identity of 'culture' and 'community' (1996). This was ostensibly a celebration of the 'Chinese community', through a celebration of the 'Chinese culture'. It also had the added element, as I identified within many recent Birmingham events, of emphasising openness, inclusivity and the welcoming of many different ethnic and cultural groups into the celebration of a specific cultural or ethnic identity. In fact, in this particular case, the idea of inclusivity almost appeared to take over from the celebration of the Chinese community as many of that 'community' were not actually present within the parade (although there were more both on stage and in the audience at the Trafalgar Square event).

Was this, therefore, a local event with global referents or was it a global event that had been given local colour? More specifically was the parade something of a pastiche or even a false (could we say 'fraudulent'?) event: something that had no direct personal relevance to any of the participants, nothing that would relate to their own identity construction, but something that aimed to make a political/ multi-cultural point?

Looked at another way there are interesting questions in this event around 'syncretism'. Given that the majority of the participants were not of Chinese origin, and that the street parade is a common part of many British events (not least the Lord Mayor's parade in London that also travels down the Strand) then we perhaps need to ask how much of the event was of Chinese origin and how much was a western reinterpretation, or re-representation, of what they thought to be Chinese. Whose identity was being proclaimed within the event and what kind of identity was being suggested? This is probably not the place to answer these questions but I could not help thinking about them as I watched yet another banner proclaiming the Ju-Jitsu Society of Croydon (or whatever it was) with yet more white, black and south Asian youngsters marching past to celebrate the 'Chinese' New Year.

I now wish to turn to the second space, Chinatown itself, and the street festival that was taking place within this space. The first point to note is that the two spaces are not entirely distinct as the parade, having left the Strand, did end its journey within Chinatown. In practice, however, the crowds and the messages associated with each of these two spaces were very different. Picking up on a theme from the previous chapter there is a real sense in which the space of Chinatown is a much more 'private' space than that of the Strand or of Trafalgar Square. The enclosing nature of the buildings, the almost gated nature of the streets, the emphasis on Chinese visual markers, including Chinese characters on the street signs, all make this space appear separate from the wider community, and in some senses more 'private'. This is, however, still a public space, open to anybody who wishes to enter; it is not a shopping mall or even a pedestrian precinct. For all that the semi-private, or pseudo-public (Mitchell and Staeheli 2006, 152–3), nature of the space is significant in the construction of the street festival as 'commercial' activity.

In the following section I will investigate the visual imagery of the streets that make up Chinatown in more detail and ask what makes this specifically Chinese. For now my interest is more on global and local elements, and more specifically the declaration that this part of the event was sponsored by the Bank of China, something that was proclaimed from a range of banners and posters all round the Chinatown area. If the City Council's sponsorship of the parade along the Strand and the show in Trafalgar Square led to a clear statement of the 'dominant discourse' as understood and proclaimed by the Council, does the Bank of China's sponsorship of the street festival lead to a different dominant discourse, as articulated by the sponsor, being proclaimed within this space?

When looking at the possible 'dominant discourse' that might be endorsed by the Bank of China then we are immediately led back into questions of 'syncretism', although of a very different kind from those related to the parade. The issue here is about the commercialisation of public events and the combination of messages of 'culture' with those of 'commerce'. The event within Chinatown was not simply a celebration by the 'Chinese community' of a cultural event that was of central importance to them, it was also a commercial opportunity, clearly designed to draw in large crowds of both Chinese and non-Chinese people and having, as one of its main purposes, to make as much money as possible. Chinatown is the visible heart of the Chinese business community with many stores and restaurants sited within these few streets (Luk 2008). These businesses all expanded onto the streets, with stalls and marketing being placed in front of each business. It was the trade and the exchange of money for food or souvenirs that formed the heart of what was going on within that space. The sponsorship of the Bank of China only reinforced that this was a commercial event, with commercial sponsorship. The Chinese cultural identity was almost lost within this wider syncretic message.

Gerard Aching, following a number of other scholars talking about a range of festivals across the world, discusses the increasing commercialisation of the Trinidad Carnival (2002). He dates this from the 1960s and independence but sees the process accelerating in recent years. For Aching, however, it is not just the growth of commercial interests in the Carnival that is important, or the fact that the government has chosen to sell it as a central element of their tourism agenda, it is the fact that the Carnival itself has been colonised by the middle classes. Aching almost appears to be suggesting that it is the middle-classiation of the Carnival that has led in turn to the growth of commercial sponsorship and promotion by the national tourism office (2002, 89–98). He quotes Richard Burton who says; 'the active masquerader of old is giving way to the passive spectator-consumer of today. Carnival has been exoticized and commodified for foreign consumption, and Trinidadians allegedly confront it as tourists in their own land' (1997, 208). This middle-classiation is linked with a growth in what the Trinidadians refer to as 'pretty-mas', floats and dance troupes that emphasise the aesthetic element over the political, and the growth of the number of women involved within the Carnival itself.

Carnival has always been both a space of protest, or counter-culture, and a means of supporting the status quo through regulated licence, as we saw in the previous chapter. The Chinese New Year, at least as it has been celebrated outside of China, has never really had this double element, as protest, or licence, plays little or no part in the event (there may be a playful challenge or licence on the part of dragon and lion dancers but this is very tame when compared to carnival antics). We can, however, still talk about an increasing commercialisation and even, perhaps, middle-classiation of the Chinese New Year within the UK. This comes in part through the increasing wealth of the Chinese businesses themselves and perhaps a class shift among people with Chinese origin within the UK (Luk 2008). It also comes from the official sponsorship of these events by city councils and their opening up to a wider (often middle-class) population from within the cities where they are held. This was clearly obvious in both parts of the London festival, and was also present in recent Birmingham-based celebrations.

The sponsorship of the Bank of China, however, speaks to commercialisation in a rather different way, and a different kind of syncretism, beyond the middle-classisation within the UK. It is significant, I would suggest, that it is the Bank of China rather than some more obviously Chinese government cultural organisation that is sponsoring the event. This speaks much more to the development of China itself in recent years. In this case the Chinese authorities have chosen a bank to be the sponsoring body, a symbol of Chinese economic development and power, rather than a cultural organisation. This suggests that the Chinese government itself sees such events as part of an economic marketing process rather than a simple celebration of 'Chinese culture'. This takes us back to the idea of a dominant discourse within the street festival, as proclaimed by the sponsoring body, and the power that is at play within many syncretic, or so-called syncretic, events. The dominant discourse of the London festival was of China as an economic power, of the economic influence of Chinese people within London, and of the event itself as a primarily commercial activity. This also speaks to contemporary views of China and the way in which an event such as New Year celebration presents, reinforces, challenges and otherwise plays with stereotyped notions of what it is to be Chinese among the wider British population.

Hyper-reality, On Being Chinese

Fenggang Yang makes the point that populations in the West tend to see China as a cultural unity but that this, of course, is far from being the case: 'Many observers are fascinated by the magnetic unity of the heterogeneous Chinese people' (1998, 333). Despite this, however, the range of images and stereotypes that come together, from many different sources, to form the Western view of that cultural unity is surprisingly large and diverse. The West has had a long and complex history of encounter with China and the Chinese and this is reflected in many of the images and discourses that surround and mould the celebration of the Chinese New Year itself (Jespersen 1996).

We can begin, once again, with questions of space, and this time with the construction of the space that has become known as Chinatown (Anderson 1991). This is, in a very literal sense, a hyper-real space, and one that is, in a very specific sense, created by the host community to 'contain' the Chinese drawing on Western images and understandings of what it is to be 'Chinese' (Anderson 1991, 249–51). Hyper-real spaces, according to Umberto Eco, are spaces that purport to be what they are not, that are in some sense more 'real' than the original (1995). However, this is not to be seen as 'deceptive' as the markers within the environment make it very clear that the reality we are looking at is not 'real', in the traditionally accepted sense of that word. The image is only skin-deep, it is a reproduction, and in the case of many theme parks this façade is all that really exists, there is nothing behind the frontages, or the frontages lead on to spaces that bear no relation to the original forms, in most cases these are spaces for eating, shopping and other commercial activity. The visitor, however, is expected to feel as though they have been transported to the space alluded to in the façade and the impression is one of current reality. As one 'philosophy' quoted by Eco makes clear 'we are giving you the reproduction so you will no longer feel any need for the original' (1995, 19). Alongside the skin-deep nature of much of the visual elements, factors such as cleanliness, the ever smiling 'characters' (to use the Disney euphemism) or workers within this world, signage and other less obvious factors make it very clear that this is not the real 'main street' or the real pirate cove, it is a fabrication, a set through which the visitor travels (Sorkin 1992b).

Some so called 'post-modern' spaces have attempted to build on this sense of hyper-reality presenting modern buildings, with modern uses and modern interiors as pastiches of traditional styles, such as the Venetian element in some of the buildings in Brindly Place in Birmingham, or so completely over-renovating a space such that it becomes a surface pastiche of its original form, despite the fact that it is that original referent that is used to sell it. I remember walking through the Gaslamp Quarter of San Diego before presenting my paper on the Chinese New Year and feeling that this was a hyper-real space, carrying only the most superficial allusions to its traditional seafarers community, despite the historic and architecturally significant buildings, but with all the grime and the vice taken out (Mitchell and Staeheli 2006, 147). Many other seafront, canalside or riverside neighbourhoods have undergone the same rejuvenating treatment (Boyer 1992).

Chinatown in London is something of a hyper-real environment. It is constructed to communicate the idea of 'China' to visitors through a series of visual markers. There is the usual ceremonial gate, statues of lions and other figures, and the frontages of the various restaurants and other businesses with their Chinese writing and Chinese imagery. In London even the street signs have been written in both English and Chinese. The setting for the street festival, therefore, already plays on many images commonly associated with China, and provides both a global, perhaps imaginary, reference to 'China' while still being very clearly situated in the local context of London. The discussions of 'luck', in their various different forms, also play into this stereotypical, imaginary, global China among a very local, perhaps very English, all be it very diverse London crowd.

If we look at the range of stereotypical images of China and the Chinese that are played out within the space of the festival then we will find, as with all stereotypes, that there are multiple layers to the images, a wide range of diverse referent and often highly contradictory messages. A simple summary of stereotypes of China and the Chinese might include, the 'yellow peril' and referents to Fu Manchu, or alternatively martial arts and the image of Charlie Chan (or even King Fu Panda), imperial images of the last emperor or the terracotta army or images of Mao, the red book, the cultural revolution, and Tiananmen Square. There will also be images of male and female stereotypes that are at the same time over-sexualised and predatory as well as being emasculated and cold. Dragons, lions, pagodas, lanterns, porcelain, writing and many other visual markers also come together to fire the imagination. Within this maelstrom of images the various ideas of luck and their associations with biscuits, the calendar and the lighting of incense sticks swirl around, emerge and are stated within the conversations of visitors to the festival.

Sitting behind these images and stereotypes are many of the issues raised by Edward Said in his work on orientalism and, as with many of the images and assumptions that he identifies for the Middle East, it is popular fiction and increasingly film that provides the source for such images for the majority of the population (1978). In the case of China I would probably suggest that film and television (including many children's programmes and cartoons) will provide the primary source for the kinds of images and assumptions that people take with them into the New Year festival (Berry and Farquhar 2006). To be more precise than this, however, and to identify specific films or programmes as they relate to specific images and ideas would be meaningless as it is the combination of many images, and the juxtaposition or confusion between these images as they are recalled at the time, that creates the particular set of stereotypes or discourses that come into play on a specific occasion. Drawing on the kind of data that underpins this chapter we cannot, in fact, go into any greater detail than this for this particular event.

There is, however, an interesting sub-question that I want to raise, before I bring this chapter to a close, about whether martial arts groups are seen in the UK as being in any sense religious. Those who run these clubs may, perhaps, see something of the religious element and may try to express that to their students (Jennings, Brown and Sparkes 2010). For many younger practitioners, however, this is probably not something that they would consider to be important. There are rules and perhaps some elements of mystical lore underpinning many of the activities of such groups, but at the more junior end of the clubs this is rarely elaborated. Again some film images, especially the Kung Fu movies, do associate martial arts with a generalised Eastern lore (more or less entirely fictitious), and there is no doubt that this does appear to get associated in the public imagination with some aspects of the sport itself (McFarlane 1991). More significantly for my purposes, martial arts groups are very seldom seen as 'religious' in and of themselves and seeing groups of boys and girls dressed in the appropriate clothing for martial arts does not suggest ideas of 'religion' to most casual observers. This element was not in any sense part of the conversations along the route of the parade. Whether such groups were seen as 'Chinese', however, is probably a much more interesting discussion and one that I cannot really explore in any more detail within this chapter.

Conclusion: The Chinese New Year and Religious Diversity

In some ways we could say that this foray into the celebrations of the Chinese New Year has nothing whatsoever to do with the wider discussions within this book about religious diversity. There was no discourse on religions or religious diversity within or around the event, and if there was anything remotely religious involved then it focussed on the idea of 'luck'. This, however, probably misses the point. There are two conclusions that I would like to draw, one on religious diversity itself and the other around the popular British imagination as it relates to religion in general, and in this way I also want to offer some kind of answer to the two questions that I raised at the beginning of the chapter, although in reverse order; why luck is so closely associated with the Chinese New Year, and whether discourses on luck can be understood as a discourse on religion.

The first point to make is that the religions of China, and the way in which the Chinese, and perhaps the Japanese, relate to religion are difficult for many people in Britain to understand. Confucianism, Daoism and Shintoism seldom come up in any spontaneous discussion of religious diversity within the British city and these traditions are little understood except as symbols in their own right of wider Chinese and Japanese religion. Buddhism also plays an interesting, and perhaps unique, role within wider discourses on religious diversity in the UK. On the whole it did not come up in any of the conversations that I listened to as part of my fieldwork in Birmingham, although there was some sense of its presence within the super-diversity of Handsworth. Discourses on religious diversity, where they focus on specific traditions, are generally expressed through references to Christianity, Islam, Sikhism and to a lesser extent Hinduism (although that might change in, say Leicester, where there is a much larger Hindu population). At a very superficial level Christianity is associated with British tradition, while the other religions are associated with south Asia and are seen as 'foreign'. Buddhism does not fit into this simple dichotomy.

Where Buddhism becomes most clearly present is in relation to discussions of Tibet and to a lesser extent Thailand and Sri Lanka, although in these last two cases the link between these cultures and Buddhism is not nearly as strong in popular discourses as that between India and Hinduism or Pakistan and Islam. Buddhism, however, is also associated with another discourse entirely, that of spirituality and the New Age, with its roots in hippy culture, that somehow gives it a British home, even if it is seen as something rather odd and exotic in this context. There are many discussions of the way in which Buddhism has been intellectualised, spiritualised and perhaps denuded of its cultural accretions as it has come over into the West, but this is not part of the current discussion and not clearly appreciated within popular discourses (Numrich 1996, Pracharart 2004). Buddhism, therefore, somehow sits separately from Baumann's dominant discourse on culture, ethnicity and religion. This in itself makes the celebration of a Chinese festival somewhat different.

At this point, therefore, we have to come back to the idea of 'luck'. Are discourses about luck discourses about religion? The obvious answer to this is to say that it depends how one defines 'religion'. If I were to use the kind of definition I developed in my previous book, based around engagement with the non-empirical, then we would have to say that luck is part of a discourse on religion, and closely related to the elementary coping form of religion developed within that text (Stringer 2008). This is the way in which Madeline Kerr noted the place of 'luck' in her study of Ship Street in Liverpool in the 1950s (1958, 129). Whether those who refer to ideas of 'luck' in relation to the Chinese street festival see themselves as engaging in a discourse about religion is much more difficult to determine. It is certainly not a discourse about the everyday. Nor is it really a discourse about spirituality. There is something distinctive, perhaps something magical, or strange, about 'luck' (or with 'fortune' or 'the auspicious') that means that it is associated specifically with this context and with a specifically Chinese thought world. It is probably the closest most people come to identifying a specifically 'Chinese' religion.

What we find at the core of this analysis, therefore, is the idea that many of those who attend the Chinese New Year festival, who are not of Chinese origin, are in fact engaging with an imagined idea of China and its religion. This, as we have seen, is derived primarily from films, television programmes and perhaps books, but essentially from fictional accounts of one kind or another. There are plenty of elements of the event itself that reinforce this imagined China, both in the outfits of the gods and dragons in the parade and in the various elements that go to make up the street festival. Where the basic visual world of China that is recreated in these events is 'imagined', so too, I would suggest, are the different elements of Chinese religion, and most specifically the idea of 'luck'. This concept has never been taught formally to any of those present, it is part of an informal discourse, reinforced through many different fictional and media-based images and through fragments of commentary, that have come together to form a common discourse among the people involved. It is half remembered, half understood and never fully interrogated. It is all part of the festive, 'syncretic', approach to the event as a whole.

What we have seen here, therefore, are fragments of discourse coalescing around a specific event, fragments that have their origins in story and in memory. While this is true of the Chinese New Year, and of Chinese religion and its association with luck, I would also suggest that something very similar is also true of other 'religions' and 'religious communities'. Abby Day highlights that for her respondents in West Yorkshire Islam is seen as 'foreign' and associated specifically with the south Asian communities of Bradford, Keighley and other West Yorkshire towns (2011, 137–42). Hindus and Sikhs are clearly seen through the same kind of framework. Where in relation to the Chinese images and assumptions from fiction, and specifically from film, form the baseline for understandings among non-Chinese people attending the Chinese New Year festivals, the same kind of images and assumptions, the same series of fragmented views, contradictory assumptions, partial and stereotypical images, and half-remembered facts, also form the baseline for the understanding of various religious groups among the non-religious people of the city. The only additional element I would add, in relation to Islam in particular, and probably in relation to Sikhs and Hindus, is the importance of the news media within this mix. What is reported on television and radio, what appears in the newspapers and what is available on many different internet sites is added to the wider images of film and television to create a varied mix of images, assumptions and memories. I would probably even go so far as to argue that in 2012 this is also true for many people in the city when approaching Christianity, despite the central place of Christian thinking, Christian images, Christian festivals and Christian values within British society. Christianity has, for many, become a half-remembered, almost alien element of our contemporary social and cultural world.

Given this centrality of story and memory in the way that religions are approached within Britain it is important to try and understand the process by which such memories and stories are created and maintained within the discourses of the people of the city. It is to these two elements, therefore, that I want to turn in the last couple of chapters of this book, beginning with memory in Chapter 7 and then to stories, and the role of the story in the management of religious diversity, in Chapter 8.

Chapter 7
Urban Memory

The anthropologist Johannes Fabian is well known for his explorations of time and memory as these relate to the craft and content of anthropology (1983, 2007). Anthropology, according to Fabian is almost defined by its specific use of time, especially its drive towards contemporaneity in practice and in presentation. In particular he talks of the 'denial of coevalness' and the 'intent and function to keep the Other outside the Time of anthropology' (1983, xi). Where time is important, then memory is never far behind. It is, however, in the generation of anthropological data, in the practice of fieldwork, that Fabian has most to say about the role of memory (2007, 132–42). Memory for Fabian sits right at the heart of the fieldwork process, 'when one thinks about it, remembering/memory turns out to be involved in almost every imaginable aspect of ethnographic research' (2007, 132). It is central to the fieldwork notes and diaries that are kept by the ethnographer. It is central to the data that is collected from informants in interviews or in more informal contexts. These informants are often recalling stories and other information from their memories. Memory is also central for the process of writing ethnography. It is the fieldworker's reflection on the experience of fieldwork as the notes, transcripts, photos and other texts are brought together for analysis, that forms the experience of ethnography, and that experience is rooted in memory.

Anthropology, therefore, cannot be understood without memory and a detailed understanding of the role of memory within the construction of data and the functioning of society. Fabian also talks of the performative nature of ethnography (2007, 36). The doing of ethnography is in itself something of a performance, but more importantly the fieldwork interview is an encounter with an 'other' and is a performance with that other. What is performed, according to Fabian, is memory; it is the opportunity for the individual or the group to present, or to perform, that which is significant for them. This picks up a wider body of literature that sees the interview (whether part of fieldwork or not) as performative (Hockey 2002, Day 2011, 194). In my own work, however, I am not dealing with interviews as such. That does not mean, however, that the conversations I have been listening to are not performed, clearly they are. Nor does it suggest that memory can only be performed within the interview. The conversations that form the data for this book are, in many cases, performances of memory in a very direct sense. Memory, and the performance of memory, has clearly emerged as being central to my own analysis of the data that I have collected within this project and so it is important to look at the kind of memories involved in these performances in much more detail.

In this chapter, therefore, I will draw on a number of theories of memory in order to explore the role of memory in the public discourses on religion and religious diversity within the city. There are essentially three approaches that I wish to investigate. First is the understanding, developed to a large extent by Danièle Hervieu-Léger, that there is something essential to religion itself that is related to memory (2000). Hervieu-Léger connects this to the idea of a 'chain of memory' and the importance of tradition, but there are clearly other ways in which this can be developed. The second approach is at one and the same time more personal and more community-orientated and takes us back to the fieldwork in Highgate and Handsworth. The most common spontaneous discourse on religion in both these neighbourhoods occurred among the elderly reflecting back on some aspect of their childhood. This is particularly true of the Afro-Caribbean community, and the work of one of my students, Jennifer Smith, also working in Handsworth, has explored this further (Smith 2006). This will, however, also allow me to introduce the ideas of Maurice Halbwachs on 'collective memory' into the discussion (1992). Finally I want to look at what Mark Crinson and others have defined as 'urban memory' (2005). The redevelopment of the inner-city has left traces of the past within the environment that trigger memories for those who live in, or pass through, the neighbourhood. In an area like Highgate, for example, the slum housing and many of the warehouses have been demolished, but others have been adapted and reused for other purposes. Many church buildings, however, remain as beacons of memory even when they are no longer used for worship. Some of what I was saying in the previous chapter about memory, imagination, and understandings of Chinese religion also relates to these ideas of 'urban', or perhaps in this case we could say 'cultural' memory.

Underpinning all these various approaches to memory from the different theories, what I want to focus on in this chapter is something of the mechanism by which the kind of discourses that I have been investigating in this book are generated and how they might work. In Chapter 2 I tried to offer a definition of the kind of discourses that I am interested in, and in the subsequent chapters I have offered a number of examples from the data that I have been collecting. In this chapter, therefore, I want to explore the nature of these partial, and in some ways inconsequential, discourses in more detail. It is clear that these discourses have some relationship to stories and these stories are 'performed' in very much the kind of way suggested by Fabian and others. Much of what I have listened to has been fragments of anecdotes shared between respondents, suggestions of stories that individuals do not go on to tell, but are known and recognised between the parties to the discussion, or even in many cases allusions to stories that are in the public arena and are assumed to be generally known. These stories, or anecdotes, are also closely related to memory and it is often a specific memory that triggers the story, or is the primary content of that story. I will come back at the end of the chapter, therefore, to revisit Fabian's idea of fieldwork, or the discourses that I have been listening to, as the 'performance of memory' and

I will look in more detail at the form and the content of the conversations that make up my data.

The Chain of Memory

In 1992 Danièle Hervieu-Léger published an important text that aimed to explore what role religion was playing in contemporary French society (2000). As in Britain at the time, France was understood as becoming a secular society and religion, according to all the commentators, was being pushed to the margins of society and more specifically into private spaces. Much of this, Hervieu-Léger suggests, comes from the kind of definitions of religion that are used within the discussion. These are fundamentally at odds with many of the modernist discourses of contemporary French society. Hervieu-Léger, from her empirical investigations, therefore wanted to challenge this secularisation narrative and, in the process, find a definition of religion that was helpful within the modernist framework of a nation such as France. Her fundamental question was to ask whether religion had any place within the modernist narrative. In order to answer this, however, she needed first to define what she meant by religion and then to look at its role within contemporary France.

Having reviewed a number of different definitions of religion, and having shown how each definition leads, in its own way, to secularism within the modernist framework, Hervieu-Léger draws on the work of Jean Séguy who suggests that we can understand other elements of society, such as sport, celebrity and so on, as 'metaphors for religion' (Séguy 1989, Hervieu-Léger 2000, 66–71). Hervieu-Léger turns this concept around and asks what it is that these metaphoric religions take from the concept of 'religion' and focuses eventually on the idea of tradition. Tradition, for Hervieu-Léger, is central to an understanding of religion in the sense of a series of narratives and ideas that are passed down through the generations, or that are perceived to be passed down through the generations, that are understood to be normative and that are used to give meaning and legitimation to contemporary existence (2000, 81). This can be taken for granted within pre-modern society where most aspects of society derive their meaning and legitimacy from the past. Within modernism, however, this is no longer the case as the very essence of modernism, for Hervieu-Léger, is the desire to derive meaning and legitimacy from rational thought, from first principles as it were, and to question all kinds of assumed historical meaning. This inevitably means that religion, based as it is in tradition, can have no a priori role within a modernist perspective. This does not mean, however, that religion itself has no role at all.

Before exploring how religion can have a role within modernism, Hervieu-Léger links the idea of tradition to collective and individual memory to explore how normative religion has fared within modernist societies (2000, 83–100). It is, she argues, the breaking of the chain of memory, on which tradition relies, that accounts for the crisis of religion within modern France, and other western secular societies (2000, 130–40). This exists at the very individual level, the passing on of the stories and ideas that form the tradition, at the level of the family, where this transmission is most commonly found, and on the level of society, where the breaking of the chain leads to a collapse of collective memories. The situation, however, is not quite as simple as this suggests. The memory itself, the idea of religion and the stories of religion, including many symbols and images, remain active within society. It is not the memory as such that is lacking, what is broken within the chain, is the sense of meaning and legitimacy that is derived from that memory. Here ideas of collective memory from Halbwachs become important for Hervieu-Léger's analysis. For Halbwachs collective memory consists of those elements of a society that are recalled because of the meaning and emotive force that they hold (1992). Collective memory is more than simply a shared memory, it is a living force within society. It is this move, therefore, from collective memory, or tradition, to shared memory, or fragmented elements of narrative and image, that has led, according to Hervieu-Léger, to the decline of religion. What has not been passed on from one generation to the next is the meaning and significance of the memory, even when the memory itself is maintained through various different forms or media. This is an important point that I will return to later in the chapter.

This, then, leads Hervieu-Léger to ask where religion can be found within modern society and here she comes back to the idea of tradition, and the collective memory of stories, ideas and images, with emotive and legitimising power in the contemporary world. Hervieu-Léger identifies three possible sources for such 'tradition' within modern society. The first is through 'effective fraternities', communities of people with shared interests who meet through networks rather than through the established geographic and familial communities (2000, 149–57). There is the potential within such effective communities, Hervieu-Léger argues, to construct new 'traditions', to tell stories of a possible past that can give meaning and legitimacy to the group in contemporary society. Within established religious communities, such as the Catholic Church, the same process of the construction of tradition with new meanings for the contemporary Catholic can also be seen to construct new religious significance, and Hervieu-Léger finds this primarily in the growth of pilgrimage devotion to figures such as the Curé D'Ars within modern society (2000, 156). Finally Hervieu-Léger looks to the new immigrant communities within France that bring their own religious narratives and traditions with them and establish the significance of these traditions over and against the modernism of the society within which they find themselves (2000, 157–62). In each of these cases it is a sense of community that leads to the need for tradition, whether invented or recovered, and to the power of religion within modernism, not the assumption of tradition, with the legitimation and meaning that this implies, as was the case in pre-modern societies. In these new religious communities memory is shifted, once more, from the shared to the collective through an act of will and it is in the new collective memory that religion finds its home within modernity.

Within the context of this book, however, it is not these reconstructions, or survivals, of religion within the modernist society that are of primary interest, it is those people for whom the chain of memory has been broken, those people who have lost the power and meaning of tradition while still, probably, retaining some memory of specific aspects of religious language and imagery. What is important here is the twofold process. The first element is the fragmentation of the tradition, and of the memories associated with that tradition. This is seen in many different contexts and was a process that I explored in more detail within my discussion of situational belief in a previous book (2008, 37–52). In that work I argued that individuals in contemporary Britain seldom hold beliefs as a systematic whole, rather they tend to draw on individual belief statements (about the importance of requiems, about reincarnation or about the presence and accessibility of dead relatives for example) as and when they needed them. Once again it is fragmentation that is highlighted as the primary feature of this approach to belief. The second stage of the process, therefore, is the divorcing of meaning, or significance, from the fragments of memory as they exist. It is not, therefore, as a series of significant and meaningful statements that people generally approach religion, rather it is as curiosities, as images, nostalgic thoughts, a series of unrelated facts, elements of their lives and their past experiences that have little or no immediate emotional value. The first of these processes, I think, is easy to document and demonstrate, the second is much more difficult to show, not least because the elements involved may actually have different meanings, and different emotional values, depending on circumstances. This is something that I want to explore in a little more detail in the next few sections of this chapter.

Personal, Collective and Public Memory

Rex and Moore, in the 1960s, caught something of the importance of memory within discourses about religion when they wrote that 'in following this pattern of worship the congregations are in fact virtually parading the values of the old Sparkbrook when it was a 'respectable area' closely identified with the gentry. The ritual goes beyond this; by drawing in old Sparkbrookians and pulling together members of the old 'respectable' working class, it recreates the old community (as far as this is possible), which corporately asserts its values. For the hour of worship and the time before and after when old friends meet to gossip, it is if nothing had changed, as if the congregation were still living in the Sparkbrook they remember from their childhood' (1967, 184).

This extract resonates directly with the story I told in Chapter 2 about the elderly Caribbean lady who, on looking out at the building of a new Sikh educational and community centre in Handsworth, remembered the chapel that had sat on the site many years before, and the video games parlour that inhabited the same site more recently. It was in relation to memory that she was able to say 'God always claims his own'. This story came from a study that one of my postgraduate students, Jennifer Smith, undertook of a Methodist Church in Handsworth with a majority black congregation (2006). In that study Smith was concerned primarily with the idea of holiness. However, as part of her fieldwork she also discovered the very powerful role that memory played in the lives of the elderly black women who made up the majority of the congregation. While there were many aspects of their story, their reception within the UK and even the attitude of the church over the years, that they found difficult or even distasteful, the religious upbringing that many of them had experienced in the Caribbean and the hymns and bible passages that they had committed to memory at that time saw them through and moulded their current identity.

Smith notes two kinds of memory that were important to the women of the congregation. The first related to the specific space in which they were worshipping at the time as they had been forced to move out of their church into a neighbouring school room. The church building had some memories of old friends and neighbours who had worshipped with them in the past and the women's need to sit in the same pattern within the schoolroom as they had inhabited within the church struck Smith as significant (2006, 73). What was more significant, however, was the inability of many of the women to see their church as a 'black' church despite the current make up of the congregation. The memory of their own arrival, the powerful presence of white members in the history of the congregation and, over time, their own marginalisation within the congregation led most of the women to talk of the church as a 'white' church even when all the white folks had left.

The other memory went beyond the current congregation to the women's earlier years in the Caribbean. Smith notes that this memory was maintained through language, specifically as that language related to scripture, 'the language people used about and from Scripture made a bridge for what they brought with them … woven into a common story' (2006, 73), and from hymns, 'the choice of hymns is certainly linked to the cultivated memory of any congregation' (2006, 102). However, it was objects in the lives of the individuals, blue envelopes for the collection, the membership list, and even flowers in church, that Smith associates most closely with memories of childhood and the Caribbean: 'Explaining why she provided extravagant fresh arrangements each week to sit on the examination bench that served as altar table, she talked about the fragrance of flowers blowing in through open church windows when she was a girl in Jamaica … she consciously sought to ground the worship with tangible symbols that referenced her own and other's memories' (2006, 67).

Many oral history projects also make note of the way in which those who were growing up in the early years of the last century talk in a way that assumes the centrality of religion within their childhood, even if they have not attended religious institutions since they left Sunday school, or more frequently since the birth of their own first child (Brown 2001, 143–4). Callum Brown provides an interesting survey of the oral history material relating to religion collected in the 1960s, 1970s and 1980s (2001, 115–44). While he is careful to state the difficulties with using and interpreting this data, not least because of the kinds of questions asked by interviewers over this time period, it is clear that the material itself shows that people born at the end of the nineteenth century and during the first half of the twentieth century had considerable experience of religion throughout their childhood. While the percentage of households where neither parent attended church stood at between 13 per cent in a sample of women from Stirling in Scotland to nearer 80 per cent in parts of London, the Potteries and the North Midlands, the number of interviewees that attended some kind of religious institution (church, Sunday school or church-related club) as a child was significantly higher, and in most cases was over 75 per cent (2001, 140). If the presence of religious books in the home, or other images and religious items, is added to this number then religion was still very significant throughout British society for much of the first half of the twentieth century. Brown therefore notes that religion and religious discourses were an important part of many people's childhood memory and what comes through most strongly from this material for Brown, is the level of personal commitment that is apparent within the interviews (2001, 141).

What is also interesting, from Brown's analysis, is not only the fact that most older members of society will have some memory of religion from their childhood, but the way in which that memory is expressed in oral history interviews that were collected in the 1970s and 1980s:

> The liberalisation of religious values, and the loss of the "religious life" which the vast bulk of oral interviewees experienced in their childhood and young adulthood of the later nineteenth and first half of the twentieth century, became radically "re-remembered". This becomes evident in the oral testimony in the form of laughter, self-derision, grief or even bitterness at recollections of the religious regimes they had followed without question as youngsters. (2001, 116)

Brown is keen to stress that this is not just a product of aging, but rather that it reflects a change in attitude, or in values, and what Brown calls a 'moral turn' within society in the 1960s. If this 're-remembering' is true for the interviewees when talking as part of an oral history project, then we can assume that it happens, although perhaps less consciously, within the kind of remembering that I am noting as part of the data that I have been collecting. In many of the comments, from both Highgate and Handsworth, the same indication of laughter, self-deprecation and even bitterness could be heard within the comments. Perhaps if I had listened more carefully I may even have heard the occasional expression of grief.

What might be assumed from this approach to memory is that the references to the religious childhood can only hold for people who are currently in their 60s or 70s, even among those of Caribbean and other ethnic groups. What struck me within the conversations that I was listening to was that even for much younger people, certainly those in their 30s and 40s, memory still appeared to play a role in relation to their comments about religion. And even for those in their 20s, the 'memory' of their parent's experiences clearly place religion firmly into the past. These individuals also appeared to associate such 'memories' with laughter, self-derision, grief and bitterness as Brown highlights for the older generation. The memory of those born and brought up in the first half of the twentieth century, and their experience of the moral turn of the 1960s, appears to have been passed, as memory, to the younger generation. Do we therefore need to turn to Halbwachs' ideas of 'collective memory' in order to try and explain what is going on here?

Collective memory, based as it is on the work of Maurice Halbwachs, assumes that some elements of memory are shared and can form a collective view as the basis for shared discourses. It is important to note that collective memory, as Halbwachs understands it, does not sit in some mystical place outside the individual memories of the various members of the group, rather 'while the collective memory endures and draws strength from its base in a coherent body of people, it is individuals as group members who remember' (1992, 48). Hervieu-Léger clarifies this further by saying 'of its essence fluid and evolutionary, collective memory functions as a regulator of individual memory at any one moment. It even takes the place of individual memory whenever it passes beyond the memory of a given group and the actual experience of those for whom it is a reference' (2000, 124). This passing beyond the group leads to what Hervieu-Léger refers to as 'cultural memory', something she associates very closely with the normative element of memory in religion (2000, 124–7). Fabian makes a different distinction, this time between 'collective memory' and 'public memory' (2007, 93–6). While Fabian sees political and other differences between these two kinds of memory, the main distinction appears to be in the fact that the research needs to search out, and perhaps even '(re)construct', collective memory while 'it would be in the nature of public memory to document itself' (2007, 95).

Is there a collective memory among the Caribbean migrants to the UK that is formed as much by the stories that are told among them, and therefore shared among them, as by individual experiences? For example, among the Caribbean community, could we talk about the 'collective memory' of the racist reception by the White majority in the 1960s and beyond ('No Blacks, No Irish' on boarding houses for example)? The symbolic value of the Windrush, however, and even the importance of the Notting Hill Carnival in establishing Caribbean identity, could both exist much more within the 'cultural memory' of the community as defined by Hervieu-Léger. Where, however, within this distinction, the hymns and bible passages identified by Smith as an important part of the memory, and identity of the older Methodist women, ultimately sit is an interesting question that goes beyond the current discussion.

Another example of how these different kinds of memory play out can be seen among contemporary Catholics, or perhaps I should say ex-Catholics. There is clear 'collective memory' among the Catholic community in some parts of the UK. I remember as a lay community worker in Manchester in the 1990s many of the residents of what used to be the old Irish slum would tell me, without really thinking, about the abuse they experienced as children and young adults at the hands of the priests within the Catholic Church. None of this was extreme, the kind of stories of sexual abuse that have since emerged, but these were stories of being forced to attend confession, for example, and what the people themselves defined as the mental or emotional abuse that was associated with the parish and school structures (Hornsby-Smith 1991, Ryan 1996). With the emergence of many more stories of physical and sexual abuse within the public media in the last 20 years then this 'collective memory' has emerged into, or perhaps merged with, a very 'public memory' of abuse among many ex-Catholics. In essence, however, the two kinds of memory are clearly very different.

In more recent years it may be argued that events such as 9/11 have become part of the 'public memory' of society as a whole. It is clear that people often remember exactly where they were when they heard of the news, and as the many television, radio and newspaper stories of memories associated with the tenth anniversary of the event in September 2011 have demonstrated, this event, and some of the subsequent actions that came from it is still very strong in the collective/public memory of the nation as a whole. The attitudes towards Islam, and religion in general, that were generated in response to that event can still be recalled and mobilised today, through reference to the collective/public memory as we shall see in my final chapter, and once again such public memories, if triggered within a specific context, can provide colour to contemporary discourses on religious diversity. It is arguable, therefore, that it is the public memories of religion that most clearly colour the conversations about religious diversity that I have heard around the city, rather than the individual's own personal memory, or even, perhaps the collective memory of the social group to which they belonged. In practice, however, as I look back over the data, I am not so sure that this is the case. For a start it is very difficult to distinguish these different elements of memory, especially as they are recalled by the older generations. But even among the young conversationalists it is Brown's 'laughter, self-derision, grief or even bitterness' that is more obvious in the discussions than the shock or horror of the public memory of 9/11. This may have something to do with the everyday urban context in which these conversations took place.

Urban Memory

Mark Crinson and his colleagues at Salford University do not claim to have invented the term 'urban memory', although they have perhaps done most to make it work in theoretical terms. They trace the roots of the term through Halbwachs and Walter Benjamin and want to use it to cover a range of different, if related, ideas. Crinson says of 'urban memory' that it 'indicates the city as a physical landscape and collection of objects and practices that enable recollections of the past and that embody the past through traces of the city's sequential building and rebuilding' (2005, xii). It is essential to Crinson's understanding of urban memory, and of memory generally, that it is as much about forgetting or erasing as it is about remembering. The edited volume that Crinson brings together includes papers on memorials and public art as sites of memory, but for my own purposes I am more interested in the latter part of Crinson's definition, the embodiment of the past through traces of the city's sequential building and rebuilding.

Richard Williams writes a paper for the book on industrial gallery space noting how often old industrial buildings, primarily warehouses but also other kinds of industrial space, have been redeveloped in recent years to provide leisure facilities including gallery spaces (2005). What is important for Williams is that in the redesign of the space many of the old industrial features are retained and the building is allowed to proclaim its past. The extent to which that past is either celebrated or, to use Williams' word, 'obliterated' will vary from space to space (2005, 128–9). Williams himself compares Tate Liverpool, where the dockside building retains, and in many ways celebrates, the past, with Tate Modern, where the original function of the turbine hall is all but obliterated and it is simply the vastness of the space that generates the experience for the visitor. Williams goes on, however, to qualify this by acknowledging that although the Tate Liverpool celebrates a certain vision of the industrial past it also clearly sanitises it in the process with references to slavery and the exploitation of dock workers taken out. Likewise the Tate Modern does, in the name 'turbine hall' and other features of the building, retain some memory of its past. As Williams says 'it might therefore be more accurate to say that the industrial gallery space therefore presents a scenario of simultaneous remembering *and* forgetting' (2005, 132, italics in the original). In both cases, however, there is also something of the exotic in these industrial spaces, something that Williams links with Foucault's idea of heterotopia, a space set apart that allows individuals to distance themselves from the experience of the space and ask searching questions about it (2005, 136–9, Foucault 1986). Memory, and the past uses of the space, plays a very important part in that reconsideration and reflection.

Crinson and Tyrer do something very similar in two separate papers in the collection, although they apply these ideas to whole neighbourhoods rather than to specific buildings (Crinson and Tyrer 2005, Tyrer and Crinson 2005). Once again, however, the idea of forgetting, or collective amnesia, is as important as remembering, or urban memory. Sharon Zukin and Peter Hall, writing from an American context, began to explore the way in which redevelopments of post-industrial spaces distanced, or even obliterated the history of the area (Zukin 1982, 112, Hall 1996, 348). Crinson and Tyrer take this further in their analysis of the redevelopment of Ancoats in Manchester (the old Irish slum where I listened to memories of Catholic abuse) with reference to the work of Pierre Nora on memory (2005, Nora 1996–8). 'Memory survives' they say 'if it survives at all, in the form of traces or residues, fetishes of the past, or bureaucratic orderings of certain venerated phenomena' (Crinson and Tyrer 2005, 50). In other words the memory of the industrial past is maintained through the retention of symbolic objects or buildings while the whole area is essentially redesigned – in the case of Ancoats into a canal-side marina with the proposed title of 'little Venice'.

The 'fetishistic' language of Nora is developed in the second paper, on the redevelopment of Trafford Park on the other side of Manchester city centre. Here

Tyrer and Crinson develop Freud's understanding of the 'totem' as something that symbolises that which is destroyed and at the same time erases the destruction from our collective memory (2005, 101–3, Freud 1938). So the redevelopment of Trafford Park maintains the symbolic representation of its industrial past in a way that erases the real memory of the grime, oppression and suffering associated with the area by those who inhabited it in its industrial days. As Tyrer and Crinson say 'the spatial suppression of working-class labour runs through the village redevelopment' (2005, 112). This language of fetishism or totemism is particularly evocative when we come to try and apply these ideas to urban religion.

If Freud's totemic structure can offer a theoretical frame for understanding the shift from industrial to post-industrial urban spaces, it can perhaps be even more aptly applied to the shift in many parts of the city from religious to post-religious (or even secular to post-secular if we prefer). Tyrer and Crinson say that 'new architectural forms, materials, detailing and other symbols … reproduce the industrialism that has been torn down' (2005, 102) so also similar forms, detailing and symbols that were once associated with religious buildings reproduce the religion that has generally disappeared. In the development of Ancoats the Building Preservation Trust 'regarded St Peter's Church as crucial to its policy of heritage-led regeneration' (Crinson and Tryer 2005, 60). The church had ceased to be a place of worship many years previously, but was essential to the totemisation, or fetishism of memory in the redevelopment process.

Something of this can, of course, be seen, and noted, in those areas that have been redeveloped within inner Birmingham. Brindley Place goes out of its way to remind those who use this leisure and office space of its previous industrial uses in and around the canal basin at the heart of the city. More specifically, for my purposes within this analysis, as part of this redevelopment the Second Church of Christ Scientist on Broadway (built originally as a Presbyterian Church), just on the edge of Brindley Place has been retained and redeveloped as a night club. It is now owned by a chain but originally opened as 'The Church'. Here the original use of the building, and the architectural features that denote its previous use, are deliberately maintained because of the frisson that is generated through the juxtaposition of the religious context and the new, we might say 'hedonistic', function. Other religious symbols such as old church furnishings, stained glass windows and even statues of angels and devils, were added to this attempt to manipulate memory, albeit a very selective memory of what 'religion' is at a stereotypical level.

If we return to Williams' paper, he makes a brief reference, through the work of Peter Hall, to the similarities between the industrial gallery space and Disneyland's 'Main Street USA' (2005, 131, Hall 1996, 348). The obliteration of history by redevelopment schemes, despite their attention to the historical façade, makes them no more 'historical' than a Disney theme park. Once again we can see something of the totemic or feshistic in this process, but this also links in with the work of Umberto Eco on hyper-reality that was discussed in the previous chapter (Eco 1995). These hyper-real spaces depend, in part, on urban memory, our understanding of what the areas should be like and the memories triggered by symbolic elements such as specific types of mock-Victorian gas lamps, park benches or waste paper bins (Boyer 1992, 194). Some of these spaces also play on stereotypes, not so much our memory of a place as our assumption of what it is that defines a place with a specific identity. The discussion of London's Chinatown in the previous chapter is a prime example of this process.

Memory and Narrative: The Form of the Discourse

If I go back to the data that underpins this work and look more closely at the range of comments that I have collected from the conversations that I have been listening to then they can be classified in many different ways. In trying out various forms of classification (by religious group being discussed, by positive or negative inflection etc.) one of the most significant distinctions comes from a classification on the basis of the 'form' of the comment itself. There are a very wide variety of forms or structures to the comments, and the variety of positions within the discourse is one of the things that I want to stress specifically within this work. However, two forms stand out as providing the largest quantity of material. The first I have identified as 'narrative' or 'story', the second as 'fact'. Both of these forms relate to memory, although in very different ways, and I want to conclude this chapter by just outlining some of the distinctive features of each form, its relation to the ideas of memory within this chapter and its connection with the wider discussions as developed in the last four chapters. In a very loose sense 'narrative' focuses more on structure while 'fact' tends to focus on content.

'Narrative' or the 'story' is one of the central themes in much of the work on memory. There is a whole discipline emerging around the study of 'narrative', or the use of narrative in the study of other topics. To enter fully into this discourse is beyond the scope of this text. One area where narrative has been used in interesting ways, which overlap with some of the work of Crinson and his colleagues, has been in urban studies and urban planning. Ruth Finnegan's work on Milton Keynes is an attempt to use narrative to explore some of the thoughts of residents about the city (1998). Leonie Sandercock also advocates the use of story as part of the process of planning, in order to reflect the many different voices that are inevitably part of that process (2003, 181–204). Both these texts, and many others in a similar vein, tend to treat the story or narrative as a complete unit, a whole telling, that can be responded to in much the same way as any other text (Sandercock 2003, 183–6). The fascinating thing about stories, however, is the way in which they are so often fragmented, partial and are alluded to rather than told in their complete form.

Michel de Certeau has some interesting thoughts, in a chapter on 'Spatial Stories' (1984, 115–30), that might begin to link together some of the ideas already discussed within this chapter and then to link them, in turn, to some of the discussions of the previous four chapters. It is not always easy to follow de Certeau's line of thought or to grasp exactly what point he is trying to make.

However, he does throw up some wonderful images and at times he juxtaposes images and ideas in a stimulating and thought provoking way. The discussion of stories and space in his chapter on spatial stories is a particularly good example beginning as it does with the observation that in Athens the vehicles of mass transportation are called *metaphori* (1984, 115).

The first point de Certeau makes is that stories 'carry out the labour that constantly transforms places into spaces or spaces into places' (1984, 118). In other words, to pick up the discussion of Lefebvre's work in Chapter 4, stories mediate between the abstract, or mental, idea of space and the lived space, the space that surrounds us in the city or elsewhere (Lefebvre 1991, 33). After exploring the distinction between maps and tours, setting the former within the scientific realm while claiming the later for the everyday, de Certeau goes on to show how the boundaries we create in space are established, and often fixed, through stories. Stories, in this sense, found spaces (de Certeau 1984, 123). This founding, however, is fragmented, miniaturised and polyvalent:

> This polyvalence does not affect the relational origins of narrativity, however: the ancient ritual that creates fields of action is recognisable in the "fragments" of narration planted around the obscure thresholds of our existence; these buried fragments articulate without its knowing it the "biographical" story whose space they found. (1984, 125)

What de Certeau is trying to express here is the idea that the stories that we use to define, describe and delimit spaces are seldom recalled or expressed in complete wholes. They come in fragments and it takes just a small element of the overall narrative for us to begin to reconstruct the story for ourselves. References to Prince Charming, Sleeping Beauty, or even just the prick of a finger on the spindle will recall favourite nursery stories and likewise an object or space in the environment will recall a wider narrative. The second point is that the stories that are generated may be common but they are seldom precise. The meaning that the story of Sleeping Beauty has to each one of us will be different in part due to the context in which the story was told, the elements we remember, and our subsequent life histories. Stories are personal, we inhabit them with our own meanings, and we can do that because they are polyvalent. There are elements here that relate directly to the discussion of stories and the meaning of Christian worship that I develop in my book *On the Perception of Worship* (Stringer 1999, 100–105).

From here, therefore, we need to jump back into the previous chapter in de Certeau's book, 'Walking in the City', in which de Certeau likens the act of walking to the act of speaking (1984, 91–114). What interests me here is de Certeau's discussion of stories, space and memory: 'the dispersion of stores points to the dispersion of the memorable'; 'a memory is only a Prince Charming who stays just long enough to awaken the Sleeping Beauties of our wordless stories. "*Here*, there used to be a bakery". "*That's* where old lady Dupuis used to live"'; 'there is no place that is not haunted by many different spirits hidden there in silence, spirits one can "invoke" or not'; 'places are fragmentary and inward-turning histories, pasts that others are not allowed to read, accumulated times that can be unfolded but like stories held in reserve, remaining in an enigmatic state, symbolisations encysted in the pain or pleasure of the body. "I feel good here"' (1984, 108, italics in the original). Space is story, and story is memory and all three of these are partial, fragmentary and fleeting.

David Crouch picks this up in a paper about the making of popular geographical knowledge (1998). It is in the shared space of the street that this knowledge is formed. However, it is only through the embodied practices of each individual tracing their own path along that street, noting what is important to them and engaging with others who share this perspective, that the fragmented understanding of the street is constructed. 'The street is embodied in the practice and in its memory. The street triggers recall of a contingent knowledge of values, actions, relationships and anticipations; the street is an image of solidarity, loss, and shared practices too' (1998, 174). This is what, in different ways Hervieu-Léger, Rex and More, Smith, Brown and Crinson and his colleagues are also saying in the various analyses that have made up this chapter. Our world, therefore, is inhabited by stories that are rooted in specific, or generalised, spaces and which recall or populate our memories. This is the way in which we engage with the world on an everyday basis. What, however, does this have to say about discourses on religion?

I think we can draw three conclusions from this material. The first is that we need to expect the kind of discourses that I have been listening to, conversations largely overheard and in public spaces, to be made up of fragments. These will consist of half finished sentences, of words and exclamations that are often no more than fillers, of anecdotes begun, finished or simply suggested. This is a discourse among those who share a common context, a common frame of reference and often a common source of memories and narratives associated with them. The individual statements, therefore, often refer back to other elements of an ongoing and highly fragmented conversation that may have been going on for many years. What is heard is only part of the story, in a very literal sense.

The second conclusion comes from the analysis that has been presented, but is seldom highlighted in any explicit sense. The statements that form part of de Certeau's analysis are more than mere factual statements. '*Here* is where the bakery used to be. *That* is where old lady Dupuis used to live.' The italics can be seen to stress the focus on space or place, but they also suggest an emotional charge. We would not remember the bakery or old lady Dupuis if these things did not mean something to us in the first place. Brown's reference to 'laughter, self-derision, grief or even bitterness', and the emphasis in Crinson's analysis of totemism, fetishism, Noro and Freud also suggests that there is more going on here than a simple intellectual exercise of memory. The memory recalls violence and that violence *is* 'obliterated' through the reconstruction of space. Members of the Caribbean community remember racism, the verbal, emotional and often physical violence meted out to themselves and their compatriots. Catholics remember fear, intimidation and abuse, a different form of violence, different scars within their community. We are dealing here with very significant emotions and it is this emotional element, both positive and negative, in all its complexity, that is tied up in the memories, and in the stories that encapsulate them, as in the statements that allude to them, or the spaces that trigger them. This is not a neutral discourse; it is one that relies on memory and one that brings the emotional element of that memory into the present, into the middle of the discourse itself.

Up to this point practically all that I have said about memory and religion has focused on Christianity as opposed to religious diversity as such. Hervieu-Léger is talking primarily about Christian tradition when she uses the image of the break in the chain of memory. However, she does refer to the religion of immigrant populations as one of the areas where religion can be seen to be growing within a modernist state, albeit through the planting of an external tradition over against the modernism of the state (2000 157–62). In the case of individual memories from childhood or collective memories from within specific communities, it was memories of Christian traditions that led to Brown's reflections on 'laughter, self-derision, grief or even bitterness' (2001, 116). In relation to urban memory then it has been disused churches that I have noted as the possible source of remembering and forgetting within the urban landscape. My discussion of the Central Mosque in Highgate, however, as developed in Chapter 3, and my discussion of Chinatown in Chapter 6 both suggest that there could be some element of 'urban memory' in relation to non-Christian religious spaces.

The main gudwara, the Gudwara Guru Nanak Nishkam Sewak Jatha, on Soho Road in Handsworth, with its onion dome, its use of marble and the orange flags flying from the front, can be understood in many ways as a hyper-real Sikh space. The construction of the building is far from traditional and the object is clearly to make a statement about the place of the Sikh community within the neighbourhood, and more widely as this is the base for an international organisation. It shouts 'this is Sikh' but all the elements are only skin-deep, from an architectural point of view, and the question is raised about the authenticity of the space. As Sorkin states 'the architecture ... is almost purely semiotic, playing the game of grafted signification, theme park building ... such design is based in the same calculus as advertising, the idea of pure imageability, oblivious to the real needs and traditions of those who inhabit it' (1992a, xiv). It is as much about marketing as any Sainsbury's or Tesco store and the same double view of loyalty and suspicion can clearly be generated within the wider community. The building itself, however, will generate all kinds of memory depending on the person who looks at it and their own experiences. There are individual memories of the space as it was being constructed, or in its current use. There are collective memories within the Sikh congregations associated with the gudwara and within members of the community that live and work around it. There are also public memories relating to Sikhs in general and these are perhaps the most difficult to identify, although it is also possible that the building itself is aiming to challenge, or even to obliterate, some of these public memories.

In the light of the discussions on memory and narrative it is clear that the memories of the gudwara, and the stories that are alluded to within these memories, are not expressed with quite the same sense of laughter, self-derision of bitterness that Brown identifies in memories of religion in childhood. In fact the story I retold of the woman who saw the building going up and stated that 'God always claims his own' is a very positive statement with none of the embarrassment or unease of some non-religious people remembering their past. The memories invoked by the gudwara can, however, be seen as 'urban memories' in the sense that Crinson and his colleagues have developed the term. Even the sight of a brash, confident and in some senses exotic 'religious' building recalls a time when Christian buildings, and all that they stood for, were much more prominent within the local community. It is a trigger for the memory of the arrival and growth of the Sikh community, of a developing religious diversity within our cities, but it will also, always, be something of a reminder of the decline, we might also say the 'obliteration' of the Christian presence within the wider society. The positive memory cannot exist without the negative.

Memory and Religion: The Content of the Discourse

Not all the comments that I have collected, however, take the form of stories, or even allusions to stories. When looking through the data there is one category of comment that I have tended to lay to one side during my wider analysis. These comments are as fragmented as many of the allusions to story. They consist of short 'factual' statements about one or other of the religions; 'Muslims pray five times a day' or 'Passover is the Jewish Easter' for example, or they can be identified in questions; 'all male Sikhs carry a dagger don't they?' These 'facts' relate to the practice, or less frequently to the beliefs, of the different religious groups. Unlike the stories, or allusions to stories, these statements of 'fact' were often stated in a very neutral, non-emotive, fashion. I set these comments aside initially because they did not appear to add anything to the discussion of religious diversity as such. However, in the light of this wider discussion of memory I am not so sure that they are as irrelevant as I had first thought. The statements of 'fact' I would suggest refer to another kind of memory, not that of the individual's own experience of religion, or of their encounter with specific religious people or buildings in the environment, but rather of their education as children. Sitting behind these 'facts' is a form of religious education, based on the phenomenological approach of Ninian Smart and his colleagues, in which children learnt about the religions of the world through a series of specific lenses; their beliefs, their worship, their festivals, their family rituals and so on (Smart 1969). It is the kind of 'fact', often stated entirely out of context; 'Sikhs don't cut their hair', that were learnt, almost rote fashion in school, and are now recalled whenever Sikhs, or whichever religion it might be, are mentioned.

What these 'facts', these memories, do point to, I would suggest, is a very specific way in which 'religion' is conceptualised within British society, rooted very firmly in educational practice over many decades. Where 'religion' is not owned as something that the individual is part of, or that forms part of their own identity, then 'religion' consists of a series of propositions and practices that relate to a particular community. What is more, the series of 'facts' about each religion is relatively small, clearly unproblematic, and takes no account of variations or subtleties of belief or practice within any one 'religion'. This is a relatively simplistic understanding of 'religion'. However, I would argue from the sheer quantity and frequency of such statements of fact within my data, that it is probably the most common and the base concept for many, if not most, of the conversations that underpin this project. If this is the root understanding of 'religion', therefore, then anything that we would wish to say about religious diversity within popular discourses has to engage with this central idea and with the memories on which it is founded.

If I were to go back over the last four chapters and look again at the conclusions that I drew from the different elements of the fieldwork, particularly in the light of this root understanding of religion, then I think it is possible to make a number of comments about the content of the popular discourses on religious diversity that are common across a number of different contexts. In the material from Highgate I emphasised the point that for many of the people of this neighbourhood 'religion' is spoken of in the singular and as 'other'. The idea that all religions are ultimately the same is itself part of the phenomenological approach as used within religious education. The discussion was entirely about the surface elements of the religions, a series of beliefs, practices, rituals, festivals etc. and if Sikhs had this set, then Muslims had another, and Hindus another. In essence each set was interchangeable, 'Passover is the Jewish Easter', and so 'religion' is a fundamental category and the different 'religions' are simply variations on a theme. I will come back to this in relation to recent developments in interfaith dialogue at the beginning of the following chapter.

If we focus on the 'othering' element of the comments from Highgate, the sense that all religions are not only the same, but also not of us, then again we can see some of the roots of this in the educational approach. The phenomenological approach attempted, at least in part, to objectify the religions, to present them as equally valid and as 'things in the world'. However, these were things in the world that did not connect with the young people who were studying them. As well as the range of 'facts' associated with each religion there were also the wide range of images and discourses about these religions, and the people who were supposed to follow them, from film, literature and the popular media, as I discussed in relation to Chinese 'religion' in Chapter 5. All this serves to construct an understanding of the religions, and even of religion in general, as other, exotic, belonging to people who are not like us, in other words to 'orientalise' many religious traditions (Said 1978), including I would suggest Christianity itself. Religion, like culture, is something that other people have.

This relationship between religion and culture, as features that belong to 'other' peoples, brings in the discussion of the dominant discourses underpinning the street festivals in a city such as Birmingham that I discussed in Chapter 5. I stressed in that chapter the way in which the inclusive, open, positive multiculturalism that forms the basis for the revised dominant discourse, leaves many people with the view that, within a controlled context, and if everybody can be seen to get along, then this kind of variety and diversity is 'nice', a good thing, to be encouraged. The base line, therefore, is the assumption that religious diversity (if religion is understood phenomenologically, if it is about 'other people', and if it is carefully controlled in enjoyable street festivals) should be entirely positive. In practice, of course, this cannot always be the case, and here the results of Chapter 4 become important. Religion, in the terms I have developed in this discussion, cannot be the real basis for difference (as opposed to diversity) between peoples, and while religion may have replaced 'culture' as a marker of the identity of 'others' in the context of 'diversity' it has not, fundamentally, replaced 'ethnicity' in the context of difference. It is when the challenge of religion that is not tame, neutral and 'private' intrudes into the public discourse, away from where the memory of school days has relegated it, that trouble starts to brew and people revert to the memories of religion based on guilt, bitterness and pain, to the language of hypocrisy and to the notion that all religion (all religions still being the same, of course) is 'bad'.

The final point that I wish to make, therefore, in this discussion of religion and memory takes me back to the discussion from Fabian with which I began this chapter. For Fabian memory is part of the fieldwork experience and is implicit in all interviewing and data collection. He describes such fieldwork encounters as 'performative' and suggests that what is being 'performed' is memory (2007, 36). The idea of 'performance' suggests two things. First, that there is something deliberate, perhaps even artificial, concealing, even deceptive about these 'performances'. What we see is not the real person, it is what the speaker wants us to see (however conscious that decision is). Here we are clearly in the world of Erving Goffman and the presentation of self (1969). This view, is also, perhaps seen most clearly in the statement of facts. The second point takes me back to the emphasis in my discussion of stories. There is a forcefulness, a commitment, an emotional edge to the performance that aims to communicate more than the simple content of the narrative (Stringer 1999). Having listened to so many conversations over the last ten years or so about religion and religious diversity, there is clearly an element of the 'performative' about many of these conversations. People are staking out a position, trying in some way to persuade (whether that is the listener or perhaps themselves), wanting to demonstrate that they know certain facts, or to associate themselves with a particular narrative with all the values, memories and cultural assumptions that come with such facts and such stories. In so many cases, what I have listened to are small, but often very powerful, performances on the theme of religion and it is the power of these performances standing out from the background conversation that drew me to explore this wider issue in more detail.

The conclusion that can be drawn from this discussion, therefore, is the importance of memory in the stories and facts that are being told or alluded to about religion. Religion is not a present reality for many of those talking, and even where it is the idea and experience of religious diversity is something that is coloured by previous experiences and memories. Some of these memories are personal, the individual's own place within the chain, what was passed on to them in their childhood or their experiences within their own neighbourhood. Many more are what might be called 'collective', or 'cultural', either shared memories within a neighbourhood (the building of a mosque, the closing of a church) or of events in the national or international arena, of which 9/11 is undoubtedly the most significant in recent years. Behind both of these is also the background public memory of our society, coloured by media and stereotypical narratives that suggest to whole sections of the population that religion is abusive, or all Muslims, Sikhs or whatever have certain festivals or particular beliefs. It is this complex juxtaposition of narratives, facts and memories of different kinds, interacting with the contemporary experiences, that creates the sheer complexity of the discourses that I have been outlining. The specific memory, with its particular form, that is recalled in a specific place or within a specific conversation may bring contradictory emotions into play such that attitudes to religion and religious diversity are at one and the same time positive, negative or entirely neutral. This is exactly the situation that we have seen in previous chapters and it is this ambiguity that, I would suggest, forms the basis for a possible approach to the management of religious diversity, or rather of discourses about religious diversity, that I wish to move on to in the final chapter.

Chapter 8
Managing Discourses of Religious Diversity

In a critique of work on sustainable cities, David Thorns notes that certain dominant approaches to urban sustainability share a common fault with the early writers of the Chicago School of urban theorists. The Chicago School, Thorns states, advocated a model 'based on plant ecology and the impersonal competition of the land market'. The explanations they offered for the structure of the city, therefore, 'was largely a result of unconscious processes focussed on biological or psychological rather than social or political processes' (2002, 216). As I draw on the same metaphor of 'urban ecology' in my title then it might be assumed that I could be accused of the same fault.

It is vitally important, for Thorns, that the planning and governance processes within the urban context are acknowledged and studied as part of the overall analysis (2002, 178–202). Activities within the city do not tend to happen by chance, at least not on the macro scale, and the decisions made by those who wield power within the city are essential to a complete understanding of the city. It is therefore important that I should end this particular study by moving out from the detailed, almost micro studies, of specific situations in which discourses about religion are used in the public arena to the question of the management of discourses of religious diversity within the city as a whole.

I might begin by coming back to the book that has sat beneath the whole of this study, Gerd Baumann's *Contesting Culture* (1996). The very understanding of discourse within that text, that I have specifically stated that I have lifted for this work, has power written in at the very beginning. The distinction that Baumann makes between the dominant and demotic discourses within Southall implies a power relation and this is made very explicit within the text. The dominant discourse is that of the authorities, although it is also more than this. The dominant discourse that aligns community with a reified understanding of culture was first identified by a number of academic studies of race and racism in the 1980s and was noted both among those who used racist rhetoric as well as anti-racist groups (Brah 1987, Phoenix 1988, Gilroy 1992). It is this all pervasiveness that Baumann notes as a feature of any 'dominant discourse'. Other features include that 'it is conceptually simple, enjoys a communicative monopoly, offers enormous flexibility of application, encompasses great ideological plasticity, and is serviceable for established institutional purposes' (1996, 30). Interestingly, Baumann identifies one of the primary sources for this dominant discourse as deriving from the colonial discourses of East Africa, as the colonial and post-colonial authorities in Uganda and Kenya chose to identify a range of Asian communities each with its own reified culture. With reference to the work of H.S. Morris, Baumann says 'the division of people-to-be-governed into communities is a time-honoured colonial strategy' (1996, 29, Morris 1968). Given that the terms that are used, 'community' and 'culture', are also borrowed from academic discourse, even if the content of the terms may vary, the academic is often implicated in the power relations that are identified through the analysis of discourses. If that is true for 'community' and 'culture' then it seems entirely reasonable for the same to be the case for discourses of religion and religious diversity.

Interfaith

One of the areas that Baumann identifies as an 'arena for cultural contestation' within Southall is that of the interfaith networks (1996, 173–8). Arenas for cultural contestation, in Baumann's terms, refers to those areas of discourse that challenge the dominant discourse he has identified and yet do not really follow a local demotic discourse as such. The development of the idea of an 'Asian culture' by young people in the borough and the political debate about a common 'black culture' among socialists and feminists are two other such arenas. However, it is the interfaith arena that is of particular concern to this text and it sits somewhat uncomfortably within Baumann's overall work, not least because religion as an identity or within the dominant and demotic discourses is underplayed throughout much of the rest of the book.

For Southall in the early 1990s the interfaith networks appear to have been typical of many other similarly 'multi-cultural' neighbourhoods. Baumann identifies that the two main churches, the Anglicans and the Roman Catholics took interfaith issues seriously in so far as they put resources into developing interfaith work. The fact that this probably marginalised the issues within the wider Anglican and Roman Catholic communities is overlooked, except for Baumann to note the comments of some local Christians who clearly found this work difficult. What is interesting, however, is that Baumann specifically notes that it is those religious groups that do not fit the mainstream definitions of Islam, Sikh and Hindu that are most active in the interfaith network alongside the churches. 'The local movement' Baumann comments, 'thus combines two rather unequal sets of parties: on the one hand, the most established Christian churches, each with its tradition of colonial missionization …; on the other hand, notably those segments of religious opinion which are branded heterodox by the traditions from which they once seceded' (1996, 174). This is probably a fairly fair reflection of the situation in many places, including Birmingham, at the time. Things changed, however, very dramatically with the events of 9/11 and 7/7.

The story is told in Birmingham of how, on the morning after the 9/11 atrocities the Rabbi from the Orthodox synagogue in Singer's Hill, Rabbi Leonard Tann, walked down to the Central Mosque and stood outside the door in an act of solidarity. He was joined by the two bishops of Birmingham and other faith leaders and so the Faith Leaders Group was founded, that has met regularly for discussion and common prayer, ever since. This group changed the dynamics of interfaith activity within the city and brought many of the mainstream religious groups into the arena. If there is any criticism then it might be that it is, in fact, the so called 'heterodox' groups, as identified by Baumann, that have now been excluded at this higher level, partly because they are considered to be too small for representation and partly, I am sure, because of an element of political exclusion on the part of the 'traditions from which they once seceded'.

Over the ten years since the founding of the Faith Leaders Group, the Group has worked closely with political leaders on the City Council, with business leaders and with colleagues at the University of Birmingham on a series of initiatives. One of these led to the publication of *Faiths for the City of Birmingham*, a series of essays on the contribution of the different faith communities within the city to the idea of a 'Good City' (http://www.faithsforthecity.org.uk/). Other initiatives have led to exploratory work in the field of health care and welfare provision, work on the Human City (Clark 2012), picking up an initiative that had been running for a number of years, and also engagement with the Chambers of Commerce on the place of faith in enterprise and business within the city. There is a clear sense in this work that some kind of principle of the 'management' of discourses on religion is taking place. However, given that much of this work takes place within, and among, a relatively small group of clearly acknowledged 'leaders', both within the faith groups and in the city, in industry and in public services, then this kind of activity has had little impact on the ordinary discourses on religion within the city at large.

One area where Birmingham has arguably been very successful within the wider arena of interfaith work is in education and the development of a curriculum for religious education in schools. This was led by a colleague at the University of Birmingham, Marius Felderhof, and building on previous leading initiatives in religious education, has set Birmingham apart as one of the pioneers in this area (Felderhof and Whitehouse 2010). This leads on to another area that Baumann identifies under the heading of 'interfaith', that is the increasing tendency, as he identified it, for young people to discuss 'religion' in a universalist manner (1996, 178–87). More specifically he identifies the way in which the teenagers and young adults that he talked to used English, and hence Christian, terms to discuss religious ideas and events and so began to equate them in their mind. So, for example, Devali is referred to as the Hindu Christmas, and Eid as the Muslim Easter. The Imam, the Gyanni and the Pandit are all referred to as 'priests' and the distinctions between the religions are played down. As one young person said, 'You see, the Muslims aren't allowed to drink, but they can smoke, and we [the Sikhs] can't smoke, but we can drink. So it's the same thing, only different, innit?' (1996, 180). Even God is treated as essentially the same across the main religious traditions.

This picks up a feature of my own data that I explored in more detail at the end of the previous chapter on memory. It appears that in the early 1990s within Southall, it was largely young people who held this implicit universalist position, reinforced Baumann suggests by what was occurring within the schools. What I have identified, almost 15 years later, is that this is probably the most common and most widely stated discourse on religion across the city, stated in general comments by both members of the different religions and by many of those who would claim no religious allegiance at all. Beyond this, therefore, I have identified that the most important distinction in many cases is not that between the different religious groups or ideas, but rather between 'religion' and 'non-religion'. This, however, is not the whole story and to take this discussion further I need to go back to 9/11 and the other outcome of those events to affect the management of discourses about religion within the city, the whole debate about 'community cohesion' and the implementation of the 'prevent' agenda.

Community Cohesion and Prevent

Following 9/11 and 7/7 the need, in some way or another, to 'manage' religious diversity, or at least certain aspects of religious extremism within the UK and elsewhere, became imperative. The models that the government turned to drew principally on Baumann's dominant discourse, although without any reference to Baumann's work. This can be seen very clearly in two of the central responses of the Labour government at the time, the policy of community cohesion and the specific elements of the 'prevent' strategy, although each of these policy initiatives used the dominant discourse in a different way.

Community cohesion began from the principle that the kind of situation implicit in Baumann's dominant discourse had gone too far. The roots of this policy lie not in the attacks of 9/11 and 7/7 but in the earlier riots that rocked a number of British cities in the spring and summer of 2001. This led the Blair government to set up an inquiry inside the Home Office to address possible policy responses. The outcome was *Building Cohesive Communities, A Report of the Ministerial Group on Public order and Community Cohesion* (Home Office 2001). While recognising the underlying economic and other social factors affecting the areas involved in the rioting the principle cause was identified as the fracturing of the communities on racial, generational, cultural and religious lines with little or no communication across these social divides (2001, 8). This, associated with the disenfranchisement of the people involved and their lack of engagement with civil society in any shape or form, led to the proposals surrounding the Community Cohesion agenda that was subsequently reinforced and given a specific focus on the Muslim community following the terrorist atrocities.

One of the most significant theorists, and more recently critic, of community cohesion is Ted Cantle (2005). He does not claim to have coined the term, which he argues 'was effectively created in response to the riots in the northern towns of England in 2001' (2005, 48) and has its roots in work in Canada and elsewhere. He does however explore what community cohesion adds to previous work on multiculturalism and to previous policies of integration. He distinguishes, for example, between social cohesion with its emphasis on 'inclusion' and the need to tackle 'social exclusion' in a more economic sense (2005, 49–50), and community cohesion that is focused more on 'identifiable communities, generally on the basis of faith or ethnic distinctions' (2005, 52). There are some very clear similarities between Cantle's analysis of the need for community cohesion and Steve Vertovec's analysis of superdiversity as both point to the significant role of what Vertovec refers to as the new migration, the growth in the number of countries from which migrants to the UK originated (Vertovec 2007, Cantle 2010). However, Cantle also identifies an important role for Robert Putnam's concepts of social capital and particularly the lack of 'bridging capital' or the lack of contact between ethnic and faith groups and therefore focuses much more on possible 'solutions' than Vertovec's analysis of superdiversity (Putnam 2000, Cantle 2005, 52).

In his 2005 book on Community Cohesion, Cantle ends with a chapter on 'developing a programme for community cohesion' (2005, 159–209) putting particular emphasis on a common vision and sense of belonging, on social capital, the role of leaders and conflict prevention, resolution and reconciliation. It is this programme that was taken by the government as the basis for their own initiatives, although applied in a very specific way to focus more directly onto the 'Muslim community' and the need to identify and encourage the moderate elements of that community rather than to work at integrating that community within the wider social fabric. In recent years Cantle has come back to the issue of community cohesion and has provided a very trenchant critique of the whole government policy and the idea of community cohesion as it was developed in practice, focusing more on the possibility of 'interculturalism' (2012).

In terms of Baumann's categories, the dominant discourse had suggested for some time that each ethnicity formed its own distinct community with its own identifiable culture. *Building Cohesive Communities*, and Cantle's theoretical analysis, both began from the principle that society had become divided into these distinct communities, each with their own ethnicity and culture, and that the boundaries between them had become fixed and immutable. What is more, there were, in the analysis underlying the policy, too many distinct communities and the boundaries between them were too solid. Whether this ever existed in practice is probably a moot point. The evidence from the context of the riots came primarily from Pakistani Muslim communities in northern cities where it was noted that many of the older members could not speak English, where the communities lived in clearly defined neighbourhoods and where many cultural and religious practices were maintained that appeared to separate the members of the community from the wider society. While there clearly were neighbourhoods of this kind throughout the country, this was not the whole story or the experience of Pakistani Muslims as a whole, and nor could their specific experience be read in every other community and/or culture.

Community cohesion, however, aimed to break down some of the boundaries between the communities and to bind the different communities together into a wider sense of neighbourhood. Of course the specific use of the term 'community' within this initiative carried mixed messages. The aim was to build cohesive 'mixed' communities (community is positive) but the problem was seen as strong isolated 'ethnic' or 'cultural' communities (community is negative). One form of community was prioritised over another and it was, ironically, the community of the dominant discourse that was rejected, despite this being the basis for the analysis behind the initiative in the first place. Any kind of local ethnographic analysis would have shown, as Baumann's work did, that the kind of isolated ethnic/cultural/religious community assumed by the dominant discourse was not the norm and that things on the ground were far more complex. However, considerable money was thrown at local authorities to develop community cohesion plans.

Ash Amin's response to the 2001 riots highlights a number of the concerns and contradictions that surrounded the analysis and its implementation (2003, 87–96). Amin praises the official report and recognises its strengths in many areas, but he believes that it does not go far enough. In particular he places the emphasis on the local neighbourhood and what he calls 'the city's micropublics of banal multicultures' (2002, 969). The point he is making is that there is nothing automatic about the process of shared space leading to shared values. He offers a number of examples where the simple proximity of people of different cultures to each other does not lead to any meaningful interaction and adds that 'habitual contact in itself, is no guarantor of cultural exchange. It can entrench group animosities and identities, through repetitions of gender, class, race and ethnic practices' (2002, 969). The examples offered in Chapter 4 bear this out in areas of super-diversity. What is needed, therefore, according to Amin, is some kind of catalyst, at the very local level, that can bring people together: 'Cultural change in these circumstances is likely if people are encouraged to step out of their routine environment, into other everyday spaces that function as sites of unnoticeable cultural questioning or transgression' (2002, 969). At one level this is simply the lesson that has been learnt through multi-faith work over the decades, that people come together most meaningfully if they are engaged in a shared enterprise focused on helping others rather than in endless discussion about common features or differences between the religions concerned. At another level it builds on the kind of distinction that I was making in Chapter 4 between diversity and difference, placing the emphasis very strongly on diversity but recognising that this is not something that comes about naturally, it is something that needs to be worked on.

One element where community cohesion went beyond Baumann's original dominant discourse was in the explicit role of religion in the definition of communities following 9/11 and 7/7. For Baumann the 'communities' implicit in the dominant discourse were primarily ethnic or cultural in form, with religion only playing a minor and ambiguous role in their definition. Because of the experience of Islamic terrorism religion rapidly became central to the definition of community in the dominant discourses of local authorities in the early years of the new millennium, and for the first time in many years local authorities began to take religion, religious communities and religious leaders seriously. In Birmingham, as in many other places, this initiative linked into the work already begun by the Faith Leaders and others, and has enabled many religious groups to find a place at the table alongside the city council and other leaders of the city. Much of the local expression of community cohesion, therefore, was expressed in religious terms and talked about the need to integrate the different religious communities into single, unified communities/neighbourhoods. This clearly had an impact on discourses of religious diversity although it has tended, I would suggest, to reinforce the view that all religion is the same.

The other policy initiative, the Prevent Strategy, was also rooted in Baumann's dominant discourse, but in this case the policy aimed to work with the local, cultural and ethnic communities and not against them (Home Office 2011). The original strategy was launched in 2007 and then revised in 2011 following the general election and a Home Office review. The revised strategy makes it very clear that the aim is to deal with all potential terrorist activity, irrespective of its source. However, it does recognise that the greatest threat at the time of publication came from al-Qa'ida and Islamic extremism. The basic principle behind the strategy depends on the assumption that the people who could most easily reach and engage with extremist Islamic groups and individuals were other Muslims, particularly those on the moderate end of the spectrum. To this end the strategy has three objectives: (a) to 'respond to the ideological challenge of terrorism and the threat from those who promote it'; (b) to 'prevent people from being drawn into terrorism and ensure that they are given appropriate advice and support'; and (c) to 'work with sectors and institutions where there are risks of radicalisation that we need to address' (Home Office 2011, 7).

The underlying assumption here, and in the rest of the document, is that there is something that could be defined as a 'Muslim community' and that this community was coherent enough that individuals and leaders within it could more easily influence others within the community than those outside. Again there is an assumption of strong boundaries and clear identities within the community, although rather than breaking down these boundaries the policy aims to work within them and to build on the assumed solidarity of the community itself. Anybody who had read Baumann's book, and taken note of other research at the time, would know that terms like 'community' can be very malleable, and the assumption of a single 'Muslim community' where members could have influence over other members, was probably far-fetched, although to be fair this kind of language is not used within the official statement of the strategy itself. The policy also had other implications and consequences, ranging from the nature or value of surveillance to international relations, that probably go beyond the specific issues raised by this book.

Islamophobia?

Reference to the prevent strategy leads on directly to the question of the role of Islam within discourses of religious diversity. I have touched on this a number of times throughout the book but never addressed it head-on. Whenever I talked to colleagues and others outside my fieldwork, and mentioned the focus of this research on religious diversity, the inevitable response was for me to be asked 'but isn't it all to do with Islam?' It is worth noting, therefore, that both of the government initiatives, while paying lip service to wider issues of multiculturalism and cultural diversity on the one hand, and to a range of different terrorist threats on the other, were both focussed almost entirely on Muslims within the UK, although the actual implementation of both agendas, at least in Birmingham, did make strenuous efforts to widen this scope somewhat. It is not surprising, given the events of 9/11 and 7/7 to see the focus as primarily on Islam, but it must also be recognised that these initiatives also played into a wider, more vocal, Islamophobia and this also needs to be touched on within this text.

Islamophobia is constructed along the same lines as homophobia, racism, misogyny or anti-Semitism. However, as we would expect, there are some important distinctions between all these concepts. What links them is not so much 'fear', as suggested by the 'phobia', but hate (Allen 2010). Some would argue that this hatred is to be seen as irrational, but that probably misses the point. The most important factor in relation to this hatred is that it is seen as all encompassing. Anything that is seen as Islamic or Muslim is to be included and the hatred is instinctual. In the case of Islamophobia, there may be an element of fear sitting behind the hatred, fear that something that is important to us is under threat, but this is not a necessary part of the construct. Like racism, and the other hate positions, Islamophobia is not to be seen simply in violent attacks against Muslims, it is an attitude of mind that can infect both individuals, a wider community and even institutions where structural neglect or oppression of Muslims is involved. Having said that, it is usually the violent anti-Muslim activities of organisations such as the English Defence League that are most commonly associated with Islamophobia within our society.

Whilst recognising that such virulent Islamophobia is prevalent within our society, and was obvious in a small number of the conversations that I noted as part of this research, one interesting aspect of this wider Islamophobia can be seen in an analysis of an inner urban estate within Birmingham undertaken by Chris Shannahan (2012). This example relates specifically to some of the issues that I have been raising within this book, especially in relation to fragments of narrative and memory, and suggests that we do need to be careful about what it is that we think we are seeing or listening to. Shannahan is specifically interested in what he defines as 'NEET spirituality' (where NEET stands for young people who are not in education, employment or training). He has worked on the Bromford Estate in Birmingham undertaking ethnographic fieldwork with a group of young men in their late teens or early 20s. Shannahan is particularly interested in identifying elements of 'spirituality' in the everyday discourses of these young men and is looking to a number of alternative forms of expression in order to find this. One young man in particular admitted to spraying English Defence League graffiti on a boarded up window on the estate (2012, 321).

The English Defence League itself reflects the shift in discourses that I have noted on a number of occasions throughout this text. Unlike other, older, right-wing organisations the EDL has avoided the issue of race or ethnicity. Its publicity even goes so far as to say that it is open to people of all races. Rather than race or immigration, the EDL has focussed on Islamic extremism as the basis for its rhetoric. It is Islam that is presented as the real threat to the English way of life and so the campaign is against Islamic extremists, and by implication against all Muslims as the EDL makes very little distinction between the mainstream and the extreme. This is a careful and effective choice of rhetoric as it is still permissible, especially in the light of the war on terror, to be against extreme forms of Islam, the government itself does this to some extent within the prevent agenda, while it is no longer really acceptable to be racist or against particular cultural or ethnic groupings. The EDL, therefore, can retain its own extreme right-wing position while appearing, for many of its own members at least, to be mainstream in its objections.

The Bromford Estate is a typical recruiting ground for right-wing organisations such as the EDL. It is primarily poor white and there are few south Asian residents. Shannahan does note the number of mixed heritage families on the estate but most of these relate to white and Afro-Caribbean origins, not to south Asian. The young man in question, therefore, does not come into contact with south Asians or Muslims in any significant numbers in his day to day life. The young man is also unemployed and out of education. It would seem only natural for him to tend towards a group such as the EDL to vent his frustration. However, as Shannahan notes, he is not a member of the EDL and in his own words the graffiti represents a more general protest against society and not a specific action against Muslims in particular (2012, 321). The discourses at work here are more complex and confused and we cannot easily assume that an individual such as this holds, or is actually concerned about, Islamophobic views simply because of his action. None of this, however, is to deny the extent and depth of Islamophobic attitudes in some sections of our society.

This discussion raises the question of tolerance, a value that is often invoked in discussions of religious diversity, as it is in similar discussions of multiculturalism. The problem, however, is that tolerance is not easy to define and even more difficult to impose. Walzer raises the possibility of five different modes of toleration from a 'resigned acceptance of difference for the sake of peace' to a full-blown celebration of difference and diversity 'as a necessary condition of human flourishing' (1997, 9–11). Sandercock comes close to the seventh definition in her work on Cosmopolis and, while never problematising the concept of toleration itself, sees diversity as both a reality to be lived with and a value to be celebrated (2003). Donald takes the argument in another direction by linking tolerance to the idea of consensus (1999, 164–5). In a sense tolerance is only possible, on a society- or city-wide scale, if there is a level of consensus about its value, which is almost to say, if it does not need to exist. The other issue comes back to the discussion in Chapter 4 where it was suggested that tolerance can exist in a neighbourhood characterised by super-diversity only where there is a level of indifference to difference. One implication of this might be to say that religious diversity, or perhaps we should say religious toleration, can only truly exist where there is an indifference to religion.

The young man in Shannahan's study, however, is probably indifferent to religion as a general concept, he is unlikely to be religious himself. It is the designation 'Muslim' and all that that stands for in his discursive world that he is not indifferent to, or tolerant of. However, the question here is whether the term 'Muslim' is to be seen as a religious designator in the language of this young man. The answer is probably not, it is more of an ethnic or social marker, co-terminus with south Asian or, perhaps, Arab.

A number of elements in this argument relate back to a discussion raised by Abner Cohen in a very different context (1969). When talking about post-independence Nigeria, Cohen argues that the ban on debate about ethnic categories at the national level led, either directly or indirectly, to the same discussions being conducted through the lens of religious groups, and more specifically through the conflict between Muslims and Christians. The situation in Britain today is very different, at all levels, from that of post-independence Nigeria, but the way in which race and ethnicity became something of a political no-go area in the late 1990s and into the early years of the new millennium, and the way in which religion has perhaps replaced ethnicity in discourses about difference in British cities has some very similar features to the process as described by Cohen. As I tried to demonstrate in Chapter 4 the fundamental differences that matter to people in areas like Handsworth remain ethnic rather than religious and while 'religious difference' may be the language people choose to use to describe these differences, that simply hides a deeper concern with ethnicity. One of the central conclusions of this work, therefore, has to be that many of the public discourses around religious diversity are, in fact, discourses about ethnicity dressed up in religious clothing and that is an important point for us to note. This does not, however, account for all the public discourses that I was listening to.

The Uses of Discourse

Much of what I have discussed so far has dealt with what I would describe as the 'management of religious diversity'. That is important, but not really the topic that I wished to address in this chapter. Given the focus of the book as a whole then what really interests me is not the management of the religious diversity in itself as the management of discourses about religious diversity. That takes us back, inevitably to the concept of 'discourse'. At one point in his discussion of everyday speech, de Certeau begins to use the imagery of water and of flow to try and capture the elusiveness of discourse in use (1984, 33–4). He is talking of consumerism, and in particular the way in which consumers use the language and products of consumerism for their own ends and in their own ways. These 'indeterminate trajectories', according to de Certeau, 'circulate, come and go, overflow and drift over an imposed terrain, like the snowy waves of the sea slipping in among the rocks and defiles of an established order' (1984, 34). Statistics, he goes on to say, can tell us nothing about the currents in this sea. In other words knowing the language of the adverts or the frequency of sales or particular products can tell us nothing about their actual use and the often surprising meanings that many such products can hold for specific individuals.

At a different part of the text, in a discussion of the work of Michel Foucault, de Certeau makes a somewhat different point (1984). He is discussing the way in which Foucault in *Discipline and Punish* (1979), by focussing on technologies, shows how the panopticon became the normative model for incarceration and even for society as a whole. This was not a deliberate decision by those in authority, or by any particular individual or group. Rather it was a slow development through a whole series of small decisions that led, over time, to the panoptic model becoming dominant. What de Certeau notes, however, is that all the other possible or potential technologies did not simply disappear, they remained, and still remain, as alternative forms of control, they are simply subservient to that of the panopticon. This raises an interesting possibility when these ideas are brought into discussion with Gerd Baumann's idea of the dominant discourse in relation to community and culture.

Baumann, as I have noted many times throughout this text, identifies a dominant discourse in Southall in which community and culture (and by implication ethnicity and religion) are merged. This is the discourse of the authorities and therefore if any member of the community wishes to engage with the authorities, either to work politically or to gain benefits such as community facilities, then they need to use this dominant discourse. The only other discourse that Baumann notes, however, is the demotic discourse as used by the social groups themselves, although there are suggestions in Baumann's own analysis that there are almost as many demotic discourses as there are social groupings. The problem with this is that the demotic discourses are, up to a point at least, distributed along the lines of the dominant discourse. Each social group/community not only has a distinct culture (ethnicity and religion), but also its own demotic discourse.

In practice, of course, things are far more complicated than this. de Certeau's reassessment of Foucault can perhaps provide the model here, with the dominant discourse slowly coming to the fore from the 1960s onwards, much in the way that Baumann indicates. However, that still leaves many other possible discourses on religion and religious diversity within the community and these continue to be present, and to be used, often by the same people who use the dominant discourse. In fact, picking up on de Certeau's images of flow and the sea washing over the rocks, these other discourses are as difficult to pin down and identify as a particular drop of water within the incoming tide. They flow over and through each other, informing and distorting each other, with individuals picking up on one or more elements of different discourses and using those elements that make most sense to them at any one point. To try and classify all the demotic discourses and to isolate them from each other would be impossible and would give a false impression of the real situation. Many discourses float within the wider social groups and elements of each, sometimes entirely contradictory in themselves, come to the surface within the snatched conversations heard in everyday situations. There is no common discourse that can be called 'the' demotic discourse, there are many, and all of them, in some form or another, need to be managed.

The use of discourses on religious diversity to avoid, and perhaps even to hide, discourses on race and ethnicity is one of the demotic discourses that I have identified. Another relates to the distinction between religion and non-religion with the underlying, although often unspoken, assumption that all religions are the same. I have suggested that the root of this discourse lies in the educational practices of the late twentieth century and so forms another eddy or current within the tide, or another alternative to the dominant discourse that could be drawn on if the need emerged. A further demotic discourse can be seen in what I have referred to as the indifference to religion that so many of the public discourses suggest. This indifference suggests a neutrality towards religious diversity, neither positive nor really negative, just uninterested. This may, in fact, be the default position of many people within the city who do not understand themselves as being 'religious'. What this might lead us to look at, therefore, are those discourses where this neutrality is rocked and a more specifically positive or negative strand is developed. This will happen most frequently, from my own data, with reference to current news stories. If this is the case, therefore, the management of discourses of religious diversity might ultimately be seen in the management of news. I want to end this book by exploring two specific stories that emphasised negative and positive strands or currents within the wider sea of discourses and use the way in which these stories were managed to draw my final conclusions.

Stories and Riots

Underpinning all the fragments of discourse that have made up the evidence within this book are, as I have suggested, a series of stories, longer narratives of how things are or how things could be. These narratives and the stories associated with them are always 'potential'. In everyday conversations the full story is very rarely told in all its detail. Very often the story is only ever alluded to, assumed to be known by those who are part of the conversation. The narrative itself remains submerged. The link to the story, however, from among the fragments and the allusions, remains and it is through memory that the connection can be made. Once in a while, however, when the need arises, the narrative and the story can be brought to the surface and used to bring people together, or to hold them apart.

Perhaps the narratives associated with the dominant discourses are the easiest to mobilise, they are among the most widely recognised within society, the default position. In both the cases outlined below these dominant narratives, if they had been drawn on, may well have led to divisions, to the separation and antagonism between ethnic, religious and cultural communities. In both cases, however, things moved in a very different direction and a very different narrative was developed.

My first case concerns a play, *Behtzi* (a Punjabi word meaning dishonour), written by a young Sikh woman and performed at a major Birmingham theatre just before Christmas 2004. Before the play opened leaders from the wider Sikh community had already objected to the play because it showed rape and murder taking place within a Gudwara in the sight of the holy book. Some news outlets carried this story but it was largely dismissed and relegated to a minor part of the publication. No analysis was offered at this stage about why the play might be offensive and the general consensus was that this was simply a particular religious community being defensive and secretive. In much of the media commentary surrounding the play it was suggested that Sikhs objected to the fact that possible abuse within the community was made public, even in a fictional situation. This was not the case. In reality it was the setting of the play within the Gudwara that offended Sikhs, not the acts that were taking place. For a Sikh any space that contains the Holy Scripture is a Gudwara, and for the sake of this play that also included the theatre, despite the fact that this was fiction. It was therefore the case that respect should have been shown to the text even within the context of the play. If the same actions were shown taking place in another space, even if they included Sikh protagonists, then there would have been no problems.

Some elements of the Sikh population in Birmingham tried to engage in a dialogue with the theatre before the play was shown in public and they gained some small compromises, but not enough for some other Sikh leaders. Those who were still unsatisfied mounted a peaceful protest outside the theatre during its early performances. Unfortunately the protest got out of hand on one night and a couple of windows within the theatre were smashed. The theatre then chose to cancel the final performances and the author was, according to news reports, forced to go into hiding. The whole episode caused considerable tension within the city and within a number of different religious constituencies. It also continued to rumble on in the media and in wider discussion around the city for much of the subsequent year.

The natural response of the dominant discourse should have been to see this whole incident as a 'Sikh' problem, a matter for a specific ethnic group within its own culture and religion. That element of the narrative was, however, played down considerably both by the media and within the wider comments of ordinary, non-Sikh, people within the city. Among the comments that I heard around the city at the time, and that were expressed publically within the media (both print and online), there were a range of different responses, each engaging with a different set of discourses. One prominent discourse related to 'freedom of speech' and the issue of blasphemy. This was linked to wider discourses within the media about the possibility of a law to ban all religious hatred and was related to other contexts in which religious groups have protested against plays, poems, operas, cartoons and other art forms that they have considered to be offensive. In this case the situation for Christians was compared unfavourably or favourably, depending on the individual's own standpoint, to that of other religions. Another set of discourses developed a more overtly feminist stance, seeing the situation as that of a patriarchal religion refusing to recognise the oppression of women among their own members. What is interesting, however, is how both these discourses, and others that I heard, almost deliberately refused to see the specific Sikh elements of this story and treated the whole incident as an example of 'religious' opposition to freedom of speech or 'religious' patriarchal oppression of women, implicitly assuming that all religion is the same.

At its heart, therefore, and particularly in Birmingham, the questions raised by the play and the violent reaction of some protestors became questions about the nature of religions, as opposed to religious diversity, within the city. What was seen in this context, and what was commented on by a number of local people I talked to in different parts of the city at the time, was a particular religious group stepping outside of a widely accepted discourse on religious behaviour or visibility, which suggest that ultimately all religions are the same and that the differences between religious people is minimal, that religion is something private and essentially irrelevant for many ordinary people of the city. An incident such as the reaction to the play appeared to stress the 'otherness' of one particular faith position. The discourses involved a move towards the kind of discourses that I have noted in relation to the question of dress in Chapter 2, a discourse that many older Sikhs in particular remember all too well in relation to the turban in the 1970s and 1980s. This is a discourse that presents the religious group as being entirely 'other', even to other religious communities, and gives that otherness a negative value. The language used at the time was one of 'extremism' or even 'fundamentalism', a language well known to Muslims but not heard very often of contemporary Sikhs.

The second case is more up to date and relates to the riots that swept the country as I was writing this text in August 2011. Three young Muslim men were killed during these riots in Winson Green, Birmingham, by rioters who drove cars directly at them while they were 'defending their community'. In the hours and days that followed many different potential responses to these deaths were possible. It was the words of the father of one of the young men, however, and the courage of religious leaders in the city and the local neighbourhood, who established the story that was to control events. This story was one of interreligious solidarity with the community coming together for a rally for peace in a local park to honour those young men who had given their lives for the community. The story, however, could have been very different.

It was some time before the press really got the point that the riots of 2011 were not rooted in ethnic or community hatred. The words 'race' and 'riots' have been associated in everyday discourse for a number of decades, especially in areas such as Handsworth as we saw in Chapter 4, and the default position of the media, as with much everyday conversation, is that riots are always, in part, about conflicts between different ethnic communities. This default position relates directly to Baumann's dominant discourse in its assumption that such communities exist, have clear identities and clear boundaries across which the riots can take place (1996). This dominant discourse was never very far away from many of the presentations of the riots as they occurred, even though later discussion did raise other, alternative, interpretations. In the case of the three young men killed in Winson Green, however, a different narrative, an alternative story, based on interreligious commonality, was mobilised and used in a highly effective way to bring the wider community together.

Part of the emerging discourse of the riots over the first few days, when commentators moved beyond the dominant discourse, focussed on the destruction of property and the looting of shops, the claiming, to use the phrase most associated with the riots, of 'free stuff'. The first discourse on the situation in Winson Green, therefore, was one in which the three young men (no specification of ethnicity or religion) were 'defending their community' when they were mown down by a car containing rioters. The young men, therefore, were presented as being on the 'good' side, the 'defenders', while the rioters in the car were seen as 'bad' and bent on the destruction of property, and of the community (to be understood as a geographical unity in this particular case). The question of ethnicity or religion had no relevance to this initial presentation.

Within the 'community' itself, however, a number of possible stories were available and could have been easily mobilised. The most prominent in the immediate aftermath of the killing picked up the dominant discourse on riots in the national media and referred back to previous riots in the adjoining neighbourhoods of Handsworth and Lozzells. The most recent riots in the area had occurred in 2005 and were clearly rooted in inter-ethnic tensions. Members of the Afro-Caribbean community had accused Asian men of raping one of the girls in their community. This was later found to be a false rumour, a story that had circulated because it spoke to an underlying tension and potential hatred. The result had been violent clashes between Asians and Afro-Caribbeans that had shocked the city. The presentation of the 2005 riots in the media, however, the story that was told around them, referred directly back to Baumann's dominant discourse, the presence of two ethnic, cultural and even religious communities set against each other in a series of escalating revenge attacks.

What is interesting about the hours following the killing of the three men in Winson Green in 2011 was that the father of one of the young men, who spoke on the evening his son was killed, was clearly aware of that story, and the potential that it held to engender more violence, and his words spoke directly to that story, without ever mentioning it directly. The previous story of hatred and division remained a memory, if only a fragment of memory, a collective memory that was known by all who listened, and which only needed to be referenced in the most elliptical fashion to be recalled and set against the new story that the father was telling. The father's words would clearly have been powerful in any context, but in the light of that previous story, and the widespread knowledge of that story, they held much greater rhetorical power. All those who commentated on this incident have said that it was those words, the story the father told, countering the story of the previous riots, that was instrumental in bringing the whole situation, within Birmingham at least, under control.

What occurred over the next few days, however, transformed the story and the relevant discourses from one focussed on looting and/or ethnicity to one focussed much more clearly on religion and religious diversity. There was a Parade for Peace in a local park on the following Sunday, at which the father once again spoke alongside the relatives of the other men killed and religious and political leaders, but which was presented within the press as a gathering of many different religious groups. The interreligious nature of the funeral on the Thursday was also noted, although this was primarily a Muslim event with over 5,000 people taking part in the local park. Images in the media portrayed Muslims at prayer, interspersed with others who were clearly not Muslim. Again the speeches from the front were positive and related, implicitly, to the stories of previous riots and previous racial and religious tension, as well as to the events of the last few days, reflections on policing, and a strong statement of the community nature of Winson Green. One interesting development within these speeches was the use of the term 'martyrs' for the young men who had been killed. This draws on a very different set of discourses that have their own resonances among Muslims, but for many ordinary non-Muslim people of the city carried allusions to terrorism and suicide bombers, and transformed this in an interesting and ultimately positive way.

What I found most interesting, however, with reference to this particular project, was a news report a few days after the funeral in which the father was interviewed with his 'best friend', a Sikh, and the report highlighted the point that the events of the riot and the killing of the young men had led to the most positive relations between Sikhs and Muslims within the city for many years. Reference was made to previous tensions (no cross-reference this time to the Lozells riots which had been between Afro-Carribeans and Asians) and a new dawn of positive relations between the two communities was announced. Here a new, and in some ways entirely unexpected, narrative was being presented as the outcome of the events, one that, if picked up, would have had significant impact not just on the interreligious relations within the city, but also, I would suggest, on the way those from other communities talk about religion and religious diversity.

Whatever the specific impact of these events on Muslim–Sikh relations, if I were to focus on the conversations within the city following these events then one consequence for the wider discourses on religious diversity appeared to be a reinforcement of the principle that I have come back to on a number of occasions throughout this text, that is the idea that for many non-religious people the idea of 'religions' and religious difference is declining. The images and discourses surrounding the Peace Parade, the funeral and the subsequent news item all reinforced, for ordinary people and the non-religious, the view that all religions are essentially the same and that the distinction between them is illusory. It also suggested to some that the divisions themselves are potentially dangerous and that it is the unity of religions that is the required goal, if religion is going to continue to have any role within the public arena at all. The messages about religion were actually very positive, but the specifically Muslim element was downplayed and, as with so many of the discourses we have looked at, it was 'religion' in general that was accentuated.

What then, has this to say about the management of discourses of religious diversity? Is the conclusion that we have to reach simply one that says we must do all we can to dilute differences and reinforce a new 'dominant discourse'? Should we highlight only those discourses that play down 'otherness', or at best give that otherness a positive value? Should we encourage more festivals, more open, welcoming and community minded buildings, focus on the positive messages and try to bury the bad news stories? One reading of this research could suggest such a position, and if there is a 'dominant discourse' on the management of discourses of religious diversity in a city such as Birmingham at the present time then this is probably it: let us celebrate the diversity and see the differences as little more than surface decoration, the costumes we wear at the festivals, the architecture we choose (in good post-modern fashion) to clad our buildings; underneath, we are all the same really. This is certainly one reading of the evidence. I would want to suggest, however, that the discourses surrounding the play and the potential of further violence sitting just beneath the surface in the discourses surrounding the riots, shows up the shallowness and inadequacy of such a reading.

Taking this line simply recognises and reinforces those discourses within the popular debate that happen to suit the manager's purpose. They fail to hear the full story and to recognise that these are simply a small selection of the wide range of discourses that are actually present within ebb and flow of the wider society. When the situation changes, when events bring otherness and the negative valuing of religion to the fore then more separatist discourses can just as easily be brought into play and used for more malign purposes. Those who simply stress the positive often do nothing specifically to counteract the negative; they tend to just ignore it. This does not help. We need to spend more time, I would suggest, out there among the ordinary people of the city, listening more carefully to the range of different discourses people use, observing those discourses at play in different situations, recording and analysing the differing underlying messages of the different discourses, and then, and only then, based on this more sophisticated analysis should any kind of policy for the management of religious diversity be devised. At that level, I would suggest, this is still very much a work in progress.

Bibliography

Aching, G. (2002) *Masking and Power, Carnival and Popular Culture in the Caribbean*. Minneapolis: University of Minnesota Press.

Albrow, M. (1997) 'Travelling Beyond Local Cultures: Socioscapes in a Global City' in J. Eade (ed.) *Living the Global City, Globalization as a Local Process*. London: Routledge, 37–55.

Aldridge, A. (2000) *Religion in the Contemporary World, A Sociological Introduction*. Cambridge: Polity Press.

Allen, C. (2010) *Islamophobia*. Farnham: Ashgate.

Amin, A. (2002) 'Ethnicity and the Multi-cultural City, Living with Diversity'. *Environment and Planning A* 34:6, 959–80.

Anderson, A.B. and Pickering, G.W. (1986) *Confronting the Color Line, The Broken Promise of the Civil Rights Movement in Chicago*. Athens, GA: University of Georgia Press.

Anderson, K. (1991) *Vancouver's Chinatown, Racial Discourse in Canada 1875–1980*. Montreal: McGill-Queen's University Press.

Anderson, N. (1923) *The Hobo*. Chicago: Chicago University Press.

Austin, J.L. (1969) *Philosophical Papers*. Oxford: Oxford University Press.

Baker, C. (2009) *The Hybrid Church in the City, Third Space Thinking*. London: SCM Press.

Bakhtin, M.M. (1984) *Rabelais and His World*. Bloomington: Indiana University Press.

Bauman, R. and Sherzer, J. (eds) (1974) *Explorations in the Ethnography of Speaking*. Cambridge: Cambridge University Press.

Bauman, Z. (2000) *Liquid Modernity*. Cambridge: Polity Press.

Bauman, Z. (2001) *The Individualized Society*. Cambridge: Polity Press.

Baumann, G. (1996) *Contesting Culture, Discourses of Identity in Multi-Ethnic London*. Cambridge: Cambridge University Press.

Beaumont, J. and Baker, C. (eds) (2011) *Postsecular Cities, Space, Theory and Practice*. London: Continuum.

Beck, U. and Beck-Gernsheim, E. (2002) *Individualization: Institutionalized Individualism and its Social and Political Consequences*. London: Sage.

Bell, O. (2009) 'A Blurred InterFaith, InterCultural Experience, A Kidderminster Story' in C. Baker and J. Reader (eds) *Entering the New Theological Space, Blurred Encounters of Faith, Politics and Community*. Farnham: Ashgate, 47–56.

Bernstein, B. (1967) 'Open Schools, Open Society'. *New Society*, 14 September 1967, 351–3.

Berry, C. and Farquhar, M.A. (2006) *China on Screen, Cinema and Nation*. New York: Columbia University Press.

Bhabha, H.K. (1994) *The Location of Culture*. London: Routledge.

Boon, J.A. (1981) *Other Tribes, Other Scribes, Symbolic Anthropology in the Comparative Study of Cultures, Histories, Religions and Texts*. Cambridge: Cambridge University Press.

Boyer, M.C. (1992) 'Cities for Sale: Merchandising History in South Street Seaport' in M. Sorkin (ed.) *Variations on a Theme Park, The New American City and the End of Public Space*. New York: Hill and Wang, 181–204.

Brah, A. (1987) 'Women of South Asian Origin in Britain: Issues and Concerns', *South Asian Research*, 1:1, 39–54.

Brown, C.G. (2001) *The Death of Christian Britain, Understanding Secularisation 1800–2000*. London: Routledge.

Burgess, E.W. (1967) 'The Growth of the City, An Introduction to a Research Project' in R.E. Park, E.W. Burgess and R.D. McKenzie (eds) *The City*. Chicago: Chicago University Press, 47–62.

Burke, P. (1994) *Popular Culture in Early Modern Europe*. Aldershot: Ashgate.

Burton, R.D.E. (1997) *Afro-Creole, Power, Opposition and Play in the Caribbean*. Ithaca, NY: Cornell University Press.

Cameron, D. (2001) *Working with Spoken Discourse*. London: Sage.

Cantle, T. (2005) *Community Cohesion, A New Framework for Race and Diversity*. Basingstoke: Palgrave Macmillan.

Cantle, T. (2010) 'Community Cohesion in an Era of Super Diversity'. Podcast from the Institute of Community Cohesion, Coventry University, http://www.cohesioninstitute.org.uk/Resources/Podcasts

Cantle, T. (2012) *Interculturism, The New Era of Cohesion and Diversity*. Basingstoke: Palgrave Macmillan.

Caro Baroja, J. (1965) *El Carnaval*. Madrid: Taurus.

Casanova, J. (1994) *Public Religions in the Modern World*. Chicago: University of Chicago Press.

Castells, M. (1977) *The Urban Question, A Marxist Approach*. London: Edward Arnold.

Castells, M. (1996) *The Rise of the Network Society*. Oxford: Blackwell.

Cheetham, D. (ed.) (2011) *Interreligious Hermeneutics in Pluralistic Europe, Between Texts and People*. Amsterdam: Rodopi.

Çinar, A. and Bender, T. (eds) (2007) *Urban Imaginaries, Locating the Modern City*. Minneapolis: University of Minnesota Press.

Clark, D. (2012) *Building the Human City, The Origins and the Future Potential of the Human City Institute (1995–2002)*. Birmingham: Human City Institute.

Cohen, A. (1969) *Custom and Politics in Urban Africa*. London: Routledge and Kegan Paul.

Cohen, A. (1993) *Masquerade Politics, Explorations in the Structure of Urban Cultural Movements*. Oxford: Berg.

Cohen, A.P. (1985) *The Symbolic Construction of Community*. Chichester; Ellis Horwood.

Connor, G. and Farrar, M. (2004) 'Carnival in Leeds and London, Making New Black British Subjectivities' in M.C. Riggio (ed.) *Carnival, Culture in Action – The Trinidad Experience*. New York: Routledge, 255–69.

Cornille, C. (2008) *The Im-possibility of Interreligious Dialogue*. New York: Crossroad Publishing Company.

Crinson, M. (ed.) (2005) *Urban Memory, History and Amnesia in the Modern City*. London: Routledge.

Crinson, M. and Tyrer P. (2005) 'Clocking off in Ancoats, Time and Remembrance in the Post-industrial City' in M. Crinson (ed.) *Urban Memory, History and Amnesia in the Modern City*. London: Routledge, 49–71.

Crouch, D. (1998) 'The Street in the Making of Popular Geographical Knowledge' in N.R. Fyfe (ed.) *Images of the Street, Planning, Identity and Control in Public Space*. London: Routledge, 160–75.

Cunningham, G. (1999) *Religion and Magic, Approaches and Theories*. Edinburgh: Edinburgh University Press.

Davie, G. (2002) *Europe, The Exceptional Case, Parameters of Faith in the Modern World*. London: Darton, Longman and Todd.

Davie, G. (2007) 'Vicarious Religion, A Methodological Challenge' in N.T. Ammerman (ed.) *Everyday Religion, Observing Modern Religious Lives*. Oxford: Oxford University Press, 21–35.

Day, A. (2011) *Believing in Belonging, Belief and Social Identity in the Modern World*. Oxford: Oxford University Press.

Day, A., Vincett, G. and Cotter, C.R. (eds) (2013) *Social Identities between the Sacred and the Secular*. Farnham: Ashgate

de Certeau, M. (1984) *The Practice of Everyday Life*. Berkeley: University of California Press.

de Tocqueville, A. (2003) *Democracy in America and Two Essays on America*. London: Penguin.

Delamont, S. (1995) *Appetites and Identities, An Introduction to the Social Anthropology of Western Europe*. London: Routledge.

Deleuze, G. and Guattari, F. (1987) *A Thousand Plateaus, Capitalism and Schizophrenia*. Minneapolis: University of Minnesota Press.

Dempsey, C.G. (2001) *Kerala Christian Sainthood, Collisions of Culture and Worldview in South India*. Oxford: Oxford University Press.

Donald, J. (1999) *Imagining the Modern City*. London: The Athlone Press.

Douglas, M. (1966) *Purity and Danger, An Analysis of the Concepts of Pollution and Taboo*. London: Routledge and Kegan Paul.

Dreher, T. and Ho, C. (2009) *Beyond the Hijab Debates, New Conversations on Gender, Race and Religion*. Newcastle-upon-Tyne: Cambridge Scholars.

DuBois, W.E.B. (1996) *The Philadelphia Negro, A Social Study*. Philadelphia: University of Pennsylvania Press.

Dummett, A. (1973) *A Portrait of English Racism*. Harmondsworth: Penguin Books.

Eco, U. (1995) *Faith in Fakes, Travels in Hyperreality*. London: Minerva.

Engels, F. (1987) *The Condition of the Working Class in England*. London: Penguin Books.

Fabian, J. (1983) *Time and the Other, How Anthropology Makes its Object*. New York: Columbia University Press.

Fabian, J. (2007) *Memory against Culture, Arguments and Reminders*. Durham: Duke University Press.

Fairclough, N. (2003) *Analysing Discourse, Textual Analysis for Social Research*. London: Routledge.

Felderhof, M. and Whitehouse, S.E. (2010) 'The 2007 Birmingham Agreed Syllabus: Educating Pupils and the Community' in M. Grimmitt (ed.) *Religious Education and Social and Community Cohesion*. Great Wakering: McCrimmons.

Finnegan, R. (1998) *Tales of the City, A Study of Narrative and Urban Life*. Cambridge: Cambridge University Press.

Forster, P.G. (1995) 'Residual Religiosity on a Hull Council Estate' in P.G. Forster (ed.) *Contemporary Mainstream Religion, Studies from Humberside and Lincolnshire*. Aldershot: Avebury, 1–33.

Foucault, M. (1979) *Discipline and Punish, the Birth of the Prison*. Harmondsworth: Penguin Books.

Foucault, M. (1986) 'Of Other Spaces'. *Diacritics* 16:1, 22–7.

Frankenberg, R. (1965) *Communities in Britain, Social Life in Town and Country*. Harmondsworth: Penguin Books.

Freud, S. (1938) *Totem and Taboo, Resemblances between the Psychic Lives of Savages and Neurotics*. Harmondsworth: Penguin Books.

Gale, R. (2004) 'The Multicultural City and the Politics of Religious Architecture: Urban Planning, Mosques and Meaning Making in Birmingham, UK'. *Built Environment* 30:1, 30–44.

Gale, R. (2005) 'Representing the City: Mosques and the Planning Process in Birmingham'. *Journal of Ethnic and Migration Studies* 31:6, 1161–79.

Giddens, A. (1991) *Modernity and Self Identity*. Cambridge: Polity.

Gilroy, P. (1992) 'The End of Antiracism' in J. Donald and A. Rattansi (eds) *Race Culture and Difference*. London: Sage, 49–61.

Gluckman, M. (1958) *Analysis of a Social Situation in Modern Zululand (Rhodes-Livingston Papers No 28)*. Manchester: Manchester University Press.

Goffman, E. (1969) *The Presentation of Self in Everyday Life*. Harmondsworth: Penguin Books.

Green, S. (2002) 'Culture in a Network: Dykes, Webs and Women in London and Manchester' in N. Rapport (ed.) *British Subjects, An Anthropology of Britain*. Oxford: Berg, 181–202.

Habermas, J. (1991) *The Structural Transformation of the Public Sphere, An Inquiry into a Category of Bourgeois Society*. Cambridge, MA: MIT Press.

Halbwachs, M. (1992) *On Collective Memory*. Chicago: University of Chicago Press.

Hall, P. (1996) *Cities of Tomorrow*. Oxford: Blackwell.

Handelman, D. (1998) *Models and Mirrors, Towards an Anthropology of Public Events*. Oxford: Berghahn Books.

Harris, M (2003) *Carnival and Other Christian Festivals, Folk Theology and Folk Performance*. Austin: University of Texas Press.

Harvey, D. (1973) *Social Justice and the City*. London: Edward Arnold.

Hayden, D. (2006) 'Building the American Way: Public Subsidy, Private Space' in S. Low and N. Smith (eds) *The Politics of Public Space*. New York: Routledge, 35–48.

Hedges, P.M. (2010) *Controversies in Interreligious Dialogue and the Theology of Religion*. London: SCM Press.

Heelas, P., Woodhead, L., Seel, B., et al. (2005) *The Spiritual Revolution, Why Religion is Giving Way to Spirituality*. Oxford: Blackwell.

Henry, N., McEwan, C. and Pollard, J. (2000) 'Globalization from Below, Birmingham – Postcolonial Workshop of the World' Working Paper WPTC-2K-08, School of Geography, University of Birmingham.

Herbert, D. (2003) *Religion and Civil Society, Rethinking Public Religion in the Contemporary World*. Aldershot: Ashgate.

Hervieu-Léger, D. (2000) *Religion as a Chain of Memory*. Cambridge: Polity Press.

Hingley, L. (2011) 'Photographer as Researcher in the Project "Under Gods: Stories from Soho Road"'. *Visual Studies* 26:3, 260–69.

Hockey, J. (2002) 'Interviews as Ethnography? Disembodied Social Interaction in Britain' in N. Rapport (ed.) *British Subjects, An Anthropology of Britain*. Oxford: Berg, 209–22.

Hollinger, D.A. (1995) *Postethnic America, Beyond Multiculturalism*. New York: Basic Books.

Home Office (2001) *Building Cohesive Communities, A Report of the Ministerial Group on Public Order and Community Cohesion*. London: The Stationary Office.

Home Office (2011) *Prevent Strategy*. London: The Stationary Office.

Hornsby-Smith, M.P. (1991) *Roman Catholic Beliefs in England, Customary Catholicism and Transformations of Religious Authority*. Cambridge: Cambridge University Press.

Hymes, D. (1972) *Foundations in Sociolinguistics, The Ethnography of Communication*. Philadelphia: University of Pennsylvania Press.

Ignatieff, M. (1992) 'Why "Community" is a Dishonest Word'. *The Observer*, 3 May 1992, editorial page.

Ingalls, M. (forthcoming) 'Bringing Worship to the Streets, Music, Religion and Spectacle in Toronto's Jesus in the City Parade'. *Journal of Contemporary Religion*.

Jenkins, T. (1999) *Religion in English Everyday Life, An Ethnographic Approach*. New York: Berghahn Books.

Jennings, G., Brown, D. and Sparkes, A.C. (2010) '"It Can be a Religion if you Want", Wing Chun Kung Fu as a Secular Religion'. *Ethnography* 11, 533–57.

Jespersen, T.C. (1996) *American Images of China 1931–1949*. Stanford: Stanford University Press.

Kapferer, B. (1995) 'The Performance of Categories, Plays of Identity in Africa and Australia' in A. Rogers and S. Vertovec (eds) *The Urban Context, Ethnicity, Social Network and Situational Analysis*. Oxford: Berg, 55–80.

Kerr, M. (1958) *The People of Ship Street*. London: Routledge and Kegan Paul.

Knott, K. (2005a) *The Location of Religion, A Spatial Analysis*. London: Equinox.

Knott, K. (2005b) 'Spatial Theory and Method for the Study of Religion'. *Temenos, Nordic Journal of Comparative Religion* 41:2, 153–84.

Knowles, J.J. (2009) *An Investigation into the Relationship between Gay Activism and the Establishment of a Gay Community in Birmingham, 1967–97*. Unpublished MPhil thesis, University of Birmingham.

Kong, L. (2005) 'Religious Processions, Urban Politics and Poetics'. *Temenos, Nordic Journal of Comparative Religion* 41:2, 225–50.

Kristeva, J. (1982) *Powers of Horror*. New York: Columbia University Press.

Ladurie, E.L. (1979) *Carnival, A People's Uprising at Romans 1579–1580*. London: Scholar's Press.

Leach, E.R. (1961) 'Time and False Noses' in *Rethinking Anthropology*. London: Athlone Press, 132–6.

Lefebvre, H. (1991) *The Production of Space*. Oxford: Blackwell.

Livezey, L.W. (ed.) (2000a) *Public Religion and Urban Transformation, Faith in the City*. New York: New York University Press.

Livezey, L.W. (2000b) 'Communities and Enclaves, Where Jews, Christian, Hindus and Muslims Share the Neighbourhood' in L.W. Livezey (ed.) *Public Religion and Urban Transformation, Faith in the City*. New York: New York University Press, 133–61.

Low, S.M. (1999) 'Introduction, Theorizing the City' in S.M. Low (ed.) *Theorizing the City, the New Urban Anthropology Reader*. New Brunswick: Rutgers University Press, 1–36.

Low, S.M. (2000) *On the Plaza, The Politics of Public Space and Culture*. Austin: University of Texas Press.

Low, S.M. and Smith, N. (eds) (2006) *The Politics of Public Space*. New York: Routledge.

Luk, W.E. (2008) *Chinatown in Britain, Diffusions and Concentrations of the British New Wave Chinese Immigration*. Amherst: Cambria Press.

Lutz, C. and Abu-Lughod, L. (eds) (1990) *Language and the Politics of Emotion*. Cambridge: Cambridge University Press.

MacIntrye, A. (1985) *After Virtue, A Study in Moral Theory*. London: Duckworth.

Marston, S.A. (1989) 'Public Rituals and Community Power, St Patrick's Day Parades in Lowell, Massachusetts, 1841–1874'. *Political Geography Quarterly* 8, 255–69.

Marston, S.A. (2002) 'Making Difference: Conflict over Irish Identity in the New York City St Patrick's Day Parade', *Political Geography*, 21 373–92.

Mason, D. (2000) *Race and Ethnicity in Modern Britain*. Oxford: Oxford University Press.

McFarlane, S. (1991) 'The Mystique of Martial Arts, A Reply to Professor Keenan's Response', *Japanese Journal of Religious Studies* 18:4, 355–68.

McKenzie, R.D. (1933) *The Metropolitan Community*. New York: McGraw-Hill.

McKenzie, R.D. (1967) 'The Ecological Approach to the Study of the Human Community' in R.E. Park, E.W. Burgess and R.D. McKenzie (eds) *The City*. Chicago: Chicago University Press, 63–79.

McLeod, H. (1996) *Piety and Poverty, Working Class Religion in Berlin, London and New York 1870–1914*. New York: Holmes and Meier.

Miles, M., Hall, T. and Borden, I. (eds) (2004) *The City Cultures Reader*. London: Routledge.

Millington, G. (2011) *'Race', Culture and the Right to the City, Centres, Peripheries, Margins*. London: Palgrave Macmillan.

Mitchell, D. and Staeheli, L.A. (2006) 'Clean and Safe? Property Redevelopment, Public Space, and Homelessness in Downtown San Diego' in S.M. Low and N. Smith (eds) (2006) *The Politics of Public Space*. New York: Routledge, 143–76.

Mitchell, J.C. (1956) *The Kalela Dance, Aspects of Social Relationships Among Urban Africans in Northern Rhodesia (Rhodes Livingstone Papers No 27)*. Manchester: Manchester University Press.

Morris, H.S. (1968) *The Indians of Uganda*. London: Weidenfeld and Nicolson.

Nora, P. (1996–8) *Realms of Memory, Rethinking the French Past*. New York: Columbia University Press.

Numrich, P.D. (1996) *Old Wisdom in the New World, Americanization in Two Immigrant Theravada Buddhist Temples*. Knoxville: University of Tennessee Press.

Numrich, P.D. (2000) 'Recent Immigrant Religions and the Restructuring of Metropolitan Chicago' in L.W. Livezey (ed.) *Public Religion and Urban Transformation, Faith in the City*. New York: New York University Press, 239–67.

Park, R.E. (1952) *Human Communities, The City and Human Ecology*. Glencoe: The Free Press.

Phillimore, J. (2011) 'Approaches to Health Provision in the Age of Superdiversity, Accessing the NHS in Britain's Most Diverse Cities'. *Critical Social Policy* 31:1, 5–29.

Phoenix, A. (1988) 'Narrow Definitions of Culture: The Case of Early Motherhood' in S. Westwood and P. Bhachu (eds) *Enterprising Women, Ethnicity, Economy and Gender Relations*. London: Routledge, 153–76.

Pollock, J.S. (1890) *Vaughton's Hole, Twenty-five Years in it*. Oxford: Mowbray & Co.

Pracharart, P.L.P. (2004) *The British Practice of Theravada Buddhism*. Unpublished PhD thesis submitted to the University of Birmingham.

Putnam, R.D. (2000) *Bowling Alone, The Collapse and Revival of American Community*. New York: Simon & Schuster.

Ram, M., Jones, T., Edwards, P., et al. (2010) 'Engaging with Super-Diversity, New Migrant Business and the Research-Policy Nexus'. Paper delivered to the Institute for Small Business and Entrepreneurship Conference, London, found at http://www.isbe.org.uk/BestPapers

Rapport, N. (ed.) (2002) *British Subjects, An Anthropology of Britain*. Oxford: Berg.

Ratcliffe, P. (1981) *Racism and Reaction, a Profile of Handsworth*. London: Routledge and Kegan Paul.

Reader, J. (2005) *Blurred Encounters, A Reasoned Practice of Faith*. St Bride's: Aureus.

Redfield, R. (1960) *The Little Community and Peasant Society and Culture*. Chicago: University of Chicago Press.

Rex, J. and Moore, R. (1967) *Race, Community and Conflict, a Study of Sparkbrook*. Oxford: Oxford University Press.

Rogers, A. (1995) 'Cinco de Mayo and 15 January: Contrasting Situations in a Mixed Ethnic Neighbourhood' in A. Rogers and S. Vertovec (eds) *The Urban Context, Ethnicity, Social Network and Situational Analysis*. Oxford: Berg, 117–40.

Rogers, A. and Vertovec, S. (1995) 'Introduction' in A. Rogers and S. Vertovec (eds) *The Urban Context, Ethnicity, Social Network and Situational Analysis*. Oxford: Berg, 1–33.

Rothschild, J. (1981) *Ethnopolitics, A Conceptual Framework*. New York: Columbia University Press.

Ryan, D. (1996) *The Catholic Parish, Institutional Discipline, Tribal Identity and Religious Development in the English Church*. London: Sheed and Ward.

Said, E.W. (1978) *Orientalism, Western Conceptions of the Orient*. London: Routledge and Kegan Paul.

Sandercock, L. (1998) *Towards Cosmopolis, Planning for Multicultural Cities*. New York, John Wiley.

Sandercock, L. (2003) *Cosmopolis II, Mongrel Cities of the 21st Century*. London: Continuum.

Sassen, S. (1991) *The Global City, New York, London, Tokyo*. Princeton: Princeton University Press.

Séguy, J. (1989) 'L'Approche Wébérienne des Phénomènes Religieux' in R. Cipriani and M. Macioti (eds) *Omaggio a Ferrarotti*. Rome: Siares, Studi e Richerche.

Sennett, R. (1970) *The Uses of Disorder*. Harmondsworth: Penguin.

Sennett, R. (1994) *Flesh and Stone, The Body and the City in Western Civilization*. London: Faber and Faber.

Shannahan, C. (2012) '"NEET" Believers? An Analysis of "Belief" on an Urban Housing Estate'. *Culture and Religion* 130:3, 315–35.

Sibley, D. (1995) *Geographies of Exclusion, Society and Difference in the West*. London: Routledge.

Simmel, G. (1950) 'The Metropolis and Mental Life' in K.H. Wolff (ed.) *The Sociology of Georg Simmel*. Glencoe: The Free Press, 409–24.

Simmel, G. (1990) *The Philosophy of Money*. London: Routledge.

Smart, N. (1969) *The Religious Experience of Mankind*. New York: Fontana.

Smith, J.H. (2006) *Mary in the Kitchen, Martha in the Pew, Patterns of Holiness in a Methodist Church*. Unpublished MPhil thesis submitted to the University of Birmingham.

Smith, S. (1995) 'Where to Draw the Line, A Geography of Popular Festivity' in A. Rogers and S. Vertovec (eds) *The Urban Context, Ethnicity, Social Network and Situational Analysis*. Oxford: Berg, 141–64.

Soja, E.W. (1996) *Thirdspace, Journeys to Los Angeles and Other Real-and-Imagined Places*. Oxford: Blackwell.

Sorkin, M. (ed.) (1992a) *Variations on a Theme Park, The New American City and the End of Public Space*. New York: Hill and Wang.

Sorkin, M. (1992b) 'See You in Disneyland' in M. Sorkin (ed.) *Variations on a Theme Park, The New American City and the End of Public Space*. New York: Hill and Wang, 205–32.

Southgate, P. (1982) 'Disturbances of July 1981 in Handsworth, Birmingham, A Survey of the Views and Experiences of Male Residences' in S. Field and P. Southgate, *Public Disorder, A Review of Research and a Study in One Inner City Area*. Home Office Research Studies, 72. London: Home Office Research Unit, 41–73

Stewart, C. and Shaw, R. (eds) (1994) *Syncretism/Anti-Syncretism, The Politics of Religious Synthesis*. London: Routledge.

Stringer, M.D. (1999) *On the Perception of Worship, the Ethnography of Worship in Four Christian Congregations in Manchester*. Birmingham: Birmingham University Press.

Stringer, M.D. (2004) 'Putting Congregational Studies to Work, Ethnography, Consultancy and Change' in M. Guest, K. Tusting and L. Woodhead (eds) *Congregational Studies in the UK, Christianity in a Post-Christian Context*. Aldershot: Ashgate.

Stringer, M.D. (2008) *Contemporary Western Ethnography and the Definition of Religion*. London: Continuum.

Sultan, P. (2012) 'Living with People of Other Faiths, an Outline' in *The Sword*, February 2012, 3–4.

Suttles, G.D. (1968) *The Social Order of the Slum, Ethnicity and Territory in the Inner City*. Chicago: University of Chicago Press.

Taylor, I., Evans, K. and Fraser, P. (1996) *A Tale of Two Cities, Global Change, Local Feeling and Everyday Life in the North of England, A Study in Manchester and Sheffield*. London: Routledge.

Thorns, D.C. (2002) *The Transformation of Cities, Urban Theory and Urban Life*. Basingstoke: Palgrave Macmillan.

Tönnies, F. (2001) *Community and Civil Society*. Cambridge: Cambridge University Press.

Turner, V. (1969) *The Ritual Process, Structure and Anti-Structure.* Harmondsworth: Penguin Books.

Tweed, T.A. (2006) *Crossing and Dwelling, A Theory of Religion.* Cambridge: Harvard University Press.

Tyrer, P. and Crinson, M. (2005) 'Totemic Park, Symbolic Representation in Post-industrial Space' in M. Crinson (ed.) *Urban Memory, History and Amnesia in the Modern City.* London: Routledge, 99–117.

Van Gennep, A. (1960) *The Rites of Passage.* London: Routledge and Kegan Paul.

Vertovec, S. (2007) 'Super-diversity and its Implications'. *Ethnic and Racial Studies* 30:6, 1024–54.

Von Brömssen, K. (2003) *Tolkingar, Förhandlingar och Tystnader, Elevers Tal om Religion i det Mångkulturella och Postkoloniala Rummet.* Göteborg: Acta Universitatis Gothoburgensis.

Walzer, M. (1995) 'Pleasures and Costs of Urbanity' in P. Kasinitz (ed.) *Metropolis: Centre and Symbol of Our Times.* New York: New York University Press.

Walzer, M. (1997) *On Toleration.* New Haven: Yale University Press.

Ward, P. (2002) *Liquid Church.* Carlisle: Paternoster Press.

Warner, R.S. and Wittner, J.G. (eds) (1998) *Gatherings in Diaspora, Religious Communities and the New Immigration.* Philadelphia: Temple University Press.

Weber, M. (2001) *The Protestant Ethic and the Spirit of Capitalism.* London: Routledge.

Werbner, P. (2002) *Imagined Diasporas among Manchester Muslims, The Public Performance of Pakistani Transnational Identity Politics.* Oxford: James Currey.

Williams, R. (1965) *The Long Revolution.* Harmondsworth: Penguin.

Williams, R. (2005) 'Remembering, Forgetting, and the Industrial Gallery Space' in M. Crinson (ed.) *Urban Memory, History and Amnesia in the Modern City.* London: Routledge, 121–41.

Williams, S. (1999) *Religious Belief and Popular Culture in Southwark, c1880–1939.* Oxford: Oxford University Press.

Willmott, P. (1963) *The Evolution of a Community, A Study of Dagenham after Forty Years.* London: Routledge and Kegan Paul.

Wirth, L. (1928) *The Ghetto.* Chicago: Chicago University Press.

Wirth, L. (1938) 'Urbanism as a Way of Life'. *The American Journal of Sociology* 44:1, 1–24.

Wittgenstein, L. (1976) *Philosophical Investigations.* Oxford: Blackwell.

Wuthnow, R. (1988) *Restructuring of American Religion.* Princeton: Princeton University Press.

Yang, F. (1998) 'Tenacious Unity in a Contentious Community, Cultural and Religious Dynamics in a Chinese Christian Church' in R.S. Warner, and J.G. Wittner (eds) *Gatherings in Diaspora, Religious Communities and the New Immigration.* Philadelphia: Temple University Press, 333–61.

Young, I.M. (1990) *Justice and the Politics of Difference*. Princeton: Princeton University Press.

Young, M. and Willmott, P. (1957) *Family and Kinship in East London*. London: Routledge and Kegan Paul.

Zorbaugh, H.N. (1929) *The Gold Coast and the Slum*. Chicago: Chicago University Press.

Zukin, S. (1982) *Loft Living: Culture and Capital in Urban Change*. Baltimore: Johns Hopkins University Press.

Zukin, S. (1995) *The Cultures of Cities*. Oxford: Blackwell.

Index